ADVANCE PRAISE FOR

Injustice and Rectification

"Professor Roberts has done a masterful job of pulling together academic theory and philosophical practice. This book combines the theoretical examination of rectificatory justice with leading scholars working through its meaning and use. *Injustice and Rectification* is a book for advanced undergraduate and graduate students. Scholars interested in issues of justice will find this work very useful as both a resource tool and a focal point for discussion and research. Professor Roberts has produced a worthwhile and valuable work. Very good!"

Bill E. Lawson, Professor of Philosophy, Michigan State University

"This timely collection of well-chosen, outstanding essays analyzes major concepts of rectificatory justice—apology, compensation, and reparation—with special attention to widely-discussed claims on behalf of African Americans and Native Americans. Roberts' introduction alone is worth the price of the book. At a time when responses to atrocities are on everyone's mind, this collection is more than welcome. It will be a great teaching tool."

Claudia Card, Emma Goldman Professor of Philosophy, and Senior Fellow, Institute for Research in the Humanities, University of Wisconsin-Madison

"This is an outstanding collection in several aspects. First, it is organized around a taxonomy of justice that provides a much needed systematic framework for discussing topics of injustice and rectification, so the whole is worth more than the sum of the parts. Second, the parts are absolutely first rate—a wonderful selection of authors. Finally, this is a focus that is sorely needed to connect the usual discussion of ideal theory with the real world. It is an important contribution to the discussion of injustice."

Patricia Smith, Professor of Philosophy and Chair of the Department of Philosophy, Baruch College, City University of New York

"Rodney C. Roberts takes a novel approach to questions of justice by concentrating on the neglected topic of justice in rectification and by placing injustice at the center of his inquiry. Along with the taxonomy of justice he develops from this analysis, Roberts makes available just the right mix of important work on the question of injustice and rectification, providing readers with both systematic and pluralistic treatments of his topic. In doing this, Roberts gives us a book that combines the benefits of a monograph with the benefits of an anthology, filling two important gaps in the contemporary literature on justice."

Joan Callahan, Professor of Philosophy
and Director of the Women's Studies Program, University of Kentucky

"Rodney C. Roberts has done the areas of political philosophy and philosophy of law a great service by editing this excellent collection of important essays on the subject of injustice and rectification. The many controversies unleashed by these questions, especially in an age of euphemistic globalism in the face of callous disregard for the profits won from practices of conquest, slavery, colonization, mercantilism, and economic orders that beset pillaged populations with debts whose interest payments seem increasingly impossible to meet, demand such engagements by philosophers—the majority of whom seem to remain locked in their dogmatic slumbers. This book, accompanied by a fine introduction by the editor, will prove valuable to scholars and teachers, as well as anyone struggling to find a voice of reason in the struggle to formulate and effect a better world."

Lewis Gordon, Professor of Africana Studies, Religious Thought,
Modern Culture and Media, and Latin American Studies,
and Chair of the Department of Africana Studies, Brown University,
Ongoing Visiting Professor of Political Philosophy in the Department of Government,
University of the West Indies at Mona, Jamaica

Injustice
AND
Rectification

PETER LANG
New York • Washington, D.C./Baltimore • Bern
Frankfurt am Main • Berlin • Brussels • Vienna • Oxford

Injustice
AND
Rectification

EDITED BY
Rodney C. Roberts

PETER LANG
New York • Washington, D.C./Baltimore • Bern
Frankfurt am Main • Berlin • Brussels • Vienna • Oxford

Library of Congress Cataloging-in-Publication Data

Injustice and rectification / Rodney C. Roberts, editor.
p. cm.
Includes bibliographical references and index.
1. Justice (Philosophy). 2. Compensation (Philosophy).
I. Roberts, Rodney C.
B105.J87 I54 172'.2—dc21 2002004068
ISBN 0-8204-6100-8

Die Deutsche Bibliothek-CIP-Einheitsaufnahme

Injustice and rectification / ed. by: Rodney C. Roberts.
–New York; Washington, D.C./Baltimore; Bern;
Frankfurt am Main; Berlin; Brussels; Vienna; Oxford: Lang.
ISBN 0-8204-6100-8

Cover design by Lisa Barfield

The paper in this book meets the guidelines for permanence and durability
of the Committee on Production Guidelines for Book Longevity
of the Council of Library Resources.

Printed in the United States of America

For Willie Mae and Cornelius

CONTENTS

INTRODUCTION

This book brings philosophical analysis to bear on the idea of injustice itself, and on some important conceptual and normative issues concerning the rectification of injustice. The aim of the book is to help us answer two fundamental questions: (1) What is injustice?, and (2) What does justice require when injustice occurs?

In sharp contrast to the concern over retributive and distributive aspects of justice, Western philosophy has paid relatively little attention to questions of injustice and its rectification.[1] A recent book underscores this point. *What Is Justice?* claims to be "an exceptionally comprehensive introduction to the subject" of justice, one which "also deals with questions of retributive justice and punishment, topics that are often excluded from other volumes on justice".[2] But although the book includes Aristotle's discussion of justice (*Nicomachean Ethics,* Ch V), and so has at least some rectificatory content, readers are steered away from rectificatory concerns. According to the editors, "[i]n modern times the focus of justice has come to be more concentrated on questions of distribution and exchange and, in particular, on questions of private property and individual liberty".[3] On this view, one that is shared by many philosophers today, "the central debate about justice emerges from the text and strategy of John Rawls's monumental *A Theory of Justice*".[4] Hence, questions regarding compensation which may be due to victims of injustice, for example, are well outside the "central debate", and are, relatively speaking, of little concern to philosophers.

One serious problem with this approach is that it favors a privileged perspective on justice. Limiting our reflection on justice by focusing on the Rawlsian world of ideal theory helps to ensure that the concerns of victims of injustice, including those who are systematically oppressed in liberal democracies, have little place in our deliberations about justice.[5]

Indeed, while Aristotle's view of rectification is still discussed,[6] and while other philosophers have had something to say about rectification since Aristotle,[7] most of the relevant literature has emerged only since the latter half of the twentieth century[8]—the vast majority during the 1970's,[9] 1980's,[10] and 1990's.[11]

Much of the impetus for the rise in scholarship was surely due to the Black Civil Rights Movement. Affirmative action in particular, became a much debated topic among philosophers, and among other scholars as well.[12] Perhaps more than any other, this topic has fueled a discussion which often connects with concerns of rectificatory justice more generally,[13] and which continues to the present day.[14] However, philosophical analyses of affirmative action, like most of the work which connects with rectificatory concerns, typically do not proceed from some more general moral theory of justice.[15] Indeed, as George Sher observes, no one has yet come close to producing a "comprehensive and integrated" theory of rectificatory justice.[16] Hence, I try to accomplish the book's aim in part by suggesting a taxonomy of justice. This taxonomy sets forth an initial framework for a moral theory of justice, the focus of which is on framing a conception of rectificatory justice.

Also absent from the philosophical literature is a collection of essays in which a diverse group of philosophers address the fundamental questions with which we are concerned.[17] Hence, the taxonomy is combined with a set of essays which together provide just such a collection. Since a collection of essays can be thought of as more philosophically valuable when the collection itself is based on a theory,[18] Chapter 1 also grounds the present collection. It does so by providing the basis for the structure and content of the book.

In "Justice and Rectification: A Taxonomy of Justice", I begin by examining the notion of justice itself, including the idea of injustice. The notion of injustice, one of the most neglected of rectificatory topics, is addressed by the authors in Part Two. As Thomas Simon notes, Anthony Woozley is "one of the few philosophers explicitly to have addressed injustice as a separate concept."[19] In his essay "Injustice", Woozley offers an analysis which yields a conception of injustice as the failure to be just. On his view, injustice is conceived as not having justice where it ought to be present. In "'The Laborers in the Vineyard' and Other Stories", Phillip Montague tries to clear up some of the confusion regarding the nature of injustice. Beginning with a parable which suggests unjust behavior, and employing the principle that relevantly similar cases ought to be handled similarly, he argues that the source of some of our confusion lies in our failure to distinguish between unjust and unreasonable behavior.

In advancing my taxonomy, I apply the language of genus and species to the idea of justice. Since I find that justice is not the whole of morality, it is classified as a genus of morality. I then argue for a taxonomy which includes only two species of justice: distributive justice, and rectificatory justice. Since the remainder of the book's essays all speak to concerns which can be subsumed under my conception of rectification, they are all included in Part Three. The opening essay by Jules Coleman suggests a contrasting rectificatory concept. In "Corrective Justice and Property Rights", Coleman devotes most of his discussion to the articulation of his conception of corrective justice. On Coleman's view, even when an institution is not fully just, we can still have a moral duty to support it. He wants to show us the circumstances under which his conception of corrective justice can sustain a scheme of property rights.

A necessary part of my conception of rectification is the notion of compensation. When wrongful losses are sustained, rectificatory justice requires the rendering of something equivalent in value to that which was lost. Judith Thomson's "Rights and Compensation", and Phillip Montague's "Rights and Duties of Compensation", both address the matter of rights to compensation. Thomson begins by introducing Joel Feinberg's story of a backpacker who breaks into an unoccupied mountain cabin. Since the backpacker breaks in, helps himself to the owner's food, and burns some of the owner's furniture in order to survive an unexpected blizzard, it seems as if the backpacker's actions are morally permissible. Thomson thinks that having a right (the cabin owner's property right) and it being morally permissible to infringe that right (the backpackers actions) are compatible. In such cases, Thomson argues, the rightholder is due compensation. Montague, on the other hand, argues that it is a mistake to think that we can be morally permitted to infringe on rights, and thinks that one who infringes on a right still has a residual duty to compensate the rightholder.

Gerald Gaus, in "Does Compensation Restore Equality?", replies to Montague,[20] but not before arguing against compensatory justice understood in the Aristotelian sense of the restoration of equality between parties. Gaus's essay also includes a discussion of the commensurability of values, an idea which I bracket in Chapter 1, but one which is important to any full theory of compensation. Gaus argues that, in general, individual values are commensurable.

Apology is another necessary part of my conception of rectification. Like the notion of injustice, apology is also a much neglected rectificatory topic.[21] In "What Is An Apology?", Louis Kort begins by analyzing a general account of apology. Finding this account inadequate, he attempts to answer the question of what an utterance must be like in order to count as an apology. Kort suggests his own conception of apology by way of five conditions which are conjointly both sufficient and necessary for an apology. Kathleen Gill shows us some of the more prominent aspects of apology's moral functions in her essay "The Moral Functions of an Apology". She develops her conception of the notion by analyzing three settings: apologies which occur in the criminal justice system, apologies offered to groups, and apologies offered by groups.

The matter of rectification for injustices perpetrated against groups is raised at the end of Chapter 1. The remaining essays in Part Three address rectificatory concerns involving two social groups in the United States which are considered by many to have been historically oppressed: African Americans, and Native Americans.

In the Black Manifesto, James Foreman demanded reparations for, *inter alia,* the historic exploitation, persecution, and killing of blacks in America. Not surprisingly, the Manifesto sparked scholarly discussion,[22] including some by philosophers. In "The Morality of Reparation", Bernard Boxill holds that Michael Harrington, a critic of Foreman, opposes reparations to blacks because he finds it ineffective as a means of correcting the disparity of incomes between blacks and whites. However, Boxill thinks that Harrington might endorse the use of special compensatory programs as an alternative to reparations. Boxill objects to Harrington's suggestion that compensation replace reparations for blacks, arguing that, while both are parts of justice, since compensation and reparation have different aims, one cannot replace the other. Hugo Bedau is more concerned with understanding the Manifesto itself. Bedau thinks that the argument of the Manifesto is less than straightforward, and that it has received an insufficient amount of scholarly attention. In "Compensatory Justice and the Black Manifesto", he begins by reconstructing the Manifesto's argument, then addresses, and ultimately rejects, ten objections to that argument.

The book's final essay is by J. Angelo Corlett. In "Wrongdoing, Reparations and Native Americans", Corlett first offers a clarification of the nature of reparations. Then, focusing on the Native American experience in the United States, he analyzes, and ultimately rejects, several objections to reparations for groups which have been historically and seriously wronged. Corlett ends his discussion by providing suggestions for possible reparations policies.

PART ONE

JUSTICE

CHAPTER I

Rodney C. Roberts

JUSTICE AND RECTIFICATION: A TAXONOMY OF JUSTICE

My aim in this chapter is to set forth an initial framework for a moral theory of justice. This is accomplished by way of a taxonomy of justice, the focus of which is on framing a conception of rectificatory justice. In Part I, I examine the notion of justice itself, posit distributive justice as a species of justice, and suggest a theory of compensation. I conclude that the idea of compensation is inadequate as ground for a second species of justice. I then argue in Part II for a conception of rectification which is adequate ground for a species of justice, and which includes accounts of compensation, restoration, apology, and punishment (at least insofar as I suggest where punishment ought to be posited in a theory of justice). On this view, a taxonomy of justice consists of only two species: distributive justice and rectificatory justice.

Justice and Compensation

Justice

The idea of "justice", or of a thing being "just", always includes some consonance with principles of moral right. Since our conception of what is consonant with the principles of moral right can be rather broad, we can begin narrowing it to a conception of justice by considering the distinction Aristotle draws between the characters of individuals and their actions towards others. Aristotle thinks that "[i]n so far as we are interested in the nature of the agent, we speak in terms of excellence . . . of character; in so far as we are interested in the way his actions affect other people, we speak in terms of justice".[1] So while being frugal in one's spending, and being fair in one's dealings with others might both be said to be "consonant with the principles of moral right", only the latter is a matter of justice.

More recently, D. D. Raphael has noted that:

> There is no such thing as justice *within* an individual. When the concept of justice relates to an individual, it concerns relationships *between* him and other individuals or between him and a group (including the large group that constitutes the organized society of the State).[2]

If we distinguish between those things we say about individuals themselves (such as being frugal) and those things we say about relationships between individuals and others (such as fairness in dealing with others), and both kinds of things are within the realm of moral right, then H. L. A. Hart was correct when he said that justice "is a distinct segment of morality". Since justice is not the whole of morality, and since the issues with which it must concern itself are of considerable breadth, we can think of justice as a genus of morality. Implicit in the classification of justice as a genus, is that there are particular species of justice which come under it. I want to suggest that there are only two species of justice: distributive justice and rectificatory justice. Let us begin with distributive justice.

As the name implies, distributive justice is concerned with establishing a just distribution. But what is it that distributive justice seeks to distribute justly? Since my concern is with justice in liberal democracies, and since liberal democracies are very much concerned with civil and political rights, it makes sense to think that rights (or perhaps more specifically, rights and duties) constitute that which liberal democracies are concerned with distributing justly. According to W. D. Lamont, the ultimate standard of distributive justice is:

> the principle of equality of consideration, [the state, insofar as it embodies the notion of distributive justice] distributes rights (on the basis of proportionate equality or equity) to the pursuit of those interests [i.e., those ends which individuals and groups in a community take to be good], prescribing, at the same time, the duties and obligations implied in the distribution of rights.[3]

But while Lamont's view calls for the distribution of rights and duties in accordance with the principle of equality of consideration, and so appears to be consistent with the liberal concern for civil and political rights, it would be a mistake to think that it followed from giving equal consideration in the distribution of rights and duties that the rights and duties in question are to be distributed equally. Rather (as Lamont recognizes) rights and duties are distributed on the basis of proportionate equality *or* equity. As Raphael notes:

> The idea of justice is often, though not always, roughly equivalent to the idea of fairness or equity. Equity is frequently contrasted with equality. 'Fair shares', for example, are not the same as 'equal shares'. How do they differ? 'Fair shares' depend on merit, need, and capacity, which of course are not equally distributed.[4]

According to Raphael, most modern theorists "seem to agree with the view of Aristotle . . . that equity is entirely a matter of proportionate distribution and that it does not include any principle of strict equality." On this view

> Equity allows, or rather requires, discrimination by reference to morally relevant differences, and forbids discrimination in the absence of such differences. . . . The rule is to treat like cases alike and unlike cases differently.[5]

It is important to note that distributive justice is primarily concerned with the distribution of rights and duties to members of society by way of society's institutions. As John Rawls tells us: "the primary subject of [social] justice is . . . the way in which the major social institutions distribute fundamental rights and duties and determine the division of advantages from social cooperation". Hence, in liberal democracies, it is the species of justice known as distributive justice which is concerned with establishing a just distribution of rights and duties among the members of society.[6]

Two Senses of Compensation

Included in this concern for a just distribution of rights and duties, is a concern for those members of society who are disadvantaged insofar as their opportunity to participate in the advantages of social cooperation. As Bill Diggs notes:

> All persons should have the opportunity to participate in a cooperative society, and, within the limits of society's means, an opportunity of self-fulfillment. . . . In trying to secure these opportunities and establish them as recognized equal rights, an unequal effort must be directed toward helping the disadvantaged. In this broad sense, distributive justice itself requires that the disadvantaged be "compensated".[7]

According to Diggs, individuals who are disadvantaged insofar as their opportunity to participate in the advantages of social cooperation and in pursuing self-fulfillment, ought to be compensated as a means of removing this disadvantage. Further, this compensation is required by distributive justice.

To compensate for something is to counterbalance it; to give something equivalent to the thing. As Loren Lomasky points out, "[t]he root of 'compensate' is "to weigh," that is to weigh different things together in order to establish a balance between them . . . 'compensation' carries the connotation of providing something *equivalent* in value to that which has been lost". In what I shall call "compensation in the distributive sense", this rendering of an equivalent is done in order to alleviate some disadvantage or natural loss which is thought to pose an undue hindrance on members of society.

Bernard Boxill's view of compensation is illustrative of this idea. According to Boxill, the aim of compensation is to "alleviate disabilities which stand in the way of some *future* good, *however* these disabilities may have come about". By alleviating any disabilities, compensation ensures equality of opportunity in the competition for positions and resources. Hence, "[t]he characteristic of compensatory programs is that they are essentially 'forward looking'". According to Boxill, compensation is concerned with

> the remedying of the present situation however it may have been produced; and to know the present situation, and how to remedy it, it is not, strictly speaking, necessary to know just how it was brought about, or whether it was brought about by injustice.[8]

For Boxill, compensation is appropriate when persons are either losers in the competition for positions and resources, or when they are disadvantaged in their opportunity to compete for them by accidents or "acts of God". This is compensation in the distributive sense.

However, it is perhaps more common that when we think of compensation as a matter of justice, what comes to mind is not making up for a loss sustained as a result of something like an act of God, but rather making up for a loss that is the result of an *injustice* that has been done. When an injustice occurs, that is, when one's actions towards another fail to be consonant with principles of moral right, the victim of such an action oftentimes suffers a loss for which compensation is thought to be due. Since distributive justice does not provide a means by which we can determine when compensation is appropriate in such cases, when compensation is due as the result of an injustice it cannot be compensation in the distributive sense. Rather, when compensation is due as a matter of justice, but its justification falls outside of the realm of distributive justice, it is what I shall refer to as "compensation in the rectificatory sense".

Individual Interests

When someone is adversely affected by an injustice, we can say that the adverse effect has been upon that person's interest(s). Since the aim of compensation is to counterbalance the loss of something by providing something else that is equivalent in value to the thing lost, we can say that when compensation is being rendered because of an injustice, the aim of compensation in such cases is to counterbalance the adverse effect on a person's interest by providing something equivalent in value to the loss to that adversely affected interest. But precisely what do we mean by "interest"?

To say that one has an "interest" is to say that the person has a feeling of intentness or concern for something. An individual's interests are those things with which she is concerned. Hence, if my automobile and my position at IBM are among the things with which I am concerned, we can say that each of these constitutes an interest of mine. This does not mean, of course, that I am concerned about them in the sense that I am *worried* about the status of either of these things, at least not necessarily. However, that these things are of concern to me does imply that were the status of either of them threatened in some way, I *would be* worried about them. No worry on my part arises when some person X's automobile is stolen in a country half-way around the world from me. The disposition of X's automobile is not something with which I am concerned (although upon hearing of X's misfortune I may sympathize with X). X's automobile is not among my interests. However, since I count my automobile among my interests, I am concerned about it, and certainly would become worried should I discover that it had been stolen. In such a case I would have suffered an adverse effect to one of my interests, and it seems likely that compensation (in the rectificatory sense) would be due. Hence, we can think of individual interests in the same way that Joel Feinberg does, namely as "distinguishable components of a person's good or well-being".[9]

The aim of compensation presupposes two things. First, that individual interests have some value, so that any adverse effect on those interests represents a loss of value. Surely in order to make any sense of the idea of compensating for a loss to one's interests we must first suppose that those interests are somehow valuable. Second, that the value of any adverse effect on individual interests and the value of the thing rendered as compensation for that adverse effect, are commensurable. It seems impossible to think of counterbalancing the loss of something of value with something else of value, without having a way in which the value of both things can be measured. In short, we need a way of knowing that some particular amount of the thing being rendered as compensation suffices to counterbalance the loss. Bracketing concerns about commensurability,[10] let's suppose that Aristotle is correct: currency makes things sufficiently commensurate in relation to our needs.[11]

As to the first presupposition, we need not take on the task of proposing anything like a complete theory of value in order to make sense of the idea that one's interests have value. Rather, all that we need do is give a sense of what we mean when we take it that an individual's interests have value. On Ralph Barton Perry's view, for example, being an object of my interest is itself a sufficient condition for a thing to count as valuable. According to Perry: "*a thing—any thing—has value, or is valuable . . . when it is the object of an interest—any interest.*" Or, "*whatever is [an] object of interest is ipso facto valuable*".[12] Thus, holding that individual interests are valuable precisely because they are the things with which we are concerned, is one sense of what we mean when we say that an individual's interests have value. Further, the value of individual interests are not necessarily subjective. Among an individual's most fundamental interests are ones concerning food, clothing, and shelter. Since everyone would count these among their interests, there is a sense in which at least some of our interests can be thought of as objectively valuable.

The Package Conception of Compensation

Let us consider a rather simple compensatory scenario as a starting point for seeing what compensation looks like when its aim is achieved. Suppose that A's interest in an 18 ct. gold necklace is adversely affected when B misappropriates the necklace. If B provides A with an 18 ct. gold necklace nearly identical to the original one, we might be tempted to say that since A has been provided with a value equivalent to the value of the loss to her interest, *viz.,* the nearly identical necklace, A has been compensated for the loss. However, we should also take into account A's pain at having the necklace taken. So even though we were able to provide something which was both commensurable with, and equivalent to, the value of A's loss insofar as the necklace was concerned, some value remains unaccounted for—what is commonly referred to as "pain and suffering".

As Joel Feinberg notes, compensation for pain and suffering does not "annul or obliterate pain, or make it as if the pain or suffering never were, or make one mind the pain less in retrospect"; although in some cases such compensation "can divert competent persons from their depression". Recognizing the need to compensate for pain and suffering suggests that we may end up providing something very different from that which was lost when we try to provide an equivalent in value for it. Since we are unable to counterbalance the pain, say, with a precise amount of pleasure of the appropriate kind, we may end up, as Feinberg suggests, diverting the victim from his depression, perhaps by facilitating the pursuit of some new interest. The aim of compensation in such cases is still to provide an equivalent in value, however, in contrast to the necklace itself, the loss here is intangible.

If this is correct, then in cases like those involving both the loss of a material object, and pain and suffering, adequate compensation is likely to include two things. First, some kind of compensation that is equivalent in value to a portion or particular aspect of the adversely affected interest. In the case of the misappropriated necklace, this was accomplished by providing another necklace nearly identical to the original. Second, some other kind of compensation equivalent to any value left unaccounted for. This remaining value might represent something like pain and suffering, and can in many cases be compensated for by rendering currency when no other good will suffice.[13] This not only allows A to pursue some other interest(s), that is, one other than the interest A had in the necklace, it also gives A the flexibility to choose from a host of other interests.

Hence, what I shall call the *Package Conception of Compensation* (PCC) has the following aim: to render a package or combination of goods that is structured in such a way as to provide an equivalent in value for losses to individual interests that occur as a result of some adverse effect upon those interests due to injustice. Implementation of the PCC is achieved in two steps. First, to the extent possible, the person who has suffered the injustice is provided with an equivalent in value in the form of something identical to, or at least consistent with, the interest(s) affected by the injustice. In fairly simple cases where the loss is a tangible one, this might be a particular kind of material object which would be provided as a replacement for an object that was lost. Second, the individual who has suffered the injustice is provided with an amount of currency and/or other good(s) as a means of compensating for any loss of value that remains unaccounted for after completion of the first step. The currency or goods supplied in this second step are meant to facilitate the pursuit of some interest(s) other than the particular one(s) affected by the injustice. Hence, when an irreplaceable object is lost (say a one-of-a-kind antique), and/or when the loss is an intangible one, as in the case of pain and suffering, the remaining value of such losses will be accounted for by providing the individual with currency or some other good(s). The package of goods, then, consists of: (1) equivalent means to pursue the same interest as the one affected by injustice, and (2) currency or some other good(s) to facilitate the pursuit of some interest(s) other than the particular one(s) affected by the injustice that is equivalent to the remaining value (if any) of the adversely affected interest(s), and/or of any further loss which may have been incurred as a result of the adverse effect to that interest.

To see how the PCC might be employed, let us consider a series of compensatory scenarios, the first of which is a slightly revised version of the stolen necklace example just discussed.

Necklace 1:

> Unbeknownst to A, B misappropriates the 18 ct. gold necklace which A has recently purchased. B loses the necklace later that night, then informs A of the malfeasance the following day.

Is compensation warranted in this case? Yes, it is. Granting that A has a right against B that B not take the necklace without A's consent, B's non-consensual taking of the necklace constitutes a violation of A's right to the necklace. Given A's right to the necklace, A's interest in the necklace is therefore a legitimate one (clearly if A's interest failed to be legitimate—say in a case where A obtained the necklace by stealing it from C—then A would have no grounds for a right to compensation for the loss). If having one's legitimate interests adversely affected by injustice is a sufficient condition for establishing a claim of compensation for the resultant loss, then B, by misappropriating A's necklace, has perpetrated an injustice upon A, and owes A compensation. The question then becomes: For what is compensation due, and by virtue of what package of goods can an equivalent in value be rendered?

According to the PCC, A must first be provided with equivalent means to pursue the same interest as the one affected by the injustice, so far as this is possible by morally permissible means. Since it is a relatively common material object that is at issue in this case, the task of providing an equivalent means for A is fairly straightforward. Any other 18 ct. gold necklace of the same size, weight, design etc., would constitute an equivalent value for A. Hence, A can easily be provided with the equivalent means to pursue the same interest as the one affected by the injustice perpetrated upon him by B.

Notice that in this case step two of the PCC is not required. Since A was never even aware of the theft, there is no need to compensate A for any additional loss from something like pain and suffering. Hence, we need not be concerned with providing currency or other goods to account for such a loss. The only loss at issue in this case is that of the necklace itself. In this rather simple compensatory scenario, then, the compensation package consists only of a new necklace for A. Hence, all that justice requires of B in order for an equivalent in value to A's loss to have been rendered is for B to secure (honestly) an identical necklace to the one he misappropriated from A. So when B presents A with an identical necklace immediately after confessing to the injustice, we can say that the aim of compensating A for the injustice has been achieved.

Now consider a slightly more complex version of NECKLACE 1, call it NECKLACE 2.

> B misappropriates the 18 ct. gold necklace which A has recently purchased. B loses the necklace later that night, then informs A of the malfeasance the following day. A has been worrying over the loss of the necklace since its disappearance the day before.

The question of whether or not compensation is warranted in this case is answered in the same way, and for the same reasons, as in NECKLACE 1. The first step towards compensating A in this case is also identical to NECKLACE 1. B must provide A with an equivalent means for A to pursue the same interest as the one affected by the injustice, which can again be accomplished by providing A with any other 18 ct. gold necklace of the same size, weight, design etc. Hence, step one is completed in the same way in NECKLACE 2 as it was in NECKLACE 1. Unlike NECKLACE 1, however, NECKLACE 2 requires the second step of the PCC.

Since A was never even aware that the necklace had been stolen in NECKLACE 1, we concluded that no compensation was required for anything like pain and suffering. Moreover, since there was no remaining loss to be accounted for once a replacement necklace had been rendered, step two was unnecessary. In the case of NECKLACE 2, however, A spends a day worrying over the disappearance of the necklace. Since A has the rational belief that the necklace is missing, and since this rational belief is what gives rise to A's feelings of worry over the loss of the necklace, A's worrying represents an additional loss beyond that of the necklace itself which requires compensation.[14] Therefore, according to the PCC, currency and/or some other good(s) must be provided to A as a means of accounting for this additional loss.

Righting Wrongs and the Need for Rectification

At least two important issues remain unaddressed by the PCC. First, even though B has lost the misappropriated necklace in both scenarios, the preferred course of action would be to have B return the exact same necklace that he misappropriated from A, rather than providing a similar one. By returning the exact same necklace (assuming it is returned undamaged), we eliminate the need to determine an equivalent in value for it. Surely a substantial advantage, especially in more complex compensatory scenarios. Moreover, in so doing we also eliminate the possibility of any miscalculation in the value of the necklace. Hence, returning the exact same necklace greatly enhances the likelihood that we will be successful in achieving the aim of compensation, *viz.*: to provide an equivalent in value to the loss sustained to an individual's interests.

Second, as much as I have tried to account for the effects of the injustice done to A, that is, the effects of B's violation of A's right to the necklace, I have said nothing about addressing *the rights violation itself*. In other words, I have said nothing about "righting the wrong" which B perpetrated against A, only righting the losses which resulted from that wrong. While the preference for seeing the exact same item that was taken from someone returned and the matter of righting the wrong of an injustice both need to be accounted for in our conception of justice, given our conception of compensation, no theory of compensation (including the PCC) can adequately address these concerns. What is required, then, is a conception upon which we can ground a species of justice which includes an account of compensation, and which also enables us to address these two concerns. The conception I have in mind is one of rectification.

Rectificatory Justice

Rectification and Restoration

To rectify something is to set it right. Hence, the aim of rectificatory justice is to set unjust situations right. This aim addresses the first of our two concerns about compensation. Although we still need compensation to address any intangible losses, restoring the exact same thing that was taken ensures that no tangible loss remains unaccounted for. Hence, justice requires first and foremost that we restore the exact same thing whenever possible. Since compensation merely aims at providing an equivalent in value to the thing that was lost, there is nothing in our notion of compensation which requires that we give back the exact same thing which was taken. It makes sense, therefore, to draw a distinction between compensation on the one hand, and restoration on the other.

Rectification and Apology

Rectification also addresses the second of our two concerns about compensation. It addresses this concern via its requirement that, in addition to restoration and/or compensation, an apology from the perpetrator of the injustice must also be rendered to the victim. Rendering an apology is a necessary condition for rectification because it addresses the matter of righting the wrong of an injustice.

Rectification accounts for the losses from an injustice more effectively than does mere compensation since it requires restoration. By including the requirement of an apology, rectification addresses both the loss from, as well as the wrong of, an injustice. Rectification is therefore sufficiently robust to qualify as a candidate for grounding the species of justice that we have in mind when the need to address an injustice arises.

The idea that justice requires an apology on the part of a wrongdoer is not a novel one. For example, Christopher Arnold thinks that:

> although we tend to think of pecuniary compensation as the appropriate kind of redress in cases of injury [for example], the scope of proper remedies rightly goes beyond that, and it is often felt correct to claim an *apology* . . . in the face of some kinds of damage."[15]

But in order to show why we ought to require an apology, and how we can think of an apology as righting a wrong, we need a clearer sense of what an apology is.

Typically, someone might apologize by saying: "I'm sorry I did X" (X being some wrongful act). Hence, an apology typically consists of two parts. The first part of an apology is the expression of regret. When someone says "I'm sorry", that person is expressing a feeling of sorrow or regret. At least in cases where the wrongdoing is unintentional, it makes sense to think that individuals would feel an appropriate degree of regret over the wrong they have committed. The second part of the apology is the admission or acknowledgment of wrongdoing. When someone says "I'm sorry I did X" (X being some wrongful act) we understand that person to be acknowledging the wrongdoing. This is in contrast to utterances such as: "I'm sorry X happened", or "Too bad you were adversely affected by X, I'm so sorry". Neither of these expressions contain an admission or acknowledgment of having done the wrongdoing, only an acknowledgment that *some event* (which may or may not have been a wrongdoing, and which I may or may not have done) has taken place. In order for an utterance to count as an apology, therefore, it must contain an admission or acknowledgment of wrongdoing.

On the other hand, the expression of regret, the "I'm sorry" part of the apology, may be optional. The reason the expression of regret may be optional is that it communicates a *feeling* on the part of the apologizer, and there is nothing in our conception of justice which requires us to have particular feelings towards one another. While we might follow John Stuart Mill in thinking that the moral rules of justice "are the main element in determining the whole of the social feelings of mankind",[16] this is far from thinking that *the rules of justice themselves* require that particular feelings be held. So, while it may very well be that morality calls for feeling some regret when we have committed a wrong, there is no ground for this requirement in justice. This view is consistent with the sentiment expressed in Kant's universal law of justice, *viz.*: "act externally in such a way that the free use of your will is compatible with the freedom of everyone according to a universal law."[17] On Kant's view:

> anyone can still be free, even though I am quite indifferent to his freedom or even though I might in my heart wish to infringe on his freedom [that is, I might desire to do him an injustice], as long as I do not through an external action violate his freedom.[18]

Hence, "justice in general has as its object only what is external in actions."[19] Without any requirement in justice that a wrongdoer actually regret having committed an injustice, it hardly makes sense to think that justice could require a wrongdoer to express such a feeling as part of an apology. If we held that justice requires an expression of regret, and if the wrongdoer is absent this feeling, then we would end up holding the view that justice requires the wrongdoer to lie. Surely this is not the kind of result we want. So if justice cannot require an expression of regret, all justice can require in the way of an apology is an acknowledgment of wrongdoing. It is this acknowledgment of wrongdoing, then, which addresses the wrong of the injustice.

What is *wrong* with acting unjustly is that it is disrespectful.[20] Every individual is deserving of respect. Insofar as justice is concerned, the way we show our respect for others is by honoring their rights. Hence, anytime I act in violation of someone's rights (especially when I act in wanton disregard for those rights) and thus wrong that person, I am failing to show that person the proper respect. Acknowledging that what I have done is wrong entails an acknowledgment that the person affected by my act was undeserving of the treatment given. By apologizing I reaffirm that, like myself, the victim is a person, and so has moral standing. It is in this way that an apology addresses the wrong of an injustice. Since all injustices are wrong for the same reason, they all involve some degree of disrespect, and so all require an apology in order to be rectified. Moreover, since the requirement of an apology is grounded in the unjust act itself, an apology is due whether or not the victim has sustained any unjust loss.

Alternatively, we might follow Joel Feinberg in thinking that compensation can take the place of an apology. However, this view demands too little of the wrongdoer. Insofar as Feinberg thinks that reparation "sets things straight", his view of reparation is similar to the conception of rectification expressed here. In part, Feinberg thinks of reparation as "compensation for harm wrongly inflicted by others". However, he holds that reparation, that is, compensation for harms wrongly inflicted, functions not only to repair damage but also to "restore the moral equilibrium *as would an apology or expression of remorse*."[21] Hence, for Feinberg, part of what it means for a wrongdoer to have rendered compensation is that the wrongdoer has apologized for the wrong done. Hence, while Feinberg recognizes that compensation ought to be rendered for wrongful losses, and that wrongs ought to be acknowledged, he thinks that this acknowledgment can be accomplished by way of compensation alone.

On Feinberg's view, reparation (compensation) is analogous to reward. On the one hand, reward "is the tangible expression of one or more of a small range of such appropriate attitudes as gratitude, recognition, or approval". Likewise:

> Reparation can express sympathy, benevolence, and concern, but, in addition, *it is always the acknowledgment of a past wrong,* a "repayment of a debt", and hence, *like an apology,* the redressing of the moral balance or the restoring of the *status quo ante culpum*. In the case of mere compensation, it is none of these extra things. In either case,

however, *the proffered help implies the recognition of a loss for which the victim himself cannot be held wholly to blame*.[22]

On the other hand, while Feinberg's view may offer a more parsimonious approach to rectification, insofar as it eliminates the need for an actual acknowledgment of wrongdoing, nevertheless, it demands too little from the wrongdoer. Feinberg thinks that the reason reparation is always the acknowledgment of a past wrong, a "repayment of a debt", is because "the wrongdoer deserves to be held liable for the harm he has caused; he deserves to be forced to compensate his innocent (or relatively innocent) victim."[23] But what happens in those cases where someone has been wronged, and there is no resultant loss?

Suppose that X has agreed to give Y a ride home from work one day and promises to pick Y up at exactly 5 p.m. If X decides instead to leave work early, say to beat the rush hour traffic, and Y, after having waited for more than half an hour for X, is forced to take a cab home, we would have good reason to say that X has acted unjustly towards Y, and that Y is deserving of Feinberg's reparation. On this view, X "sets things straight" as soon as X repays Y for the cab fare, and perhaps some additional funds for the inconvenience caused, and for any other legitimate intangible losses suffered by Y. By giving Feinberg's reparation, X has both compensated for the wrongly inflicted loss, and, in effect, apologized for that wrong as well.

But suppose instead that at 5 p.m. Y discovers by way of a friend that X will not be arriving as promised. And suppose further that this friend gives Y a ride home just as X would have. In this case we would be hard pressed to identify any wrongful loss suffered by Y. Nevertheless, Y has been wronged by X: X (for no good reason) broke a promise to Y. X therefore owes Y an apology for breaking the promise. However, since Feinberg does not think that any reparation is due in this case, there is no sense in which an apology is due. But without an apology, the wrong of the injustice remains unaddressed. So at least in cases where wrongs fail to result in a loss to the victim, Feinberg's conception leaves the victim and perpetrator far from a situation in which justice obtains between the two parties. This suggests that rather than an "all in one" conception where compensating for wrongs implies an apology, what is required by justice is an actual acknowledgment of wrongdoing by the perpetrator. Hence, one must compensate *and* apologize for any wrongful losses one inflicts.

Gerald Gaus makes this same point, when he holds that "[n]o redistribution of *resources* can by itself restore moral parity between victim and aggressor". According to Gaus, "[a]lthough aggressors can repay victims for the harm done, transfer of resources cannot right a wrong."[24] This is because "the aggressor not only causes the victim a loss of *value*" by way of the injustice done, but "in addition, he has acted in a way that is *unjustifiable* and so shows a lack of respect". Gaus recognizes that "one has a residue complaint even when one has not been harmed, or even when the harm has been undone."[25] When one has been treated unjustly, regardless of any loss which may have been sustained as a result, and regardless of any compensation which may have been rendered, one still has legitimate grounds for feeling moral indignation in response to the unjust treatment. As J. R. Lucas notes:

> We are angry when we are hurt, but indignant when we are treated unjustly. . . . Indignation, which is the conceptually appropriate response to injustice, expresses, as its etymology shows, a sense of not being regarded as worthy of consideration. *Injustice betokens a lack of respect,* and manifests a lack of concern.[26]

Since Feinberg's account of reparation fails to address this lack of respect, the wrong of the injustice remains unaddressed, and the injustice unrectified. Feinberg's view, therefore, demands too little of the wrongdoer. Justice demands not only that we be given compensation for those losses which result from our having been wronged, but also that the wrongdoer apologize for that wrong.

It is important to understand that this is not a denial of the rather obvious relationship between apology and compensation in which the latter legitimizes the former. In cases where compensation is required but not given, any apology made in such a case would be vacuous, and hence morally illegitimate. At best, my actions are inconsistent with the spirit of an apology if I am acknowledging my wrongdoing and your moral worth on the one hand, while denying you an equivalent in value for the losses sustained to your interests as a result of my wrongdoing on the other. Hence, in order for any apology to count in cases where compensation is required, it must in fact be rendered. By similar reasoning, when a case is such that compensation is not possible, then it seems fair to say that this condition can be met by a reasonable attempt at achieving compensation. Generally speaking, then, the acknowledgment of wrongdoing by the wrongdoer must be conjoined with compensation for wrongful losses (where appropriate) in order for the apology to count.

In contrast to Feinberg's account, which asks too little of the wrongdoer, it is possible that we may ask more than justice requires. Richard Swinburne's focus is not on justice, but rather on removing the guilt of the wrongdoer. When an injustice has been done intentionally, Swinburne thinks there are two consequences: (1) "the harm caused by and distinguishable from the act of causing it"; and (2) "the purposive attitude of the wrongdoer towards the victim manifested in the causing of the harm". Regarding the first consequence, Swinburne rightly distinguishes the harm caused by an injustice from the unjust act itself. But while Swinburne requires that this harm be addressed,[27] he says nothing about addressing the unjust act itself. As for the second consequence, addressing it is not something which is required by justice. According to Swinburne:

> the wrongdoer has by doing the act made himself someone who has harmed the victim. He cannot change that past fact, but he can distance himself from it by privately and publicly disowning the act. The victim has been hurt, and so it is to the victim that the disowning is owed and must be shown. But the disowning which is owed

> must be sincere and so must reflect the attitude which the wrongdoer now has, and naturally expresses to himself. The natural expression to oneself is *repentance*, the public expression to the victim is *apology*.[28]

So for Swinburne, the wrongdoer must disown the act in such a way that it reflects a change in the wrongdoer's "purposive attitude" towards the victim that is a consequence of the wrongdoing. When one expresses this to oneself one repents, when one expresses it publicly to one's victim, one apologizes.

Swinburne thinks that to repent in this case involves two things: (1) "acknowledgment by the wrongdoer that he did the act and that it was a wrong act to do"; and (2) "a resolve to amend—you cannot repent of a past act if you intend to do a similar act at the next available opportunity".[29] But while justice can and does require an acknowledgment of wrongdoing by the perpetrator, since the scope of its authority does not extend to setting requirements for individual feelings, it cannot require that individuals make resolutions to change their behavior. All that justice can do is set requirements for the limits of one's actual behavior. Hence, justice cannot require that the perpetrator resolve to amend the unjust behavior. Since repentance is the private expression of that which one expresses publicly to the victim in an apology, on Swinburne's view, an apology also requires the resolution to amend one's behavior. So while resolving to amend one's behavior may be of significant moral import, it is not a requirement of justice. In other words, while justice can and does require the wrongdoer to acknowledge the wrongness of the unjust act as a means of apologizing to the victim, it cannot require that the wrongdoer express an intent to "mend his ways".

With the additional requirement of an apology, our conception of rectification thus far includes: (1) the requirement that restoration be affected whenever possible (2) the Package Conception of Compensation (PCC), and (3) the requirement that wrongdoers acknowledge when they have acted unjustly as a means of apologizing to the victim of the injustice, with compensation being a necessary condition for affecting the apology whenever there is a need to address wrongful losses.

The Idea of Full Rectification

The requirement of an apology suggests a limitation on rectification, *viz.*, the idea of "full rectification". Full rectification has been accomplished when there is no remainder following its implementation. In other words, neither the wrong, nor any wrongful loss resulting from that wrong, is left unaccounted for. Since the most obvious criterion for having achieved full rectification is that our attempt at compensation be successful, once this is done the only chance for a remainder lies in somehow having failed to adequately address the wrong of the injustice. Since an apology by the wrongdoer is the mechanism by which the wrong is addressed, any constraint on our conception of rectification will be found by reexamining the matter of an apology.

Rendering an apology and rendering compensation are very much alike when it comes to the matter of acceptance. When a wrongdoer presents a victim with compensation for an unjust loss, and the victim accepts this package of goods, the process of compensation is complete. That is, the process of rendering an equivalent in value for the value lost as a result of the injustice is complete. By the same reasoning, then, if the wrongdoer presents the victim with an apology, and the victim, under circumstances in which it would be reasonable to accept the apology, has not accepted that apology, the process of rectification remains incomplete: in other words, full rectification has not been achieved.

In the case of apologies accepted for unintentional wrongdoings, the acceptance itself implies forgiveness of the wrongdoer. Suppose I release the brake on my car while we are both waiting at a red traffic light, and I bump your car from behind. By anticipating the green light, I have unintentionally wronged you. If I am very apologetic, saying to you that "I am so sorry I hit you" as I approach your car, then it seems almost certain that when you accept my apology you are forgiving me for the offense. When we part company the matter is closed, there is a sense of finality to the entire matter of the injustice. By forgiving, the victim pronounces the wrongdoer free from moral culpability; without forgiveness there seems to be a moral remainder. If this is correct, then forgiveness is a necessary condition for achieving full rectification.

The problem with positing the acceptance of an apology and forgiving the wrongdoer as a necessary condition for achieving full rectification is that justice cannot require it. Justice cannot require a victim to either accept an apology, or forgive the wrongdoer. Outside of perhaps requiring that the victim be reasonable in deciding the acceptability of a given compensation package from the wrongdoer, the requirements of justice in cases of wrongdoing seem to rest squarely with the wrongdoer and with *what the wrongdoer must do to make things right*. And this is as it should be, for "[h]ow can my hurting you and then trying to undo the harm, actions all of my choice and not yours, put you under an obligation to do something, which did not exist before?"[30] Surely there is no way that it can. Hence, somewhat paradoxically, we end up saying that justice cannot require full rectification.[31]

Rectification and Punishment

One obvious objection to this account of rectification thus far is that nothing has been said about the matter of punishing wrongdoers. How, an objector might ask, can we think that a conception of rectification, that is, a conception which has at its core the matter of righting wrongs, has been sufficiently sketched, when the idea of punishing wrongdoers has not been addressed? And of course, the objector would be quite right—something must be said about punishment and the role it plays in the righting of wrongs, since, if nothing else, it is an important part of our intuitions about what justice may require.

Insofar as our intuitions about punishment are concerned, John Stuart Mill's idea regarding the necessity of punishment vis-a-vis wrongful acts is useful in helping us to see why we might think that there is a necessary connection between punishment and wrongdoing. According to Mill:

> We do not call anything wrong, unless we mean to imply that a person ought to be punished in some way or other for doing it; if not by law, by the opinion of his fellow creatures; if not by opinion, by the reproaches of his own conscience.[32]

Hence for Mill, there are three ways in which it may be appropriate for individuals to be punished for wrongdoing. In order of severity, they are: (1), punishment by way of the reproaches of one's own conscience; (2), punishment by way of public opinion; and (3), punishment by way of some prescription of law. Mill's idea is consistent with our intuitions about moral wrongness because when we think of having done something morally wrong, we think that one or more of these kinds of punishment ought to apply. In any case of wrongdoing it ought to be the reproach by our consciences, our sense of moral wrongdoing or guilt, which alerts us to the fact that something we have done was (or at least may have been) morally wrong. Put another way, when we suppose that one has a strong sense of right and wrong, then necessarily one will feel this reproach by one's conscience any time one has committed an unjust act. Hence, at least with regard to this weakest sense of punishment, punishment is a necessary consequence of wrongdoing, and so no act can be legitimately characterized as being wrong unless it is the case that the individual who has committed the act ought to be punished (in some way or other) for having done it.

However, while we might include Mill's weakest sense of punishment as part of our conception of morality, it is not part of our conception of justice. Since this sense of punishment is self-inflicted, and, more importantly, since it is something we think individuals ought to *feel* after having acted wrongly, for reasons already discussed, justice cannot require that wrongdoers be punished in this way. In contrast, since the two stronger senses of punishment are not feelings but actions, they are more likely to be appropriate candidates for the kind of punishment required by justice.

Hugo Bedau, for example, thinks that punishment "involves intentionally inflicting deprivations on persons by someone with authority to do so".[33] Hence, punishment is not something that is self-inflicted, rather, it is something that someone in authority does *to* a wrongdoer. Further, that which is being done is done deliberately. Authors such as W.D. Lamont make both the connection to the law, and the outcomes that ought to be associated with the punishment of wrongdoers, more explicit. For Lamont, punishment, "which is (usually) ordered by the decree of a criminal court, is the infliction of pain or suffering upon the person who has infringed a right."[34] But as Bedau notes, since we are inflicting deprivations on someone, and since these deprivations

> themselves are typically not unlike the harms that crimes cause (fines are like theft, imprisonment like kidnaping, etc.), punishment has generally been thought to need

justification, especially in a constitutional democracy committed in theory to the protection of human rights and the values of individual liberty, privacy and autonomy.[35]

Bedau suggests two ways in which punishment may be justified: "either by reference to extrinsic (consequentialist) considerations, or by reference to intrinsic (retributive) factors"; and points out that "[p]hilosophical disputes over punishment typically focus on which goal is to take priority over others and why."[36] I will discuss each of these justifications in turn, however, my aim here is not to enter into this dispute over the justification of punishment. Rather, my claim is simply this: *if* punishment is a legitimate part of a moral conception of justice for liberal democracies, then either or both of these standard approaches to its justification can fit into our conception of justice.

Randy E. Barnett describes the consequentialist justification for punishment as a "political" justification,[37] that is, a justification which has as its end the maintaining of a properly ordered society. Barnett lists three ends which may be at the heart of this political justification: (1) disablement, that is, to keep wrongdoers off the street, and thereby disable them from committing wrongs against other members of society (no doubt for some specified period of time); (2) rehabilitation;[38] and (3) deterrence, that is, to deter individuals from becoming wrongdoers by way of the threat of punishment, and so thereby prevent (to some extent) wrongdoings from taking place.

On the other hand, according to Michael Moore, the retributive justification:

> is a very straightforward theory of punishment: We are justified in punishing because and only because offenders deserve it. Moral culpability ("desert") is in such a view both a sufficient as well as a necessary condition of liability to punitive sanctions.[39]

Although for some the retributive view of punishment may lack the intuitive appeal of the consequentialist justification, certainly for others, "[n]o rule on the subject recommends itself so strongly to the primitive and spontaneous sentiment of justice, as the *lex talionis,* an eye for an eye and a tooth for a tooth."[40]

Of course, much has been said about punishment. Everything from straightforward arguments for the justification of punishment on either consequentialist or retributive grounds, to attempts at reconciling both justifications into a single theory of punishment. Still other discussions of punishment advance claims which tie punishment, in particular retributive punishment, to concepts like reparation and compensation. However, my claim, since it does not involve justification for a particular form of punishment, is much more modest. I seek only to account for either or both forms of punishment in my conception of justice. Specifically, my claim is this: If consequentialist punishment is justifiable, then it is a part of distributive justice; if retributive punishment is justifiable, then it is a part of rectificatory justice.

Two important distinctions are required here. The first of these distinctions has already been draw, *viz.,* the distinction between distributive justice and rectificatory justice. These two species of justice represent justice in its entirety. Whatever the requirements of justice are, they can be legitimately assigned to one or the other of these two species. The aim of distributive justice is to distribute rights and duties amongst the members of society in accordance with its prescribed principles. Ideally this distribution of rights and duties will be maintained, and hence, society will be well ordered. When circumstances become less than ideal, when the system of rights and duties prescribed by distributive justice breaks down, then it is the aim of rectificatory justice to set right any unjust states of affairs by requiring an apology from the wrongdoer as a means of addressing the wrongfulness of the unjust act itself, and restoration and/or compensation as a means of addressing any wrongful loss that may have resulted from the injustice.

The second distinction is made within our conception of rectificatory justice itself. Thus far in our discussion of rectification we have focused mainly on the victim; we have been primarily concerned with what the victim deserves once an injustice has occurred. However, since we are adding retributive punishment to our discussion of justice, we must also consider what the wrongdoer deserves once an injustice has occurred. The distinction is between *victim-centered rectification* on the one hand, and *wrongdoer-centered rectification* on the other hand. While both senses of rectification have to do with what one deserves following an injustice, distinguishing between what the victim deserves and what the wrongdoer deserves allows us to account for retributive punishment in our conception of rectification.

Victim-centered rectification, then, concerns what ought to be done *for* the benefit of the victim of an injustice as means towards rectifying the injustice. Restoration and/or compensation clearly benefit the victim, they are rendered by the wrongdoer as a means of remedying the wrongful loss of value which the victim has incurred. Likewise, the apology given by the wrongdoer is meant to benefit the victim. The apology is a means of remedying the wrong done to the victim when the wrongdoer failed to respect the victim's legitimate interests.

Further, when we consider this notion of victim-centeredness along with Mill's idea of punishment by the opinion of one's "fellow creatures", an idea arises which suggests an aspect of rectification which ought to be brought to light. Suppose that Mill is correct, and wrongdoers in certain cases ought to be punished by way of public opinion, that is, they ought to be condemned for their actions, perhaps both verbally and in writing. This kind of action on the part of the general public is clearly directed against the wrongdoer—it is something that the wrongdoer deserves as a result of some wrongful act. As John Locke points out: "it is easy to be imagined that he who was so unjust as to do his brother an injury will scarce be so just as to condemn himself for it".[41] But if condemnation by the public can be justified by way of a wrongful act, and hence constitutes something of which the wrongdoer is deserving, it certainly makes sense to think that demands for justice by the public can also be justified by way of a wrongful act, but in this case constitutes something of which the victim is deserving. In other words, if wrongdoers ought to be condemned by the public for their wrongful acts, then, analogously, wrongdoers ought to be subjected to demands for justice by the public when the wrongdoer is less than forthcoming in taking the necessary steps towards rectifying the injustice. Hence, we may have the makings of a ground upon which to base a duty on the part of those individuals who are aware of an injustice having taken place, to exert pressure upon recalcitrant wrongdoers as a means of prompting them to take the necessary steps towards rectification. Hence, the ascription of this duty to individuals who are knowledgeable of wrongdoings, may represent an aspect of rectification that is worth further investigation.[42]

Returning to our distinction, given the notion of wrongdoer-centered rectification, we can now account for retribution. If retributive punishment is justified, it can be accounted for in our conception of rectification, and hence in our conception of justice. One might immediately object to such a conception, however, by pointing out that: (1) we have no reason to think that retribution ought to be a part of our conception of rectification, and (2) retribution itself is sometimes thought of as a species of justice—this explains our reference to "retributive justice" when the topic of retributive punishment arises.

Taking the second objection first, we need only consider that positing another kind of justice unnecessarily complicates our conception of justice. Take compensation for example. We have no good reason for positing "compensatory justice" as a species of justice. As I hope has already been made clear, compensation is merely an important and necessary part of the more robust idea of rectification. When an injustice has occurred, we cannot reasonably assert that, once the aim of compensation has been achieved that "justice has been done". Clearly there remains the matter of righting the wrong. Given this obvious remainder, were we to posit "compensatory justice" as itself a species of justice, then we would be forced to either find a way to include the missing components, or posit something like "restorative justice" and "apologetic justice" as a means of accounting for them. Hence, it can only serve as a source of confusion to posit "compensatory justice" as a species of justice when the concept is insufficiently robust to warrant such a characterization.

Moreover, the notion of compensation plays a dual role in our conception of justice. Compensation is what we have in mind in cases of natural disaster when we think that individuals ought to be aided in their recovery from things like damage to their homes. This is compensation in the distributive sense. We also have compensation in mind in cases of wrongful loss when we think that individuals ought to be aided in their recovery from things like having their property stolen. This is compensation in the rectificatory sense. To account for both senses of compensation, we would have to consider "compensatory justice" as some kind of overarching concept under which matters of both distribution and rectification can be subsumed. Hence, positing "compensatory justice" as itself a species of justice serves as a source of confusion.

A similar argument can be advanced against the idea that we ought to posit "retributive justice" as a species of justice. If it is indeed justifiable, then retribution, like compensation, is an important and, perhaps necessary, part of rectification. Any injustice of sufficient severity would give rise to the need for punishing the wrongdoer. In such cases the wrongdoer deserves to be punished. Since the matter is one of what ought to be done in response to an injustice, the matter falls within the concerns of rectificatory justice. When an injustice has been done, we cannot reasonably assert that, once retribution has been exacted that "justice has been done", there remains, at the very least, the matter of compensating the victim for any wrongful losses which may have been incurred. So, just as in the case of compensation, given this obvious remainder, were we to posit "retributive justice" as itself a species of justice, we would have to provide a theory of "compensatory justice" as a means of accounting for this remainder, in addition to something like a theory of "apologetic justice" as a means of accounting for the remainder from mere compensation. So, like the case of "compensatory justice", positing "retributive justice" as itself a species of justice would also serve as a source of confusion. Moreover, this gives us reason to think it appropriate to hold that retributive punishment should be a part of our conception of rectification (the first objection).

So, like compensation, the notion of punishment may play a dual role in our conception of justice. If retributive punishment is justified, then it is a part of rectificatory justice. If consequentialist punishment is justified, then it is a part of distributive justice. This latter characterization might be objected to on the grounds that consequentialist punishment can take several forms, hence, it is not at all clear that each of these forms is rightly thought of as punishment in the distributive sense. A brief analysis of these various forms should put this objection to rest.

We noted earlier that, according to Randy E. Barnett, consequentialist justifications for punishment include: (1) disablement, that is, keeping wrongdoers off the street, thereby disabling them from committing wrongs against other members of society (no doubt for some specified period of time); (2) rehabilitation; and (3) deterrence, that is, to deter individuals from becoming wrongdoers by way of the threat of punishment, and thereby prevent (to some extent) wrongdoings from ever taking place. Even at first blush (1) and (3) can be seen as parts of distributive justice.

Disablement and deterrence are both pre-emptive. Both aim at maintaining the distribution of rights and duties established by of distributive justice, either by physically restraining individuals from committing wrongs, or by giving potential wrongdoers strong incentives not to commit wrongful acts. Since both disablement and deterrence pre-empt (at least some) injustices from occurring, they are both properly construed as concerns of distributive justice. By "maintaining the distribution" I mean of course "maintenance" in the sense of preventive maintenance, not reparatory maintenance. Were it the latter, we would probably be talking about a rectificatory sense of punishment. It is in this reparative sense of maintenance that some might construe rehabilitation. However, this idea is mistaken.

First, the idea that we ought to associate rehabilitation with a reparative sense of maintenance is mistaken because punishment in such cases is being justified on consequentialist grounds. In other words, whatever reasons we have for punishing in this way are grounded in some end result or consequence which we hold to be just. Of course the earlier objection to this characterization might now be renewed with added force. One might point out that, while this premise of a consequentialist grounding seems to make sense, and may be convincing to some, we have ignored the etymology of the term. The prefix 're', in words like 'rectification' and 'retribution', implies that something is taking place after the fact. Rehabilitation is restorative: it helps to restore an individual who is defective in some way. Hence, rehabilitation is reparative, and backward-looking. It would be a mistake, therefore, to characterize it as part of our (mostly) forward-looking conception of distributive justice. Although this view has some merit, it unfortunately misses the point. While the points regarding the etymology and restorative character of rehabilitation are well taken, the *justification* for employing rehabilitation is consequentialist. This is analogous to the case of compensation in the distributive sense. When some individual has suffered a loss due to a natural disaster, we of course must take a backward-looking perspective in order to ascertain precisely how the damage was caused. Further, compensation, like rehabilitation, is also restorative: we are attempting to provide the individual with an equivalent in value to the loss suffered. However, the means by which we justify compensation in such cases is forward-looking. We might, for example, ground such a justification in a principle of justice which holds that all individuals in society be given equality of opportunity. Hence, like rehabilitation, compensation in this sense is distributive in its aim; and it is so because in cases where it is appropriate, we justify its employment on distributive grounds.

A second, and perhaps more compelling reason for rejecting the idea that we ought to associate rehabilitation with a reparative sense of maintenance is the fact that rehabilitation is a benefit to the person being rehabilitated, and to society as well. Rehabilitation helps to restore an individual who is defective in some way, and so aids the individual. This aid to the individual is also a benefit to the society in which that individual lives, since it helps to ensure that the individual will act reasonably, and so act in accordance with the principles prescribed by a just system of distribution. This makes sense because the granting of individual benefits, like in the case of compensation for losses incurred as a result of natural disaster, is a function of distributive justice. Moreover, just as is the case with disablement and deterrence, the benefit to society is preemptive. Surely once a just system of distribution has broken down, and an injustice has occurred, we are not looking to benefit the wrongdoer for having committed the unjust act as a means to rectifying the unjust state of affairs which the wrongdoer has caused. The claim that rehabilitation maintains the distribution of rights and duties established by the principles of distributive justice, means that it does so in the sense that it is preventative, that it pre-empts wrongdoing by helping to ensure that individuals will act in accordance with those principles in the future.

Since all three forms of consequentialist punishment can rightly be construed as forms of punishment in the distributive sense, we can now see how the conception of justice I have been advancing can account for punishment on consequentialist grounds, on retributive grounds, or both.

A Taxonomy of Justice

The taxonomy of justice which emerges from the foregoing discussion is illustrated below. It consists of the two species of justice, and includes those concepts required by rectificatory justice (or, in the case of punishment, *may* be required). Of course, this is just a beginning. Since only the most homogeneous of liberal democracies could even hope to avoid accounting for the rights of social groups,[43] and hence for a group right to rectification, further advancement toward a full theory of rectificatory justice must account for group rectification *(inter alia)*. However, since any account of group rectification I might offer is to proceed from the general moral theory of justice I have begun here,[44] and will require, at the very least, the incorporation of a conception of social groups and an account of group rights, I shall leave this task for another occasion.[45]

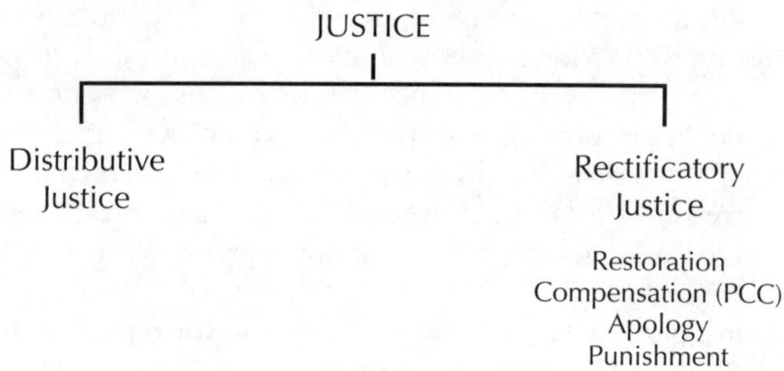

PART TWO

INJUSTICE

CHAPTER 2

Anthony D. Woozley

INJUSTICE

Although philosophers and non-philosophers alike have written much about justice, they have not always observed the distinction between questions of analysis and questions of criteria, i.e., the distinction between what justice is and how to determine instances or non-instances of it. Thus, claims to characterize justice (a) in terms of fairness, and (b) in terms of equality are not merely different claims but claims of different kinds. That a given distribution is unequal among the recipients may be, and, depending on the context, is a good reason for saying that it is unfair, but it is not identical with its being unfair. We can ask whether a distribution is fair, and whether it is equal. But when we go on to ask why it is fair and why it is equal, we are asking questions that are very different from each other: in the first case we are seeking a justification of the claim that the distribution is fair; in the second case we are accepting that the distribution is equal, and seeking a justification of it being so. In short, even if it were true that the only way to treat men fairly is to treat them equally, treating them fairly, although it would consist in treating them equally, would not be conceptually identical with treating them equally. The core meaning of "fair" is a moral meaning, the core meaning of "equal" is not. "It is unfair to treat men unequally" is a significant assertion, and a moral assertion. "It is unequal to treat men unfairly" is not a moral assertion, and would need some torturing even to make into a significant assertion. And the proposition that all men are created equal is so conspicuously false if regarded as a factual proposition that it has to be interpreted as a moral proposition *about* equality if it is to have the ghost of a chance of being true, let alone be the self-evident truth that Thomas Jefferson proclaimed it to be.

Again philosophers have had comparatively little to say about injustice—which is surely the more interesting of the two. Here, perhaps, we have a case of what J. L. Austin used to call "trouser words," with "injustice" wearing the trousers. Justice is

This essay originally appeared in *American Philosophical Quarterly Monograph Series,* Monograph No. 7, Nicholas Rescher, ed., Oxford: Blackwell, 1973, pp. 109–122. Reprinted by permission of *American Philosophical Quarterly.*

the least and the most anaemic of the virtues, about which it is difficult to get excited except where it is refused or threatened. We, are liable to think of "unjust" as the contradictory of "just." Here we are wrong, for it is a contrary, but, as it is the only morally interesting contrary, the error is understandable and has no serious consequences: it is not the absence of justice that we get excited about, but the absence of justice where it should be present. Failure to be just, not merely not being just, is what matters, and failure to be just is injustice.

We might start by saying that injustice is unfair discrimination between persons or classes of persons in the distribution of advantages or disadvantages, and that discrimination is unfair if and only if it is based on factors which are not relevant to the distribution. (This will soon need some qualifying.) The injustice of second-class citizenship consists in discriminating between whites and blacks, Aryans and Jews, in general *A*'s and *B*'s, where the dissimilarities between the *A*'s and the *B*'s, although they may be many, obvious, and considerable, are not relevant to the rights and capacities of citizenship; and it is not merely that there is nothing about white pigmentation or black pigmentation which is relevant, but that there is nothing about being a white or being a black which is relevant.

To justify something, such as a practice or an institution, is to show that it is right, or at least that it is reasonable to suppose it to be right; and one way of being right is to be just. But it is not the only way, for the just is a species of the right. It is further in my view possible (although many would dispute this) for a practice to be right, even [though] it is unjust. Treating people unjustly can sometimes be right and be shown to be right, to be justified in terms of social utility. Because "justify" has come to bear this wider meaning, of showing to be right (or, from another aspect, making right), we need another word with the more limited scope of showing to be just, or making just; perhaps "justicise" would do.

This first step of analyzing injustice as unfair discrimination, and unfair discrimination as discrimination based on factors not relevant to the distribution of the advantages or disadvantages involved, is only a first step.

Next, can we either list or give any general characterization of the factors which are relevant to questions of discrimination? Clearly they are factors about the patients in the case, those being treated unjustly, not factors about either the agents in the case or others who may be affected. If General Electric is treating its employees in Waynesboro, Virginia unjustly by paying them lower rates than it pays its employees in Schenectady, New York for doing exactly the same work, the injustice derives from facts about those employees, e.g., that neither the needs nor the merits of those in Virginia are different from those in New York; it does not derive at all from facts about the agent, e.g., that General Electric does not have to keep its wage rates as low as job demand permits in order to stay competitive with rival manufacturers; and it does not derive at all from facts about others affected, such as the selling trade or the consumer. It may be unjust to the latter that G.E. lower cost products from Virginia are sold at the same price as the identical, but higher cost products from New York; but, even if it is, then not reflecting lower costs of production in a lower selling price is no part of the injustice to the employees at the Waynesboro plant. This is the important distinction between "justify" and "justice" coming in again. If G.E. can be charged with unjust discrimination against its Waynesboro employees, it is not the beginning of a rebuttal for the company to say that it must keep wage rates down to the lowest level that local conditions will permit—although that might be the beginning of a rebuttal of the charge that discrimination against Waynesboro employees is not justified. Again, maintaining a uniform selling price to the trade may or may not result in unjust treatment of the consumer, and it may or may not be justified. But whether or not it is unjust to the consumer, and whether or not it is justified, has nothing whatever to do with the question whether paying a lower wage rate to employees in Virginia than to those in New York is or is not unjust to the former.

As a beginning of a list of relevant factors, I have mentioned merits and needs. I am sure they are both relevant, but I am not sure that they are alike in the way that they are relevant. If a number of men have equal needs, if you are in some way such as that of an employer or a welfare agency responsible for meeting those needs, if you have sufficient resources available to meet them, and if you then give some men more than they need and (whether consequentially or not) others less than they need, you are treating the latter unjustly. In that situation you have a double duty and they have a double right: you have the duty to respond to their needs and the duty not to discriminate in meeting their needs; and they have the two correlative rights. In the case where you do not have the first duty you may still have the second. Even if you do not have the duty to respond to their needs, then, if you do respond to their equal needs but do not respond equally, you are being unjust. Having a duty not to discriminate in responding to equal needs does not imply having first a duty to respond to the needs. A father does not have the duty to meet the needs of his neighbor's children which he has to meet the needs of his own; but if he does respond to the former, discrimination, if it leaves the needs of some but not others inadequately met, is unjust. But the principle of treating like cases alike, if it is not to be vacuous, needs careful handling. If the needs of the recipients are equal, failure to meet them equally is unjust. That is to say, a pattern of distribution which gave some more than they needed, but others less than they needed, would be unjust: the latter could justifiably complain that they had been treated unfairly. It is less obviously true that a pattern of distribution which gave some more than they needed, but none less than they needed, would be unjust. No doubt the latter would often protest that they had been treated unfairly, but it is not clear that they would be right; and, indeed, I do not think they would be. We thus have to distinguish between a weak version and a strong version of the principle of treating like cases alike.

Weak version. It is fair (not unfair) to treat like cases alike. This version does not entail that it is unfair to treat like cases unalike. Fairness permits the treating of like cases alike.

Strong version. It is fair (only fair) to treat like cases alike. This does entail that it is unfair to treat like cases unalike. Fairness demands the treating of like cases alike. The weak version clearly is true, i.e., it is never the case that it would be unfair to treat like cases alike. "Like" has to be understood as "relevantly alike": *A*'s being like *B* in any old respect at all, regardless of the nature of the distribution, will not do. And equally clearly the weak version does not entail that it is unfair to treat like cases unalike. From the proposition that it is not unfair to treat like cases alike, nothing whatever follows about the unfairness (or fairness) of treating like cases unalike.

The strong version on the other hand, that it is only fair to treat like cases alike, clearly does have the entailment which the weak version does not: if it is only fair to treat like cases alike, then it is unfair not to, which is to say that it is unfair to treat like cases unalike. And it is the strong version of the "treat like cases alike" slogan which we are inclined to hold (of course it carries the weak version with it) and which we appeal to in what we think to be cases of injustice, viz., the injustice of treating like cases unalike. But, unless it is modified, the strong version is false: it is *not* always the case that it would be only fair to treat like cases alike—or that it would be unfair not to. If *A*'s and *B*'s needs are equal, then while it would be unfair totally to disregard that fact in making your distribution to them, it would not be unfair, having given equally to each what will satisfy his needs, then to give the whole of the surplus to *A*. *B* might protest that it was unfair that *A* got more than he himself did—many beneficiaries under a will have so protested—but he would be wrong, unless there was some further respect, other than need, in which *B* (possibly *A* also) had a claim on your distribution. If a father in the bequests which he makes to his two sons *A* and *B* has fairly met their needs, he does no injustice to *B* if he leaves the whole of the rest of the estate to *A*—unless there is some further respect, other than need, in which the distinction between like cases is unjust.

What this brings out is that the strong version is more complicated than the weak version. A modified strong version would be true, viz., that, if *A*'s and *B*'s needs are equal, it is only fair not to treat them as if they were unequal before reaching the point of meeting their needs. But the unmodified strong version summarized in the ambiguous slogan "treat like cases alike" is not true.

From Aristotle on it has seemed natural to think of injustice within the context of distribution of advantages or disadvantages (e.g., on the one hand emoluments, tax reliefs, exemptions; and on the other fines, taxes, military conscription), and of discrimination in the distribution which was not based solely on relevant factors about those who came out well or badly from the discrimination. This makes us think of injustice as something between the treatment of one individual and that of another, between the treatment of some individuals and that of others, between the treatment of one class and that of other classes, etc. The basic cry of injustice thus seems to be the child's "He has got more than I have" or "He has got one and I have not" or, on the other side of the account, "I was punished and he was not." It looks as if the only question we have is that of determining what are the justicising factors, of only one of which I have so far talked, viz., need. That is one question, but not, I think, the only one. There is also the question whether it is correct at all to define justice and injustice in terms of distribution and discrimination. I doubt whether it is; I do not doubt that the most conspicuous cases of injustice are those involving discrimination, but I am inclined to think that there is something more fundamental, that it is not so much the discrimination itself that is offensive as what is involved in the discrimination.

I find the second question more interesting than the first, the question of justicising factors, but I think the second can usefully be approached through the first. I am not going to attempt to make a complete list of justicising factors, but shall mention some that are commonly propounded and that have been held to be in one way or another relevant to the question whether discrimination is essential to injustice. The three sources that I have had primarily in mind are: Henry Sidgwick, *The Methods of Ethics* (6th Edition, 1901), Book III, Chapter V; A. M. Honore, "Social Justice," *McGill Law Journal,* vol. 78 (1962) revised and reprinted in Robert S. Summers (ed.) *Essays in Legal Philosophy* (1968); and Nicholas Rescher, *Distributive Justice* (1966), Chapter 4. Not surprisingly, there is a high degree of agreement between these sources (and others, too, which could be added) about the justicising factors. I give what is substantially, although not precisely, Honore's list (not in his order):

1. Need
2. Desert—Achievement
3. Desert—Ability
4. Transaction
5. Special Relation
6. Conformity to Rule

In every case the person to be treated, justly or unjustly, has a claim on the agent, and the agent in not meeting the claim is guilty of injustice. This accords with the distinction made by Kant and again by Mill between justice and the rest of morals, the duties of justice being those which have correlative rights in the other party, other moral duties being those which do not: we have a duty to keep our bargains, e.g., contracts, wage agreements, conditions of service, etc. (= Honore's *transactions),* and the other party has a right that we should; we may also have a duty of benevolence to others, but they have no right that we should be benevolent towards them. Failure in either would be moral failure, but only failure in the first would be injustice.

From the fact that we have a plurality of justicising factors it does not logically follow that there will be conflicts between them. It could be the case that they fell into an order which could be numbered from 1 to *n,* such that any factor outranked any other factor with a higher numeral; and I am not sure that Honore, for example, does not believe that *need* outranks all the rest. But it seems to me clear that neither that particular claim, nor the more general claim that some hierarchical ordering is possible, can in fact be sustained. And even under a single heading there can be conflicts, e.g., conflicting needs. Perhaps it is not necessary to stress that the issue is not always justice versus something else, say utility, but it seems at least worth pointing out, because in practical issues where questions of justice and injustice arise there is a human tendency to oversimplify. For example, in the school issue over busing children to achieve integration it is surely over-simple to suppose that justice points in one direction only. What follows in the remainder of this chapter should be understood as being acknowledged to be subject to possible conflicts, not only between the different factors, but also under the heading of a single factor.

Need

This is the factor which I have so far used in my examples, and I do not think more requires to be said about it now. If you have the duty of meeting needs, and you do not match distribution to needs, you are treating unjustly those to whom you give too little or nothing. We should distinguish between

> (a) the criticism we might want to make of a society which, say, prefers to expend its wealth on missionary wars, or space spectaculars, or conspicuous consumption than on welfare and poverty programs,

and

> (b) the criticism we might want to make of the inequitable legislation for, and operation of, welfare and poverty programs.

In (a) we are complaining about wrong priorities but not directly about injustice (although wrong priorities may breed injustice); in (b) we are complaining about injustice. Meeting the needs of some families, but failing to meet those of others, because they are hesitant to apply or ignorant how to, is clearly unjust. But even in this category of needs it should be noted that, although discrimination (whether intentional or negligent) nearly always is an element of the injustice, it does not have to be. The injustice of failing to pay a living wage is not conditional on discrimination, i.e., on paying some people better; it is possible to treat *everybody* unjustly by paying them less than they need. Fat cats among executives or stockholders are not necessary to the validity of a union's claim of injustice to the workers.

Desert—Achievement

That a man has got less for what he did than he deserved, e.g., by way of payment or reward, or more than he deserved, e.g., by way of damages awarded against him or punishment, is perhaps the oldest cry of injustice. If not getting what you merited by your performance is not a paradigm case of injustice, what could be? Failure here is failure in Aristotle's distributive justice and the feeling for desert as a justicising factor is what lies at the root of objections to the views of penal and social reformers such as Barbara Wootton, who would have us in the area of crime give up thinking in terms of responsibility and punishment and think instead in terms of social utility. The objection to Barbara Wootton is less that for what he did the convicted man deserves to be punished than that he does *not* deserve to be submitted to therapy however securely beyond the stage of uncertain experiment the therapy may be.

Note that, as in the case of need, injustice in responding to the deserts of achievement does not require unjust discrimination, although very often that is the injustice that will be complained of. A man's getting less than he deserved for what he did is doubly unjust if somebody else got more than he, but it would still be unjust if nobody else got more, even if nobody else was involved at all.

Desert—Ability

I have separated ability from achievement as a justicising factor (although neither Honore nor Rescher does) because it seems to me far less clearly a justicising factor at all. They both find it unjust to a man to deny him what by ability he is qualified for; and so also does J. Feinberg in his "Justice and Personal Desert" *(NOMOS,* vol. VI). Incidentally, being qualified must not be confused with being eligible. One can be well qualified, moderately well qualified, poorly qualified, etc.; and in considering rival candidates for an appointment, we *weigh* their qualifications. Eligibility, on the other hand, is an either/or, on/off business. I may be excellently qualified to be president of the United States of America, but I am not, and never can become, eligible; and of the millions of those who are eligible few are qualified. Again, the fact that I am qualified for a job is a good reason for appointing me (provided that, if there are eligibility conditions, I meet them); the fact that I am eligible for the job is, at most, a good reason for considering me. Nepotism in making appointments may be objectionable, but I doubt whether it is objectionable on the ground that it is unjust to the better qualified candidates for the job—unless other factors than simply ability are to be taken into account (as I think they normally are). If an employer in appointing a new secretary cares to disregard the excellent qualifications of Miss *A* in favor of the attractions of Miss *B* whose talents are strictly those of a businessman's playgirl, has he been unjust to Miss *A*? Not, I think, unless other factors are involved such as (1) a statement or an implied statement in the advertisement for the job that the candidate judged to be best qualified in secretarial skills would be appointed or (2) the existence of a convention or a rule that in competitive appointments the candidate judged to be best qualified is the one appointed. But then the injustice is, not failing to treat according to ability, but failing to act according to a specially or generally authorized expectation that you will treat according to ability. It can be imprudent not to appoint according to ability and it can be morally objectionable, but I doubt whether the moral objection can be that it is unjust *simpliciter* to disregard ability.

An objector might cite as counterexamples the injustice of denying civil rights to blacks or to women; that (to state the case at its mildest) plenty of blacks who have been prevented from registering as voters have been as well qualified to vote as plenty of whites who are registered; or that women have had it made difficult or even impossible for them to get into jobs and positions for which their ability is no less than that of male competitors. I do not deny the injustice of these examples, but I question whether they are always and clearly counterexamples. The fight for such rights has, on the whole, been the fight against discrimination, not the fight against nonrecognition of ability by itself. Nonrecognition of ability can be unjust, viz., where on the one hand the ability is claimed or is so conspicuous as to stand in no need of claiming and where on the other hand it is denied through hypocrisy or prejudice. What lies at the base of this is, I think, the injustice of affront or insult to which I shall be coming back shortly. The treatment of suppressed minorities (or majorities) whether they are blacks, women, Catholics in Northern Ireland, Jews in Russia, or whatever, is an affront in a way in which merely not to get a job because the boss has a weakness for dumb blondes is not.

I wonder whether the view that ability carries desert, which is a view that is widely held, with the consequences that it is unjust not to treat according to ability, does not perhaps rest on a confusion between ability and demonstration of ability. In many cases, where a choice has to be made between candidates, it is made on the basis of competition in a test or examination; and the choice is made on the performance or display of ability therein. If the man who has performed best does not get the job, he can protest at the injustice of it, because by his achievement, by his showing his superior ability, he deserved the job. There are, of course, possible complications to this: for example, it might be that, although *A* performed best, *B* showed more promise; in such a case it might be imprudent, or even wrong, not to, appoint *B*, and, as showing promise is a way of showing ability, it might even be unjust to *B* not to appoint him. Again, *B* may have performed better than *A* over part of the examination, but not over the whole because he was taken ill during it, or from some other uncontrollable cause; in this case it might be unjust to *B* not to appoint him. And the method of selecting the performances that are to count as demonstrating ability may be open to criticism. This is especially liable to happen in situations where what matters is not just having an ability but also being on form or on a winning streak; for example, the method of selecting professional golfers either in this country or in Great Britain to play against each other in the Ryder Cup is frequently criticized on these grounds. But here it does seem to me more a matter of inefficiency or plain bad luck, rather than injustice. What is unjust is the denial of an asked-for opportunity to display an ability, if there is some evidence of its possession. So, it can be unjust to be refused an opportunity of displaying your ability, and it can be unjust not to be treated in accordance with your achievement in displaying it: but I am still unconvinced that it is unjust simply not to be treated in accordance with your known ability—unless, as I have hinted already, the failure to treat you so can reasonably be described in terms of affront.

Transactions

The justice of transactions is approximately Aristotle's diorthotic justice: the justice of restoring the *status quo* exemplified by payment for services, compensation for harm done— and on the view generally taken by Anglo-American law that promises require consideration, the keeping of bargains and fulfillment of contracts. The injustice of transactions is simply the injustice of taking something for nothing, of getting something at somebody else's expense when he was not a willing party to your doing so. I have nothing more to say about it until I come back to asking whether there is any common thread running through the list of justicising factors.

Special Relations

This is on Honore's list but not on Rescher's. I am strongly disinclined to accept it. No doubt special relationships, contractual (e.g., husband-wife) familial (e.g., father-son), official (e.g., ruler, judge, policeman, etc., those over whom they have authority) and others produce special duties, but only where they also produce special rights do they make possible justice and injustice. A father who does not provide in his will for his son, where there is no special reason why he should not, may be open to moral criticism for not doing so, but unless the son has a claim under another heading such as need, or transaction, or rule, unfairness does not seem to enter into it. The special relations such as the contractual and the official that do make possible fair or unfair treatment clearly do fall under other headings, and I see no reason to retain this one. That the world would be a worse place if familial duties were not accepted and discharged is not identical with its being a more unjust place if they were not. Old people may be treated thoughtlessly, carelessly, heartlessly by their self-centered sons and daughters, but not in the absence of other factors unjustly.

Conformity To Rule

This either is itself or comprehends the most important factor of all. It is not merely that each of us has a claim that our society's rules should both be fair and be fairly operated, but also each of us has a claim that they should be observed. If the rule in question, whether being one of law, of positive morality, of custom, or of convention, serves a beneficial social purpose, it does so only provided that it is generally observed. For any individual to gain whatever advantages he does from breaking the rule or from treating himself as being exempt from it, it is in general necessary that others should not be breaking it: the situation has to be seen not just as the simple situation of *A* gaining an advantage by breaking a rule, but as the complex situation of *A* gaining an advantage by breaking a rule, which all (or most) others are keeping. Consequently the strongest argument against such a would-be rule breaker is neither that his conduct will, or is liable to, through its consequences undermine society (for in the case of most individuals its chances of doing so are negligible), nor that society would be undermined if everybody did the same (for it well might not), but simply the unfairness of his securing an advantage which depends on his breaking a rule in circumstances in which most others are keeping it. So the claim that we should conform to the rules does not depend on their being either legal or moral rules; it depends on those being the rules by which the game is being played. (It is not easy to be precise about what constitutes something being such a rule. But it can be as little as its being a matter of reasonable expectation, which is enough to create a rule, and to open the way for just and unjust treatment of others.)

What I want to suggest is that the notion (or notions) of reasonable expectations, or of the right to expect, is the basic notion of justice, and that injustice consists in treating people differently—more accurately, worse—than they have a right to expect. What treatment a man can reasonably expect, or has a right to expect, sometimes depends on the existence of rules, sometimes does not. We have thus two different types of case; we also have an ambiguity in "reasonable expectation" which we have to be careful about.

We can expect *that* people will in given circumstances behave in a certain way, and we can expect people in given circumstances *to* behave in a certain way; and expecting that they will . . . and expecting them to . . . are very different things.

(Certainly the range of use of each of these expressions does overlap the range of use of the other, so that within that overlap they are interchangeable; I am in this chapter concerned with the non-overlapping portions of their respective ranges, e.g., the case where *A* can expect *B* to behave in a certain way at the same time as he cannot expect that he will.)

We can expect that people will behave in a certain way because there is a rule prescribing such behavior.

(a) At its weakest this is simply a regularity type expectation. We can and do expect that people will go on obeying this rule just because they always/usually have; or, as in the case of a new rule, we can expect that they will obey it because they always/usually have obeyed the rules. What makes this expectation reasonable or one which we have a right to or are entitled to hold is its inductive backing. (Note that "can" in "we can expect" does not mean "are able to" or even "are allowed to," but "are entitled to," "have a right to," "would be justified in," etc.) A simple illustration of the regularity type expectation (although not one depending on rules) would be that of Kant's neighbors setting their watches by his walking habits. These were so regular day after day that they could expect that they would continue, and they would be entitled to feel that something had gone wrong if he suddenly changed his walking schedule. They might feel, if they had really come to rely on his walking habits to determine the accuracy of their watches, that he had let them down if he suddenly changed, although they would not be *entitled* to feel so if there was nothing more to their relationship with Kant than I have supposed.

They would be in the same position as the son who received far less under his father's will than he had counted on getting (provided, that is, that his counting on getting much more had been based just on evidence and not at all on promises or even strong hints by the father).

(b) Then we can introduce the notions of people accepting a rule, of feeling committed to it, or feeling bound by it. These are notions which are perhaps different from, although related to, each other. The differences do not matter to the present topic so I will use "feeling bound by" to stand for them all. We can expect that people will behave in a certain way as prescribed by a rule, not just because they always/ usually have, but because we can expect them to feel bound by it, and consequently because we can expect them to behave as prescribed. We are entitled to expect them to behave that way, or to demand that they should, for various possible reasons such as undertakings given, explicitly or implicitly, or society's dependence on reciprocity of sacrifice. Expectation that they will behave in the prescribed way is vulnerable to counterevidence, but expectation-to is not, or not directly, since it can be vulnerable to counterevidence showing *incapacity* to behave that way. We can have evidence about their past conduct or about their present plans and intentions such that we cannot expect that they will keep to the rule; but consistently and simultaneously with that we can expect them to keep to the rule. And in the absence of such counterevidence we can expect that . . . because we can expect them to. . . .

(c) Thus we can expect a man to behave in a certain way even though we cannot expect that he will because we know too much about him for such an expectation to be reasonable. A demand on a person does not fail to be reasonable just because the expectation that he will meet it fails to be reasonable. Because what we can expect a man to do is what we can rightfully demand of him, not only are there situations in which we can expect him to do what we cannot expect that he will do, but also there are situations in which we can expect that he will do what we cannot expect him to do. Kant's neighbors again illustrate the latter: they could expect that Kant would stick to his walking habits but they could not expect him to stick to them. They would not be entitled to complain of his letting them down if he suddenly changed his schedule; for them to be entitled to complain, not only would Kant have to know that they were relying on him as their watch-regulator, but they would have to know that he knew, and he would have to know that they knew that he knew.

The claim of justice within the context of rules is the claim that reasonable expectations of conformity to rule should not be disappointed. And the basic claim is that of expectation to, which may range up from expecting a man, or an official, or a government, etc., not to depart from the regularities and customs upon which we are known to be depending, to expecting him or them to behave in the way prescribed by the rule because he or they can be expected to feel bound by it. Injustice consists in failing to treat the victims of it in the way in which they can expect to be treated, at the same time, perhaps, as treating them in exactly the way in which they can expect that they will be treated.

This can be generalized to any case where one can expect to . . . including, that is, cases where even in the absence of rules one can expect to. . . . And there certainly are such cases. I can expect *A* to keep his promise to do *x* because he authorized me to expect that he would. The fact that by promising he authorized an expectation is the reason why he has the obligation to do what he promised to do. His obligation is not logically dependent on promises being a practice (in J. Rawls's sense), although the fact that they are such a practice may reinforce the obligation. Breaking a promise is unjust because it is somehow an affront or an insult to the promisee as a human being, in this case the insult of first conferring a right on him and then behaving as if you had not, and that I suggest is what injustice fundamentally is—the affront done to a man as a human being by not treating him in the way that he can expect to be treated. It is, I suspect, no accident that it is indignation rather than merely anger that we feel at injustice, whether we or others are its victims, and that indignation is still true enough to the etymology of the word to be dependent on viewing the treatment that arouses our indignation as somehow belittling or affronting the worth of the victim. Even where we are justified in treating people unjustly (and unhappily we sometimes may be) we are not to be admired for growing the calluses which make us insensitive to the affront we are doing them. The injustice which is done by discrimination when it is unjust (and not all discrimination is unjust) is the insult given to those discriminated against, the insult being rubbed in by letting them see others not relevantly different being better treated. The injustice done to women or to blacks does not absolutely consist in, although it is compounded by, their being discriminated against; the injustice is the insult of being held to lack the capacity or the qualifications which they clearly do not lack.

It is an affront to have a crying need denied or ignored, to have shown your worth by achievement and to have it belittled. It is inefficient, and socially wasteful, not to treat people according to their abilities, but it is not obviously unjust, unless on other grounds they could expect to be so treated. What is insulting about discrimination against, for example, women or blacks is not so much the failure to allow them to develop and exercise their abilities as the implied denial that they possess them. The boss who employs dolly girls rather than competent stenographers simply because he finds the former easier to look at is not being unjust to the latter; he would be, if he pretended that they were not as good stenographers as the dollies, and gave that as his reason for not employing them.

In this chapter I have said nothing about canons or maxims of justice and injustice. I have been concerned solely with making some suggestions about the notion of justice, or rather the notion of injustice, itself. It seems advisable to be clear about that before going on to discuss the practically more demanding and emotionally more charged questions about canons. It may, for instance, be true that justice demands equality; but that truth, if it is one, should not be confused with the falsehood that justice *is* equality.

CHAPTER 3

Phillip Montague

"THE LABORERS IN THE VINEYARD" AND OTHER STORIES

In Chapter 20 of the Gospel according to St. Matthew, Christ relates the following parable:

> For the Kingdom of heaven is like a householder who set out early in the morning to hire workers for his vineyard, and when he had agreed with the workers for one denarius a day he sent them into his vineyard. Going out about nine o'clock he saw other men standing idle in the market place and said to them, "You go into my vineyard, too, and I will give you whatever is right," and so they went. Going out again at midday, and at three o'clock, he did the same. About five o'clock he went out and found others standing. He said to them, "Why do you stand here all day idle?" They answered him, "Because no one has hired us." "You too go into the vineyard," he said. When evening came, the owner of the vineyard said to his steward, "Call the workers and give them their wages, beginning with the last, and so up to the first." When those who were hired at five o'clock came, they each received a denarius. When the first came, they supposed that they would receive more, but they each received a denarius. On receiving it they grumbled to the owner, "The last only worked an hour, but you have made them our equal, and we have borne the burden and heat of the day." But he answered one of them, "My friend, I am not doing you an injustice. Did you not agree with me for a denarius? Take what is yours and go. I choose to give to the last what I also give to you. Am I not allowed to do what I wish with my own property? Or is your eye evil, because I am good?" So the last shall be first, and the first last.[1]

It is easy to sympathize with those laborers who bore "the burden and heat of the day," and to regard them as having been treated unjustly. And yet from a different

This essay originally appeared in *Journal of Social Philosophy* 16 (Summer 1985): 2–10. Reprinted by permission of Blackwell Publishing Ltd.

point of view the householder not only appears innocent of any wrongdoing, but deserving of praise for an act of generosity. The story generates a genuine puzzle, the source of which, I am convinced, is a confusion regarding the nature of justice. I will attempt here to clear up this confusion, and by so doing to reduce if not eliminate entirely the puzzling aspects of the parable.

I

There are several ways in which our householder *might* have acted unjustly in his treatment of the workers, but each of these misses the essential bothersome point in an important respect. For example, a payment of one denarius for a full day's work might simply be an unjust wage; if it were then those who worked an entire day for one denarius would surely have a right to complain. But they would have this right regardless of the amount paid to those who spent less time in the vineyard; and yet the parable suggests that their discontent was caused by a comparison of their wages with those received by the other workers. Moreover, the scent of injustice continues to rise from the parable even if we assume that one denarius is a fair wage for a day's laboring in the vineyard.[2]

Even less satisfactory as a possible solution to our problem is the suggestion that the injustice was actually perpetrated on those who worked the single hour and were paid an inordinately high wage. One possible source of this idea might be a comparison of the parable with the following case: when handing out final grades in a course I give everyone what he or she deserves save for one individual to whom I assign a grade higher than he deserves. I think I could be rightly accused of doing that individual an injustice in that, for example, I have given him a false idea regarding his mastery of some subject matter, and this might lead him to enroll later in courses he cannot handle. In line with this example, it might be suggested that in paying some workers more than a fair wage, the householder is providing them with false expectations about their future work, and is thus doing them an injustice. But such an account is surely inadequate as a solution to our problem. In the first place, we can assume that the overpaid laborers know full well that they are unlikely to receive so high a wage on any future occasion, and yet even on this assumption the idea lingers that some sort of injustice occurs in the parable; and secondly, it is not the overpaid workers who have apparently been treated unjustly, but rather those who received an assumedly fair wage.

The major shortcoming of the above suggestions as possible solutions to our problem is that they ignore the essentially *comparative* aspect of the case. What strikes us as unjust about the householder's treatment of those who labored all day is the way this treatment compares with that given to those who worked much less. And this fact calls to mind the familiar principle (call it P) that relevantly similar cases ought to be handled similarly.[3] That is, we might regard the householder as having violated this principle, and in so doing as having committed an act of injustice. Indeed this conclusion appears so obvious that one might wonder why this discussion should go any further. But this point of view assumes—incorrectly I think—that the parable is really not puzzling at all, that the householder's act of injustice is a rather obvious one. More importantly, it assumes that the householder has in fact violated P; and I will argue here that this assumption is simply mistaken.

According to P one ought to treat relevantly similar cases similarly (with the implication that to do otherwise is to act unjustly). In the parable the comparison cases are the laborers who worked all day for one denarius on the one hand, and those who worked one hour for the same amount on the other. The cases can surely be regarded as having been handled differently by the householder since he paid the two groups of workers at different rates; so let us consider whether the cases are relevantly similar.

It is worth emphasizing that P is being regarded here as a principle of *justice*. I mention this point because a principle formulated exactly like P is sometimes invoked as a norm of reasonable behavior. As I have argued elsewhere,[4] these principles are essentially different, and the difference lies in what counts as relevant similarities in the two cases. What we are concerned with here is whether two cases are relevantly similar *for the purposes of deciding a question of justice*. Whether the cases might be relevantly similar for some other purpose is not at this moment relevant, though the question will be raised again later.

Our inclination to think that the two groups of workers are relevantly similar in the required sense is based on considerations like these: both groups were involved in the same sort of work, under the same conditions, there was no agreement to pay the two groups at different rates, and their respective financial needs are presumably the same. And all of these considerations apparently support the idea that one group of workers has as much right to be paid a denarius per hour as the other group. Indeed, I would like to suggest that the notion of relevant similarity as contained in P (interpreted as a principle of justice) must be spelled out in terms of equality of rights: two individuals (or groups) are relevantly similar with respect to being treated a certain way *only if* their rights to being treated in that way are equal.

If, however, we examine the parable case under the assumption that one denarius per day is a fair wage, I think we must conclude that the rights of the two groups to one denarius per hour are equal only in the sense that neither group has the right to that wage. That is, one group has as much right to a wage of one denarius per hour in that neither group has any right whatsoever to being paid that amount. We must now ask whether differential treatment of individuals or groups who are relevantly similar in *this* sense is in fact a violation of P and an act of injustice.

Suppose I encounter a group of beggars, give some money to one of them and give none to the others.[5] None of the beggars has a *right* to receive money from me,[6] and hence, following the above line of thinking, each one has as much right as any other to receive a donation. If we conclude on the basis of these considerations that the beggars are relevantly similar for the purposes of applying P, then I have committed an act of injustice in failing to give money to all of them. But this is a very peculiar result, in that it suggests that any charitable contribution which fails to benefit all possible recipients involves an act of injustice. If, for example, some philanthropist donates one hundred thousand dollars to Harvard, he has committed an act of injustice unless he also contributes to Yale, Stanford, the Vietnamese refugees, and every other needy group or individual.

One might attempt to counter this kind of result, I suppose, by claiming that injustice is avoided if charitable contributions are spread in a way that will maximize the number of those benefitted within the limits of the contributor's available resources. Thus, in deciding how to deal with the beggars in my example, I would have to consider both how much money I have available for contributing to them, and how to distribute it so as to benefit the greatest number of them. I may have only one dollar available for donating, there may be a hundred beggars, and I may decide that giving each of four of them twenty-five cents is the right thing to do, since giving the hundred a penny each will really benefit none of them.

The notion that my decision in this case is correct would presumably be based on the following principle: charity should be dispensed so as to benefit as many (needy?) individuals or groups as possible. Now let us recall how we arrived at this point. We considered the possibility that, for the purposes of applying P, two individuals could be relevantly similar with respect to receiving certain treatment in that neither has the right to the treatment, and hence one has as much right as the other to be treated in the way in question. But this assumption about P evidently leads to undesirable results: whenever anyone contributes to charity he acts unjustly towards those to whom he does not contribute. As a possible solution to this problem we considered the principle mentioned above about maximizing the number benefitted when making charitable contributions.

But even if this last principle is acceptable (which I seriously doubt), I don't see how it saves P under the latter's problematic interpretation. Even if I maximize benefits by contributing twenty-five cents to each of four of the hundred beggars, and even if donating to four instead of only one increases the chances that any given beggar will receive *some* money (thus removing one possible source of objection), each of the other ninety-six would presumably object to my not choosing him as a beneficiary of my largess. And the objections of the ninety-six are as justified—and for some of the same reasons—as would be the objections of ninety-nine if I donated the entire dollar to only one of them. In both cases each of those who received no money could claim to have as much right to a donation as the lucky recipient(s); and we are right back where we started with our laborers in the vineyard.

It is possible, of course, to reconstruct the above example in such a way that my giving money to only one of the beggars is wrong—indeed even morally wrong. Suppose, for example, I give a million dollars to one beggar and nothing to the others. Clearly the amount donated far exceeds the needs of the recipient, and I think I could be rightly accused of doing something wrong. After all, I could have done much more good by distributing the money among several—or all—of the beggars; to give so much to one is surely a waste of resources which could have been put to much better use. But even if correct, these conclusions do not show that I have committed an act of *injustice,* and in particular that I have acted unjustly in virtue of violating P.

I think we must abandon the idea that, for the purposes of applying P, two individuals can be relevantly similar with respect to receiving certain treatment when their rights to that treatment are equal only in the sense that the rights are non-existent. To see what "relevantly similar" does mean when employed in P, let us consider a case to which P clearly does apply.

Suppose a man dies, leaving money to his sons without specifying that any particular amount should go to any one of them. If it turns out that one son receives a greater amount than another, or even that one is somehow afforded a greater opportunity than another to attain a larger amount, P would have been violated and an act of injustice would have been performed. But there is a crucial difference between this case and that of the beggars. Even though in both cases we might say that no one person has any more right to the available money than any other, in the inheritance case this "equality" of rights among those concerned does not consist merely in the absence of rights on everyone's part. The sons do have rights regarding the inheritance; the fact that they have these rights is what is *relevant* for the matter of justice. They are relevantly *similar* in that their rights to the money are equal. Because they are relevantly similar in *this* sense, to treat them differently in distributing the money is to act unjustly through violating P.

What I am suggesting, then, is that P, as a principle of justice, be interpreted in this way: If x has the right to y and z has the right to y; and if x has as much right to y as does z; then x ought to be granted (in the sense that it would be unjust not to) as much of y as is z (or x ought to be granted as much chance at attaining y as is z). Under this interpretation P, it is applicable neither to the beggar case nor to that of the workers in the vineyard. In the latter instance, neither group of workers has the right to a wage of more than one denarius per day (given our initial assumption that this is a fair wage); so even if we can make sense of the idea that the rights of each group to the higher wage are equal, the two groups are not relevantly similar in the sense required for an application of P. Hence, in paying the two groups at different rates the householder has not violated P. If he has committed an act of injustice, it is in virtue of violating some other principle of justice; and quite frankly, I cannot think of what this principle might be.

II

To conclude—even if correctly—that the parable involves no acts of injustice by no means eliminates its puzzling aspects. There is still a strong inclination to regard the householder as having done something which is in some way objectionable, and I should like now to explain what I see as the source of this feeling.

I mention above that the principle that relevantly similar cases should be handled similarly can be interpreted not only as a principle of justice, but also as a principle of reasonable behavior. Indeed, some philosophers have argued that there is really only one principle involved and that principle provides an important link between the concepts of justice and of reasonableness.[7] Although I believe that this view is mistaken, it is not obviously so, and its plausibility partially explains our puzzlement about the parable.

According to Chaim Perelman, "A form of behavior or human judgement can be termed just only if it can be subjected to rules or criteria. . . . Just behavior is regular. It conforms to rules, to standards."[8] Without rehashing here points I have made elsewhere[9] in connection with Perelman's views on this matter, let me simply note that, if he is correct, we can see some basis for regarding the householder as guilty of injustice in his treatment of the workers. For there is a real sense in which his action, which involves paying different groups of workers at different rates is not rule-guided, not regular. The same can be said of the beggar case where some individuals were singled out—for no apparent reason—to receive donations. In both instances there is a tendency to ask "Why them rather than the others?" In both instances, choice as to whom to benefit is apparently without rhyme or reason.

Now let us forget the idea—as I am convinced that we must—that some special connection exists between just behavior and rule-guided or regular behavior. Let us assume instead that there is *some* sense in which *reasonable* behavior takes place according to "rules or criteria," and manifests an element of regularity. Then, by the same line of reasoning as used above in connection with the idea that *just* behavior is rule-guided and regular, we could conclude that the householder's behavior with respect to the laborers (and my behavior with respect to the beggars) is unreasonable.

It is this apparent unreasonableness—what we might on occasion regard as inconsistency of behavior or arbitrariness—that we find objectionable about the householder's actions. We are convinced that, if we asked the householder why he paid one group of workers at the rate of one denarius per day and the other group at the rate of one denarius per hour, he would be stuck for an answer. We are convinced of this because, without reading a great deal into the parable about reasons which the householder *might* have, it seems clear that whatever would count as a reason for paying one group of workers at the higher rate would also be a reason for paying the other group at that rate. Thus, the householder's decision to pay one group rather than the other the higher wage (or perhaps his decision not to distribute his largest equally among all the workers), is evidently without reason. It is from this point of view that we see *something* wrong with the householder's treatment of his workers, though I seriously doubt that we could build a case for his being guilty of moral wrong.[10]

I should like to consider one more example in order to underscore the point I am attempting to make here regarding the difference between unjust behavior and unreasonable behavior. Suppose a mother is confronted by her two children asking for candy, and that in response to their request she gives one child two pieces of candy and the other a single piece. Suppose further that the children are approximately the same age, have essentially the same tolerance for candy, like candy equally well, etc. Under these assumptions there would be a strong tendency on the part of most people to regard the mother's action as unjust treatment of one of the children. Yet it is difficult to see how anyone's rights are violated, unless we want to say—implausibly I think—that the children have a right to the candy.

I would like to suggest, however, that to the extent that we are inclined to regard the mother's action as unjust, to that extent we are assuming that her unequal treatment of the children is evidence of a preference on her part of one child over the other. And *this* is unjust, since children are entitled to equal affection, care, etc., from their parents.

On the other hand, if we were to discover that the mother prefers neither child over the other—that her attitudes towards them are essentially the same—then our feeling of outrage at an evident injustice yields to one of puzzlement. The differential treatment of the two children is apparently without reason; and though we might continue to regard the mother's actions as objectionable, I think the basis for this attitude must be the action's unreasonableness itself, and not any alleged injustice.

The parable is puzzling, then, because we tend to confuse behavior that is unjust with behavior that is unreasonable. And this tendency exists because it appears as if both sorts of behavior can occur when relevantly similar cases are treated differently. But, as I have argued above, relevant similarity as it pertains to making determinations of justice involves the existence and equality of rights, while these considerations play no necessary role in deciding questions of reasonableness. And thus while our householder can be regarded as acting unreasonably even though perhaps generously, his unequal payments to the two groups of workers involve no acts of injustice.

PART THREE

RECTIFICATION

CHAPTER 4

Jules L. Coleman

CORRECTIVE JUSTICE AND PROPERTY RIGHTS

Suppose the prevailing distribution of property rights is unjust as determined by the relevant conception of distributive justice. You have far more than you should have under that theory and I have far less. Then I defraud you and in doing so reallocate resources so that our holdings *ex post* more closely approximate what distributive justice requires. Do I have a duty to return the property to you?

There are many good reasons for requiring me to return to you what I have taken. One is that while you may have no right in justice to all that you own, it does not follow that I do, or that I have a right to take it. Thus, requiring me to return the property to you is a way of recognizing that I had no right to take it from you in the first place.

If I have no right to take your property, then justice might require that I give up my unjust enrichment. It hardly follows, however, that I should turn over my gains to you, since, *ex hypothesi*, you have no "right" to them either.[1] Perhaps I should be made to deposit my ill-gotten gains in a public coffer created for the purpose of general redistribution. One thing we might be tempted to say about a practice of compensation, then, is that it cannot be a requirement of justice if the underlying property rights that are sustained by it do not themselves conform to the requirements of distributive justice. Compensation is a matter of justice only if the underlying property rights scheme that is sustained by such a practice is itself required by justice.[2]

If compensation is demanded by justice only if the underlying property rights are themselves required by distributive justice, it will be difficult to understand important legal practices, especially tort law, as expressing or implementing demands

This essay originally appeared in *Social Philosophy & Policy* 11:2 (Summer 1994): 124–138.

of justice. That is because the prevailing distribution of property rights is probably not the one required by the best conception of distributive justice. Perhaps our tort practice is best understood on, broadly speaking, consequentialist grounds. How is that?

Even if doing so has the effect of sustaining an unjust distribution, making compensation or repair can be justified in order to discourage individuals from making matters worse by taking redistribution into their own hands. To be sure, sometimes agents are in the best position to reallocate resources privately. This occurs in the typical voluntary exchange, sanctioned by the law of contract, in which individuals have adequate information about, among other things, their preferences. On the other hand, individuals may not be in the best position to *force* transfers in the name of distributive justice, since most individuals lack the information necessary to produce "justice-enhancing" forced reallocations, and many are poorly motivated to try. Worse, efforts to force private redistribution are likely to be met with private resistance, with its attendant injury, loss of additional property, and loss of life. Therefore, someone who takes from another has to make repair even if the taking in a particular case makes matters better (from the point of view of distributive justice), simply because individuals cannot be counted on to make matters better in the aggregate or over the long term. Requiring compensation discourages private redistribution.

Interestingly, requiring compensation does not discourage private redistribution altogether. Suppose that the "taker" values the property more than does the property right holder. Then, the taker will be better off even after he compensates the property right holder than he was before the taking. Because he gains by the taking, the "injurer" will not be discouraged from engaging in private redistribution by a practice requiring him to compensate for his taking. A practice requiring compensation for harms to property rights will not fully discourage forced, private redistribution.

Moreover, it is not obvious that coercive private redistribution should be stifled completely. In the typical voluntary exchange, adequately informed individuals reallocate resources between or among themselves. This private reallocation is normally justified because it is voluntary and the participants are sufficiently knowledgeable about their preferences to insure that the transaction is mutually advantageous. Voluntary exchanges among informed, rational agents are generally welfare enhancing. One way of looking at an exchange is to view the parties to it as "taking" but compensating *ex ante,* where the terms of compensation are set by agreement. Both contract and forced, but compensated, transfers involve the same elements: "taking" and "compensation."

From the welfare-maximizing perspective, the difference between contract and forced, but compensated, exchange, is that in the latter case, compensation occurs *ex post* and its terms are set by a third party (typically a court), whereas in the former case, compensation is established *ex ante* by mutual agreement. As long as the compensation is adequate, both kinds of transfers produce net gains.

By requiring compensation for takings, each potential taker (or "forced transferrer") is put in the position of determining whether he will benefit sufficiently by harming another to make it worth his while to do so. In order for someone rationally to decide, he will need sufficient information about his benefit schedule and the damage schedule of his victim. When he has the relevant information, he may find it rational to force a "mutually advantageous transfer."[3]

If individuals have the kind of information about their private interests and preferences that justifies allowing them to reallocate resources voluntarily (via exchange), then a practice of requiring takers to compensate property right holders will encourage individuals to gather information regarding benefit and damage schedules. It will also allow those with adequate information about their preferences and the damage schedules of property right holders to force transfers that, because they are welfare enhancing, are justified on certain kinds of consequentialist grounds. What the practice of compensation does is discourage wealth- or welfare-reducing transfers: precisely those forced transfers that are, from this perspective, undesirable.

From the welfare-maximizing perspective, the choice between exchange and forced transfer depends on the difference between transaction and compensation costs, not on the relative voluntariness of the transaction. Typically, but not always, voluntary exchanges are less costly than forced ones, and are preferable on those grounds.[4] There is a natural connection between our practices of voluntary exchange and forced, but fully compensated, transfers. Under differing empirical circumstances, both practices allow resources to move to more highly valued uses. If this is correct, then the best way of looking at our prevailing practice of requiring individuals to compensate the victims of their takings is that doing so allows the value of those resources to rise when circumstances do not permit voluntary exchange, or when the costs of voluntary transfer exceed the costs of *ex post* compensation.

It would be a mistake to deny the power of consequentialist arguments for our current legal and moral practices. On the other hand, we should not abandon the possibility of understanding our current practices as reflecting or implementing certain demands of justice. The plausibility of this line of argument depends on the claim that individuals can have a moral duty to support institutions that are not themselves fully just. And that is precisely the argument I want to make. Repairing certain loses can be a requirement of justice even when the net effect of doing so is to sustain a less than fully just allocation of property rights.

Not every distribution of property rights, however, can be sustained by a practice of corrective justice. Thus, the burden of this chapter is to set out the conditions under which a property rights scheme can be sustained by corrective justice. This will require quite a few preliminary distinctions and substantial groundwork. Indeed, the bulk of the argument sets out the relevant conception of corrective justice. I reach the problem of specifying the relationship between corrective justice and property rights only in the last section, and then only in a preliminary fashion.

Corrective Justice

What are the conditions that a scheme of property rights must satisfy in order for it to be sustained by a practice of corrective justice? Answering this question, even in a preliminary fashion, requires a conception of corrective justice; I will draw on the conception of corrective justice I have defended in my recent book *Risks and Wrongs*.[5] According to corrective justice, individuals have a duty to repair the wrongful losses for which they are responsible. Thus, any conception of corrective justice requires conceptions of *loss, wrongfulness,* and *responsibility*.

Loss

A *loss* is a diminution in an individual's welfare or well-being as judged relative to an appropriate baseline.[6] So conceived, a loss is the kind of thing that can give rise to reasons for acting. The fact that you have suffered a diminution in welfare—that you have been rendered worse off than you otherwise would have been (as determined by the relevant baseline)—is the sort of fact about you that could provide me with a reason for acting, for doing something with respect to alleviating your current state. Sometimes, losses give everyone reasons for acting. Thus, in a community of a certain type, the fact that all your family possessions have been destroyed by a flood, or by some other natural disaster that you could have neither guarded against nor otherwise anticipated, may give everyone else in the community a reason for contributing to a general fund that will help you get back on your feet.

On other occasions, the losses you suffer may give some individual a reason for acting, a reason that no one else has to come to your aid or to alleviate your condition. If I have caused your loss, then I may have a reason to do something about alleviating your condition that no one else has.

Different principles and practices connect individuals with the losses that others have suffered. In order for a particular person to be connected with another's loss via the principle of corrective justice, the loss itself must be *wrongful* and the individual in question must be *responsible* for it. Other practices can give rise to agent-specific reasons for acting in which neither the wrongfulness nor the responsibility condition may be satisfied. Thus, if I unintentionally knock you down as the result of an unanticipated, involuntary muscular twitch, then I may have a duty to lift you up, to apologize, or, if necessary, to assist in finding emergency help, and so on. I may have these agent-specific reasons for acting even though your loss is not wrongful in any obvious way, and even though it is at least arguable that I am not morally responsible for it.

The duty imposed by corrective justice—namely to render compensation—requires not just a loss, but a wrongful one, and not just causation, but responsibility. This means that we need an account of what makes a loss wrongful as well as an account of what it means to be responsible for a wrongful loss.

Wrongfulness

A loss is *wrongful* in the sense required by corrective justice if it results either from *wrongdoing* or *a wrong*. Wrongdoing is conduct that falls below the relevant norm or standard of behavior. If individuals ought to exercise reasonable care, then failure to do so constitutes a kind of wrongdoing in this sense. Individuals can fail to exercise reasonable care without harming anyone, without invading anyone's rights. In contrast, someone wrongs another whenever he invades that person's rights. Thus, wrongdoing is a failure to comply with a relevant norm; a wrong is an action contrary to another's right. Conduct that is wrongful because it involves either wrongdoing or a wrong can give rise to wrongful losses, losses for which those responsible can incur a duty to repair in justice.[7]

Wrongs are invasions of rights. Whether a particular act constitutes a wrong depends on the content of the relevant right. If I take something of yours over which you have the power to exclude and alienate, then I wrong you. On the other hand, if I take something of yours over which you have a power only to demand compensation, then (provided I compensate you) I have not wronged you.

If I act contrary to your right then I wrong you *whether or not I am justified in doing what I did*. I may dock my boat at your slip to protect my family from an impending storm even if I have no right to do so without your permission. Suppose you refuse me permission. Then it is possible that I could be justified in my action even though it is invasive of your rights. There are many examples of this sort, including the famous torts case of *Vincent v. Lake Erie*.[8] This suggests a distinction between two ways of invading rights: *violating* and *infringing* them. Infringements are justifiable or permissible invasions of rights; violations are wrongful invasions of rights. Violations are not only wrongs; they are wrongdoings as well. That is, they fall below the relevant standard of acceptable behavior, and that is just another way of saying that they are unjustifiable departures from the background norms. Infringements are wrongs; but they are not wrongdoings. An infringement involves conduct that is permissible, sometimes justifiable, and, perhaps, even laudatory on balance.

We also distinguish between rights and interests. Rights are special ways of protecting legitimate interests. Not all interests rise to the level of rights. Both rights and interests can be set back or harmed. The harming of a legitimate interest can create a wrongful loss only if it is the result of another's wrongdoing; the harming of a right can occasion a wrongful loss whether or not the conduct of another is wrongful or at fault. Wrongful losses can result either from wrongs, that is, invasions of rights, or wrongful harming of legitimate interests. The latter kind of wrongful loss depends on the injurer having done something wrong or unjustifiable, the former does not: indeed, it is compatible with the agent's conduct being morally desirable on balance.

There is a normatively significant feature of the difference between interests that are rights and those that are not. If you set back an interest of mine that is not a right, I have been harmed; I may well suffer a loss, but not necessarily a wrongful one. In order for my loss to be wrongful, you would have had to set back my interest unjustifiably, impermissibly, or wrongfully. Only then would the loss I might suffer as a consequence be wrongful.

If, in contrast, you were to harm an interest of mine that is a right—in other words, if you were to wrong me—then whatever losses resulted would be wrongful in the sense required by corrective justice. More importantly, it would be no defense against your duty to make repair to point out that you were justified in what you did. So if I had a right to a successful career, pointing out that my work is full of mistakes would be honorable, but would nevertheless constitute a wrong to me. In the case of interests that are rights, it is not part of my claim to repair that you acted impermissibly, whereas in the ordinary case in which I have a legitimate interest, but no right, that is precisely what I need to show. By the same token, you can free yourself of the duty to make repair by showing that you acted permissibly or justifiably in the case of a harm to a legitimate interest, but your efforts will be to no avail if my interest is a right.

Responsibility

The concepts of wrongdoing and wrong implicated in corrective justice are not those of *moral* wrongdoing and *moral* wrong. Consider the latter first. A person can wrong another by acting in morally justifiable ways, by permissibly invading the rights of others. The conception of a wrong, therefore, does not suggest that the agent has acted in a morally reprehensible fashion. If the point of offering an *excuse* is to show that one's conduct is not morally blameworthy or reprehensible, then such an excuse is irrelevant to determining whether conduct is a wrong—at least from the point of view of corrective justice. If it is irrelevant to determining whether conduct is a wrong, it is irrelevant to determining whether a loss is, in that sense, wrongful. The same is true of conduct that is wrongdoing. Recall that conduct is wrongdoing if it falls below the relevant standard of conduct. It is one question whether conduct falls below the relevant norms; it is another whether the actor is to blame for this failure, whether the fault in his conduct marks a moral fault in him. The point of corrective justice is not to penalize or punish the agent for his conduct, but to recognize the *victim's loss* as wrongful and worthy of repair. The question is whether the victim's loss is morally significant; it is not whether the injurer's conduct is morally culpable. The primary role of wrong and wrongdoing bears on assessing the kind of loss the victim has suffered, not the kind of character the injurer has exemplified.

Culpability is not a condition of corrective justice; responsibility is, however. Corrective justice imposes a *duty* of repair on those *responsible* for the wrongful losses of others. And does not the notion of responsibility presuppose that the agent has no excuse for his conduct, for his wronging or wrongdoing?

Once again, we need to draw a distinction—this time between two different kinds of excuses: those that, if sound, defeat ascriptions of *blame,* and those that, if sound, defeat ascriptions of *agency*. Excuses of the first sort are typically offered to show that the agent's action does not exemplify a defect in his character or motivation. Excuses of the second sort are designed to show lack of volition. So if I hit you, but only because I was pushed by someone else, then although it was me who hit you, my doing so was the result of no action of mine. The consequences of my *actions,* in contrast, are my responsibility even when they do not evidence a defect in my character or motivation. I am, in the normatively interesting sense, responsible for them even if I am not to blame for them. Thus, excuses that defeat agency are relevant to corrective justice, even when those that defeat culpability or blame are not. Corrective justice *connects* agents with losses by the criterion of responsibility. Excuses that defeat agency sever the relationship between loss and agent. Other excuses that admit agency while denying culpability, are therefore irrelevant.

The next question is whether agency is all that is required to connect an actor with a wrongful loss—whether agency is enough in the sense of sufficient under corrective justice to make another's loss the agent's responsibility. It is not. To see this, consider a rather straightforward counterexample to the claim that it is.

Suppose the actions of both Mike and Ike are causally necessary for the loss that Pike suffers, but that only Ike is at fault: only Ike, in other words, has failed to exercise due care. In that case, Pike has suffered a loss owing to the wrongdoing of another (Ike). His loss, therefore, is wrongful. That loss is connected by the principle of agency with the conduct of both Mike and Ike, in the sense that it would not have occurred but for the conduct of both. There is wrongful loss and there is agency (in both Mike's and Ike's actions). Were causal agency sufficient to connect actors with others' wrongful losses under corrective justice, Mike, as well as Ike, would then be connected to Pike's loss in a way that would impose a duty to repair on both of them. And this seems wrong. Mike's conduct contributed to Pike's injury, but he did nothing wrong. It is not Mike's conduct that makes Pike's loss a wrongful one. It is Ike's. This suggests that more than agency or causal power is required by corrective justices as a link between injurers and wrongful losses.

Someone can be *responsible* for a loss in the sense required by corrective justice only if the loss is *his fault*. So what we need is an account of the truth conditions (or assertability conditions) of sentences of the form: Such-and-such harm is so-and-so's fault. My tentative suggestion is the following.

A loss *L* is some individual *S*'s fault if and only if:

(1) *S* is at fault (that is, his conduct falls below the appropriate norm).

(2) That aspect of *S*'s conduct that is at fault is causally connected in the appropriate way to *L*.

(3) *L* falls within the scope of the reasonably foreseeable risks in virtue of which *S*'s conduct is at fault.

(4) *S* does not have an agency-defeating excuse for his conduct.

This analysis is surely controversial, but let me briefly say something about important aspects of it. First, in the Mike-Ike-Pike example, the possibility of holding Mike liable in justice to Pike is eliminated by (1): Mike is not at fault. Therefore, Pike's loss cannot be his fault; and if it cannot be his fault, he cannot have a duty to repair it. Clauses (2) and (3) are designed to rule out perverse cases of the following sort. I go out driving and in the course of doing so my car hits yours. Now suppose that my driving is at fault because my rear brake-lights were broken. If my driving is otherwise flawless or reasonable, then your loss is connected to my driving, but it is not connected to that aspect of my driving that is negligent.[9] Moreover, there might be cases in which your loss is connected to that aspect of my driving that is negligent, but in which it is not the sort of loss that falls within the scope of the risks that lead us to think of the conduct as negligent or at fault in the first place. This analysis attempts to remove those cases from the realm of responsibility.

This analysis of responsibility for loss cannot apply in all cases involving wrongful loss. The reason is that in some cases—those involving infringements—there is no fault in the doing. Clause (1) is never satisfied. Instead, we need to focus only on whether the loss results from a rights-infringement and on whether the loss falls within the scope of the risks protected by the right. In other words, the questions we need to ask are: "Did the injurer's conduct invade the victim's right, that is, was it action contrary to the demands or constraints imposed by the right?"; and "Was the loss of the victim suffered within the scope of the interests protected by that right?"

Local Justice

We have accounts of both wrongful losses and the principle of responsibility. We do not yet have a complete conception of corrective justice however. The reason is that corrective justice, unlike other principles of justice, is said to constitute a form of "local justice"—justice between the parties. We need to give some content to this aspect of corrective justice.

Suppose I make you a promise to meet you for lunch tomorrow, and suppose promises give rise to rights and duties of a certain sort. Then if I fail to show up, other things being equal, I have wronged you. I have not only done something wrong, in the sense of violating the norms governing promising, I have wronged you. If the wrong was simply breaking a promise, it would be problematic, some might say, that you should have a claim against me. No particular person can have a claim against me just because I have done something wrong. Some might say, then, that the reason you have a claim against me—whether to insist that I apologize or otherwise make amends—is that I have *wronged you*. And that is the essence of local, as opposed to global, justice; that is the essence of justice between us: I owe you something—I have a duty to you—because I wronged you.

This suggests that in order for a duty (or a right) in corrective justice to arise, there must be some sort of first-order right that already governs (normatively) the relationship between the parties, a right whose invasion provides the grounds for a claim in corrective justice to repair. Corrective justice is justice between the parties because it builds on, or is layered on, rights that already govern the relationship between the parties.

This conception of local justice is too narrow, however. It explains why certain private rights-violations give rise to duties in corrective justice, but it does not explain the connection between *wrongdoing*—in which no rights are involved—and corrective justice. The problem, then, is to square this fact about wrongdoing with the prevalent view of corrective justice as "local." In what sense can violations of "general" norms create local duties of repair?

My suggestion is that the *locality* of local justice does not have to do only with the *parties;* rather it has to do with the baseline or background norms governing wrongdoing within a particular community, and with "local understandings" of more general norms.

Norms that are general may depend on local practices and understandings for their content. In our culture, there is a general practice of restricting one's behavior so that it is not unreasonably risky to others. But the content of the norm varies; it is partially given by norms and conventions that arise within "local" communities of risk-takers. The actual standard of care imposes different substantive requirements depending on the community's conventions and local practices. So, to use an obvious example, reasonable risk-taking on a football field is different from reasonable risk-taking in a schoolyard during recess; and reasonable risk-taking during recess differs from reasonable risk-taking in the classroom.

American legal practice also recognizes this distinction by its reliance both on customary practice as a criterion of reasonable risk-taking and on the role of criminal statutes in setting *per se* negligence standards. The idea in the first case is that manufacturers in a particular industry, for example, are in the best position to determine what is reasonable practice among themselves. In the second case, the legislature is presumed to speak as the representative of the community as a whole over a relevant domain.[10]

It should be clear from these remarks that the notion of a "local" community is not a geographic one. It should also be clear that the notion of community is not identical with affective or intentional communities. It refers to groups of individuals whose interests bring them together in relevant ways—ways that make it important for each of them that all of them abide by certain reliable and enforceable practices. Such communities are defined by the norms that govern interaction among their members. They may be smaller or larger, more or less tightly knit, and so on. The sorts of norms whose violation can give rise to claims to repair in corrective justice are local in this sense. They are typically conventions and norms that arise within communities. It is in this sense that corrective justice is local justice, or justice between the parties.

If I fail to do what *distributive* justice requires of me, and if you, therefore, have less than you ought to have under the principle of distributive justice, and I have more than my share, then *distributive* justice says I have too much and you too little.

It is distributive justice that says a correction is in order, not corrective justice as an independent moral ideal. By the same token, if I act inefficiently and impose inefficient costs on you, then it is efficiency that says a correction is in order, not corrective justice as an independent ideal. Not every justified correction is itself required by corrective justice. Corrective justice, in other words, grounds a subset of justified corrections. Put another way, all corrections are forms of *redistribution*. The case for redistribution can be grounded in distributive justice, efficiency, benevolence, utility, or corrective justice. (There may be other justifications as well.)

The norms enforced or sustained by corrective justice are local norms and conventions of the sort mentioned above. It is likely that these norms will be efficient since their stability depends in part on the extent to which they are mutually beneficial, that is, wealth maximizing.[11] It is also true that they will be sufficiently fair or equitable to be stable within the community. Since the primary means of enforcement of informal norms within a community are also informal, reliance is typically placed on internalization and reciprocal private sanction. Thus, it would not be surprising to find that the norms governing, for example, reasonable risk-taking, within most liberal, nonoppressive communities are both relatively efficient and fair. But it is neither their efficiency nor their fairness that gives rise to the duty in corrective justice to repair losses resulting from their violation.

The problem is that corrective justice imposes *moral* reasons for acting. If neither the efficiency nor the fairness of the norms is necessary in order to sustain duties in corrective justice, what is? Put another way: What conditions must be satisfied in order for norms to be sustained by the imposition of duties in corrective justice? In order to be sustained by corrective justice, the norms must be local, that is, part of the background or baseline norms governing behavior within communities. But it hardly follows that "local norms" or conventions will necessarily give rise to moral reasons for sustaining or protecting them. What else must be true of them in order that a practice of corrective justice should apply to them? To answer this question, let us focus primarily on the local or conventional norms governing property rights or holdings.

Property Rights and Corrective Justice

One thing someone might hold is that corrective justice does not reach the underlying property rights or holdings. It applies only to the norms or practices governing the *transfer* of holdings. Suppose that the underlying property rights are both unfair and inefficient. Even so, we will need norms to specify the conditions of their transfer. These background or baseline norms are the ones sustained by a practice of corrective justice, not the norms that specify the property holdings themselves. This is just another way of saying that corrective justice is a dimension of *transactional* justice. The rights, wrongs, norms, and losses that are its concern are those governing transfer, not those governing the justice of the underlying claims. So it is simply a mistake to phrase the problem of corrective justice as we have: that is, as the question of what conditions must be satisfied in order that a scheme of property rights be sustainable by a practice of corrective justice.

Corrective justice only indirectly affects property rights schemes. It sustains transactional schemes or norms. We should have asked a different question: namely, "What must be true of a scheme of transactional norms in order that they be sustainable by a practice of corrective justice?"

However plausible this line of argument may be, I reject it for at least two different reasons: one conceptual, the other normative. To the conceptual concern first: I reject the distinction between underlying rights and transactional "rights." On the account of rights given above, rules governing their transfer are part of the content of rights; transactional rights are part of the underlying rights, not distinct from them. Second, and more importantly, the normative concern: Corrective justice imposes *moral reasons for acting*. If it happens that applying corrective justice has the effect of sustaining a distribution of resources that is simply unjust, then how can an individual have a duty in morality to do so? To this question, it may be no answer to say that one does not have a moral duty to sustain an unjust system of property rights, but that one does have a duty to sustain a just system of transfer, even if sustaining the just system of transfer has the effect of sustaining an unjust system of property rights. Indeed, one might wonder whether a system of transfer could be just if sustaining it under normal circumstances had the effect of entrenching an unjust system of property rights.

I do not want to suggest that no arguments on behalf of some such position can be constructed. My point is the more modest one that in order to determine the conditions of being under a moral duty to make repair, we must determine what conditions, if any, would justify the practice of making repair in such cases. Thus, we cannot simply dissociate the duty to make repair from the status of the underlying entitlements and treat the latter as if it had no bearing on the grounds or content of the former.

Here is a schematic answer to the question of what conditions must be satisfied in order for a scheme of property rights to be sustainable by a practice of corrective justice. The rights sustained by corrective justice must be ones that justify their enforcement against infringements and invasions by the actions of others, *even if they would not be enforceable against the actions of a state seeking to implement the correct allocation of property rights under the best available theory of distributive justice*. This schematic answer is not without content, however. It implies, among other things, that the state has an authority—to redistribute for the purposes of implementing a just distribution of property holdings—that private individuals do not have. Suppose there exists a set of holdings that satisfies this condition. Then it would follow that even if an individual could further distributive justice by not paying compensation for a loss he wrongfully caused another (either by keeping his gain or by redistributing it in some other way), he would have no authority to do so; indeed, he would have a duty to repair in justice, whereas the state would be justified in not paying compensation. Of course, part of the reason the state would be free of the burden of compensation is that, unlike the private individual, it can implement the demands of distributive justice *systematically,* over the community as a whole. And part of what that means, at least implicitly, is that the state would be authorized to infringe a property right to implement distributive justice without owing compensation, provided it did so in a reasonably systematic fashion. And that is part of the reason why the state, in the United States at least, would have a duty of compensation under the "takings clause" of the Fifth Amendment to the Constitution even if the property it takes is not one that would be held by the "victim" under the best theory of distributive justice, and even if the point of the taking is redistribution according to that theory. The typical "taking" is not part of systematic redistribution aimed at implementing the correct distribution of resources.

The fact that the liberal state has an authority that private individuals do not have, and that it is one that depends in part on the state's ability to implement redistribution systematically, might help us to fill out the content of the principle stated above. Whatever their ultimate justice (or efficiency), schemes of holdings, and the norms regulating them, help to create stable expectations on which individuals can rely in coordinating their behavior with one another. Coordination allows individuals to create a framework of norms and institutions within which individuals formulate and execute projects and plans and pursue goals. Norms and institutions are essential, in other words, to personal autonomy and to individual and collective well-being. A scheme of property rights, of holdings secured by enforceable powers of exclusion and alienation, provides a good example. There is a wide range of possible principles according to which property rights might be allocated. Some of these are likely to be more just than others. A range of these, however, will serve reasonably well in providing the framework within which individuals can formulate meaningful projects and plans, and make the necessary investments to execute them.

The very idea of tying together autonomy in the formulation and pursuit of individual projects and goals with the framework of property rights suggests some constraints on the kinds of property rights schemes that are justifiable. They must provide individuals with an adequate range of opportunities and with the capacities to successfully pursue them (other things being equal). The scheme of norms cannot, moreover, be incompatible with the concept of autonomy; and part of what that means is that the scheme of holdings cannot be oppressive, or enforceable only through oppressive means. Beyond that, practical considerations, especially those of stability, will constrain the set of enforceable (by moral duties in corrective justice) property rights schemes.

In short, the basic idea I am reaching for is this: The set of property rights enforceable by duties in corrective justice need not itself conform with any abstract ideal or demand of distributive justice. The norms, and the rights they create, however, must be central to individual autonomy and well-being. The roles norms play in this regard are complex and connected. First, they create a framework within which individuals formulate and pursue their projects and plans. Second, they provide part of the wherewithal necessary to formulate and pursue those plans. Thus, any distribution sustainable by corrective justice must be stable and facilitate coordination, and it must provide the ingredients required by the liberal conception of autonomy. Any set of underlying property holdings that satisfies these substantive constraints is, I suggest, enforceable by duties of corrective justice.

Two final remarks: The first seeks to connect these substantive constraints with the notion of locality implicated in the principle of corrective justice. The norms that evolve among individuals within various communities allow coordination. Coordination provides individuals with a framework of reliable and stable expectations that, I have argued elsewhere, is necessary if investments in one's private projects are to be rational.[12]

The second seeks to connect these remarks about property rights with our initial concern about the relationship between corrective and distributive justice. At the outset, I said that I would defend the position that corrective justice could sometimes impose a moral duty to make repair even if doing so had the effect of sustaining a less than just distribution of resources. What I have argued is that distributions of resources that are less than ideal can be sustained by corrective justice. One way of interpreting my argument is that it is based on a distinction between "first" and "second" best conceptions of distributive justice. Corrective justice does not apply only to cases of first-best distributions of resources, nor will it apply to all second-best distributions. It will apply to some second-best sets of holdings, those in which certain threshold requirements are met. Those threshold requirements are themselves to be determined, at least in part, by the relevant first-best or ideal theory. If one has a theory of distributive justice of the sort I do—a theory that emphasizes human well-being and autonomy—then a practice of corrective justice can sustain a scheme of property rights provided that scheme sufficiently allows for individual autonomy, the possibility of human development, and the like. Instead of saying that corrective justice can sustain a property rights scheme that is not just, we might say that practice of corrective justice can sustain second-best distributions of holdings or property rights that meet or satisfy threshold requirements of allowing for adequate autonomy and the possibility of achieving significant levels of well-being.

CHAPTER 5

Judith J. Thomson

RIGHTS AND COMPENSATION

1. Suppose, following Joel Feinberg,

> that you are on a back-packing trip in the high mountain country when an unanticipated blizzard strikes the area with such ferocity that your life is imperiled. Fortunately, you stumble onto an unoccupied cabin, locked and boarded up for the winter, clearly somebody else's private property. You smash in a window, enter, and huddle in a corner for three days until the storm abates. During this period you help yourself to your unknown benefactor's food supply and burn his wooden furniture in the fireplace to keep warm.[1]

Feinberg thinks it is morally permissible for you to do all these things, and he is surely right.

"Yet," as he also says, having done them, "you have infringed the clear rights of another person." Why does he think that if you act as he imagines you to act, you infringe another's "clear rights?" Well, as he said, that cabin is "clearly somebody else's private property."

It seems to me that Feinberg is right in thinking that in so acting you infringe the rights of the cabin owner. It seems to me that if I own a piece of property, then, unless and until I give you permission, I have a right against you that you not burn it. In Feinberg's story, the cabin owner did not give you permission to burn his furniture: the cabin owner was not there to be asked for permission. So it seems to me that in acting as Feinberg imagines you to do, you infringe at least this right of the owner's: the right that you not burn his furniture.

Let us go in for a closer look. Suppose that I am the cabin owner, and that you have just broken into my cabin, and that you have not yet burned any of the furni-

This essay originally appeared in *NOUS* 14:1 (March 1980): 3–15. Reprinted by permission of Blackwell Publishing Ltd.

ture. Among the bits of furniture is an old wooden chair, Feinberg's view is that I have a right against you that you not burn that chair—a claim, of course, rather than a privilege, in Hohfeld's sense of these terms. Let us abbreviate "x has a claim against y that p" as "$C_{x,y}$ p." Then we may say that it is Feinberg's, and my, view that

(1) $C_{I,you}$ You do not burn the chair

is true.

But some people would say that if you burn my furniture in circumstances of the kind which Feinberg describes, then you do not infringe any right of mine. They would remind us of the fact that

(2) It is morally permissible for you to burn the chair

is true in circumstances of the kind which Feinberg describes; and if (2) is true, how can (1) also be true?

In fact, some—perhaps all—of them would say that (2) *entails* that (1) is false. They would say, quite generally, that the question what claims one person has against another is settled by the answer to the question what it is morally permissible for that other person to do; so that, in particular, if he *may* burn my chair, then it is not the case that I have a claim against him that he not burn it.

Our theory of rights would, after all, be considerably simpler if we could adopt the general view that the question of what claims one person has against another is settled by the answer to the question about what is morally permissible for that other person to do. No puzzling clashes: i.e., no cases in which A has a right against B which B may permissibly infringe.

One would have to pay something for that simplification. In particular, one would have to allow that ownership is a little more complicated than might have been thought. But ownership is already, and on any view, a complicated business—more complicated, certainly, than a hasty first thought suggests. To own something is to have a cluster of rights in respect of it. Which rights? I own a certain chair. One's hasty first thought is that it follows that I have a right to sit in it whenever I choose. A second thought makes clear that this does not follow. For I might own a chair, and yet have rented it to Jones—and if I have rented it to Jones, then, though I still own it, I do not (for the duration of Jones' lease on it) have a right to sit in it whenever I choose. Again, does it follow from the fact that I own a chair that I have a right to sell it? I should think not: it seems to me eminently possible that I should own a chair and have committed myself to not selling it—i.e., waived my right to sell it.

It is clear that the range of rights included in ownership of a piece of property is constrained by rental or loan or other kinds of commitment. And we *can* say that the range of rights included in ownership is narrower even than these considerations suggest it is. I said that if I own a piece of property, then, unless and until I give you permission, I have a right against you that you not burn it. But we can say that this is just a mistake. If you are in circumstances of the kind which Feinberg describes, you are in dire need; that is what makes (2) true. We *can* say that that also makes (1) false. Perhaps we should say that (1) *was* true, but became false when you stumbled onto my cabin, needing to burn the chair; perhaps we should say that (1) is not now true, and never was true—that I at no time have a claim against you that you not burn it, but only a claim that you not-burn-it-when-you-are-in-no-need-of-burning-it. In any case, we *can* say that, though I do still own the chair (1) is now false. And isn't a simpler general theory of rights worth buying at the cost of a more complicated theory of that small branch of it which has to do with ownership?

2. A number of people have suggested that there is yet another reason to suppose (1) is false. What they would draw our attention to is the fact that it is not morally permissible for me to *prevent* you from burning the chair. Suppose, that is, that I have been watching you stumble toward my cabin via television. Suppose that I have a device in place, by the activation of which I can prevent you from burning my chair—e.g., pressing the switch will cause all the furniture to be coated with fire-proof foam. Would it be morally permissible for me to activate that device? surely not; surely it would be wrong to prevent you from burning the chair.

If Jones is drowning, Smith cannot pull his rope out of reach and say "Mine!" Now friends of the simplification can easily accommodate the truth of

(3) It is not morally permissible for me to prevent you from burning the chair,

for on their view, (1) is false since (2) is true. But how are Feinberg and his friends to accommodate it? If (1) is true—if I really do have a claim against you that you not burn the chair—how can it be morally impermissible for me to prevent you from burning it? We Feinberg-friends thus seem to be committed to further puzzling clashes, for we are committed, not merely to there being cases in which A has a right against B which B may permissibly infringe, but also to there being cases in which A has a right against B that B not do a thing, though it is not permissible for A to prevent him from doing it.

But we ought not let this sail by too quickly. *Does* the truth of (3) cast doubt on (1)? Suppose I own a concrete garden gnome. Is

(1') $C_{I,you}$ You do not smash my gnome

true? Well, why would you want to smash it? Let us suppose that no one is in need of its being smashed; let us suppose that you simply dislike me, or my gnome, or both. But let us suppose also that I can prevent you from smashing my gnome only by killing you. (You are bigger than me, but I have and anti-tank gun.) Surely I cannot, surely it would be bad, wrong, morally impermissible for me to prevent you from smashing it in those circumstances. Thus

(3') It is not morally permissible for me to prevent you from smashing my gnome.

is true in this case. Should we say that since (3') is true (1') is false? Really? So that out of moral compunction I do not kill you, and thus do not prevent you from smashing my gnome, you infringe no right of mine in smashing it?

I think we really must grant that (3') is entirely compatible with (1'). No call for puzzlement *here:* it is perfectly possible that A have a right against B that B not do a thing, and that it not be permissible—the circumstances being what they are—for A to prevent him from doing it.

It is a good question why people have thought otherwise. *Why* has it seemed to people that the truth of (3) casts doubt on (1)? One possible, and I think interesting, source of the idea that it does comes out as follows.

It is a very plausible idea that if I have a *claim* against you that you not burn my chair, then I have the *privilege* as regards you of preventing you from burning it—i.e., that (1) entails

(4) I have the privilege, as regards you, of preventing you from burning the chair.

I'll call the thesis that (1) entails (4) "the claim/privilege thesis".

Now as I said, our theory of rights would be considerably simpler if we could adopt the general view that the question what claims one person has against another is settled by the answer to the question what it is morally permissible for that other person to do. And shouldn't what is true of claims have an analogue true of privileges? And don't we obtain a comparable further simplification if we suppose also that the question what privileges a person has is settled by the answer to the question what it is permissible for *him* to do? So shouldn't we say, not merely that (2) entails that (1) is false, but also that (3) entails that (4) is false?

The argument now emerges. Suppose you like this simplification. Then you accept that (3) entails that (4) is false. To accept that is to accept that (4) entails that (3) is false. Suppose you also like the claim/privilege thesis that (1) entails (4). It would be no surprise if you drew the conclusion that (1) entails that (3) is false, and therefore that (3) entails that (1) is false.

I am inclined to think that this is not merely a *possible* source of the idea that the truth of (3) casts doubt on (1): I am inclined to think that those who think it does have reached that idea in just this way.

The simplification to be got in this way is very attractive indeed. It is worth noticing that if we say both that the question what claims a person has is settled by what it is permissible for others to do, and that the question what privileges a person has is settled by what it is permissible for him to do, we do not merely have a simpler theory of rights, we have a simpler moral theory, for to take this line is to commit oneself to the view that rights do not have an independent bearing in moral assessment of action.

And isn't the claim/privilege thesis plausible?

Unfortunately, we cannot have both the simplification and the claim/privilege thesis. An argument exactly analogous to that which we just went through yields that (3') entails that (1') is false, which simply is not so—for in the case I imagined (3') and (1') are both true.

Which should be given up? Feinberg and his friends say: Alas, the simplification must be given up. They say: (1) is entirely compatible with (2) and (3) with (4). They say: the question what claims a person has is not settled by what others may do, and the question what privileges a person has is not settled by what he may do—rights do have an independent bearing in moral assessment of action, so we must learn to live with whatever moral clutter that fact produces.

Indeed, they have an argument to the effect that the simplification must be given up—for they have an argument to the effect that we must suppose that (1) is true. We should now turn to it.

3. Let me remind you of what is being supposed. You were caught by a blizzard; you stumbled onto my cabin; you broke in, and have it in mind to burn my furniture for warmth—among other bits of furniture, an old wooden chair. As Feinberg says: if you go ahead and burn that chair, you will later owe me compensation for doing so.[2] Feinberg says:

> [You will later owe] compensation here for the same reason one must repay a debt or return what one has borrowed. If the other had no right that was infringed in the first place, one could hardly have a duty to compensate him. Perhaps he would be an appropriate object of your sympathy or patronage or charity, but those are quite different from compensation.

Thus Feinberg thinks that if you go ahead and burn that chair, I will have a claim against you for compensation—thus that if you go ahead and burn the chair,

(5) $C_{I,you}$ You compensate me for the loss of the chair

will be true. Moreover, Feinberg things (5) will be true *because* (1) is now true, and that (5) would not become true if (1) were not true now.

The proposal is of considerable importance, since accepting it blocks accepting that attractive simplification I drew attention to. It seems plain that Feinberg is right in thinking that if you go ahead and burn the chair (5) will be true. What we must ask first, however, is whether he is right in thinking that if (1) were not now true, then (5) would not become true when you burned the chair. In other words, is there no other way of explaining the fact that (5) will be true than by supposing (1) to be true now, and appealing to *that* fact to explain it?

4. Robert E. Keeton's discussion of similar cases in tort law suggests an alternative explanation.[3] On this view, we do not need to suppose that (1) is now true. We

need not suppose that I have a claim against you that you not burn the chair; it is enough if we suppose that I have a claim against you that you not do something complex, viz., burn-the-chair-without-compensating-me-for-the-loss-of-it. More precisely, it is enough if we suppose that

(6) CI, you (If you burn the chair, then you compensate me for the loss of the chair)

is now true.

And why should we think that enough? it is a very natural idea that the conjunction of (6) with

(7) You burn the chair

entails (5). So the alternative explanation goes like this: why will (5) be true if you make (7) true? Well (6) is true, and the conjunction of (6) with (7) entails (5).

This *is* a very natural idea—and it is therefore most unfortunate that we cannot make a permanent home for it.

What I have in mind is this. There is a principle governing the relations among ascriptions of claims, viz.,

(P_1) '$C_{A,B}$ p' entails '$C_{A,B}$ q' if 'p' entails 'q',

which I think we really ought to accept. I do not have space to defend it here; I shall simply assume it true. Suppose that

(CP_1) '[$C_{A,B}$ (p→q)] & 'p' entails '$C_{A,B}$ q'

were also true. ("CP_1" is an abbreviation for "first candidate-principle.") Then

(α) [$C_{A,B}$ (-p)] & p

would entail

(β) $C_{A,B}$ q-

for '$C_{A,B}$ (-p)' entails '$C_{A,B}$ (p→q)' by (P_1), and the conjunction of that with 'p' entails '$C_{A,B}$ q' by (CP_1). But we really cannot have it that (α) entails (β). For if (α) entails (β), then if A has a claim against B that B does not kick A, and if also B *does* kick A, then for any sentence S you choose, A has a claim against B that S be true—the sentences "B murders A's father," "B starts World War III," and so on. This is, to say the least, an unacceptable consequence. You do not give me a claim against you to anything and everything simply by bringing about some one thing which I have a claim against you that you not bring about.

So we may not accept (CP_I); and I should imagine we must, therefore, reject that very natural idea that the conjunction of (6) with (7) entails (5). So this putative alternative explanation of what will make (5) true if you burn the chair is a non-starter.

5. There is a possible source of worry about what I just said which is worth attending to. What I have in mind is that if we reject (CP_I), we may seem to be in trouble elsewhere in ethics. There are cases and cases, and in some there is a duty to compensate where there is no plausibility whatever to the idea that anyone infringed anyone's rights. Suppose, for example, that A owns a restaurant. B enters, and sits down at a table. A hands B a menu, and let us for simplicity imagine that there is only one thing written on it, viz., "Stew. . . . $1.50." B says "Yes, please." A brings B some stew, and then, later, when B has eaten the stew, a bill for $1.50. It is now surely true to say:

(5*) $C_{A,B}$ B pays A $1.50.

What makes (5*) be true? It is a plausible idea that

(6*) $C_{A,B}$ (If A gives B stew, then B pays A $1.50)

was true, and by hypothesis,

(7*) A gives B stew

is true. But if the conjunction of (6) with (7) does not entail (5), then the conjunction of (6*) with (7*) does not entail (5*). How *are* we to account for the truth of (5*), if we cannot suppose that (CP_I) is true?

Such situations are common enough, and it is—quite apart from our concerns here—an interesting question how the debt gets generated in them. One thing which is plain is that no one infringes anyone's rights in such situations: e.g., we plainly cannot say that what makes (5*) true is the fact that B infringed a right of A's.

A and B seem to have made a deal. Neither *said* anything about a deal; they did not have to, the custom in such things being what it is. What they made was an unwritten, unspoken contract.

How precisely did they do that? The most plausible account of what happened is, I think, H. A. Prichard's.[4] On Prichard's view, we must take A and B to have made promises to each other. What promises? It cannot be supposed that in handing B the menu, A was promising (all simply) to give B stew; A wants to give B stew only if he can suppose B to be committed to paying for it if he gets it. On Prichard's view, A was, in handing B the menu, making an (unspoken) promise reportable in the words

(8) A promises B that [if B promises A that (if A gives B stew, then B pays A $1.50), then A gives B stew];

and B was, in saying "Yes, please," making an (unspoken) promise reportable in the words

(9) B promises A that (if A gives B stew, then B pays A $1.50).

I think this is a plausible account of what went on between them. In any case, it is easy to see *roughly* how B's debt got generated under this account of what went on between them. By making the promise reported in (8), A commits himself to the truth of what is in the square brackets in (8); by making the promise reported in (9), B makes its antecedent true, and commits himself to the truth of what is in the parentheses in (9). Since B made the antecedent of what is in the square brackets true, A must give him some stew. By giving him some stew, A makes the antecedent of what is in the parentheses true, and B must therefore pay A $1.50.

But this *is* rough. We must look at it a little more closely. I shall concentrate on the second half of the drama, i.e., on the source of B's debt to A.

Suppose B has made the promise reported in (9). I said B thereby committed himself to the truth of what is in the parentheses in (9). I might have put it: B thereby gave A a claim against him to the truth of what is in the parentheses in (9). It seems a plausible idea, that is, that we should accept

(P_2) '$\text{Prom}_{A,B}$ p' entails '$C_{B,A}$ p',

and thus take (9) to entail (6*). After B made the promise reported in (9), A gave him some stew; so he made (7*) true. I said: by giving B some stew, A made the antecedent of what is in the parentheses true, and B must therefore pay A $1.50—i.e. (5*) is now true. But without (CP_1) in hand, we cannot deduce (5*) from the conjunction of (6*) with (7*). So what warrants my use of that word "must"? How does the debt reported in (5*) get generated?

It seems to me we need, and should adopt, a second principle governing the relations between promises and claims, namely

(P_3) '[$\text{Prom}_{A,B}$ ($p \rightarrow q$)] & p' entails '$C_{B,A}$ q'.[5]

Let us first see that if we can adopt (P_3), all is well. Suppose B has made the promise reported in (9), and that A has therefore given B some stew. The conjunction of (9) with (7*) is now true; and (P_3) tells us that it entails (5*). So if we have (P_3) in hand, all is well: what generates the debt reported in (5*) is the fact that B made his promise, and that A gave B stew.

Can we adopt (P_3)? Compare it with (CP_1). They look very like—and yet we had to reject (CP_1).

We would have to reject (P_3) for analogous reasons if

(CP_2) '$Prom_{A,B}$ p' entails '$Prom_{A,B}$ q' if 'p' entails 'q'

were true. For if (P_3) and (CP_2) were both true,

(α^*) [$Prom_{A,B}$ (-p)] & p

would entail

(β^*) $C_{B,A}$ q.

And we can no more have it that (α^* entails (β^*) than we can have it that (α) entails (β).

Fortunately, however (CP_2) is on its face a false principle. I may promise you that a state of affairs S will obtain without having promised you that every state of affairs S* will obtain such that S's obtaining entails S*'s obtaining. Compare some other "speech-activities." Suppose 'p' entails 'q'. I may say that p without thereby having said that q; I may tell you that p without thereby having told you that q; I may ask you whether p without thereby having asked you whether q; and so on. Claims are different. If you have a claim against me that S will obtain, then you have a claim against me to the obtaining of every state of affairs which must obtain if S is to obtain. Promising, like other "speech-activities," involves intentionality; the generating of claims does not.

So I think we *can* adopt (P_3). Moreover, it really does seem a plausible principle. If I promise you that if p then q, and it turns out to be the case that p, then I surely am committed to you to its being the case that q—you have a claim against me that it be the case that q, and can complain to me if it is not.

If so, then we do not make trouble for ourselves by giving up (CP_1). We *can* explain B's debt to A without it.

6. Let us go back to the case we began with. If we could suppose that you promised me that if you burn my chair, then you will compensate me for the loss of it, we could explain the fact that (5) will be true if you burn my chair in the same way as we explained B's debt to A. But we cannot suppose this. If memory serves, nobody has ever made me a promise, written or unwritten, spoken or unspoken, to the effect that if he burns any of my furniture, he will compensate me for the loss of it. So what makes it be the case that if you burn that chair (5) will be true?

I gather that some legal writers would say that if you burn the chair, you will have "unjustly enriched" yourself, and that that is why you will have to compensate me for the loss of it. Unjust enrichment? I am taking it to be a datum that it is—in the circumstances—morally permissible, not bad, not wrong for you to burn that chair. It could be said that if you burn the chair then, although you act permissibly, you do nevertheless act unjustly—since I have a right that you not burn the chair, which right you therefore infringe in acting. If they take this line, they are friends of Feinberg's: they explain the fact that (5) will be true by appeal to the fact that (1) is now true.

The idea of unjust enrichment could enter at a different place. It could be said that burning my chair would not be a case of unjust enrichment, but that burning-my-chair-without-compensating-me-for-the-loss-of-it would be. As I said, Robert E. Keeton is one who takes this line. Unfortunately it does not succeed.

7. Feinberg says that (5) will be true if you burn the chair because (1) is now true. I think he must be right. I certainly have not canvassed all the possibilities, but it does seem to me that there is no way of explaining the fact that (5) will be true which does not, somewhere, pass through the truth of (1). It is perhaps just worth saying explicitly that to take this view is not to commit onesself to the view that (5) entails (1). (5) plainly does not entail (1). (5) does not even entail that you infringed any right of mine. Compensation may be owed in cases in which no one infringed anyone's rights: see, for example, B's duty to compensate A for the stew he ate in A's restaurant. The duty to compensate is at best a sign of an infringed right—and probably not even a very good one at that. What has been in question here is only this: what could explain the fact that (5) will be true *in those circumstances* if we cannot suppose that (1) is true.

There remains a second question, namely *how* the fact that (1) is true—supposing now that (1) is true—explains the fact that (5) will be true if you burn the chair. It is not obvious how it does. I am sorry to have to leave this question for discussion elsewhere.

8. My main aim has been to give ground for thinking that we cannot have that simplification in moral theory which I drew attention to earlier. If, as I think, we must suppose that (1) is true if we are to be able to explain the fact that you will have a duty to compensate me if you burn the chair, then we must suppose that (1) is compatible with (2). More generally, we cannot have it that the question what claims a person has is settled by the answer to the question what it is permissible for other people to do. Moral theory is more cluttered than we might have wished for it to be.

CHAPTER 6 *Phillip Montague*

RIGHTS AND DUTIES OF COMPENSATION

I shall be concerned here with two propositions about the moral significance of infringing another's rights, and will suggest that both rest on mistakes. The first (which should be regarded as an obvious truth by most moral and social philosophers) is that infringing rights is sometimes morally permissible; the second is that even permissible infringements produce residual duties to the rightholder on the part of whoever infringes his rights. In discussing these propositions I will focus on a class of cases which seem to provide clear occasions for their application, namely, those in which individuals cause others property losses and owe compensation as a result.

I

If x vandalizes y's property, then x owes y compensation for what he damages or destroys. The duty of compensation here evidently falls within W. D. Ross's category of duties of reparation—"Those resting on a previous wrongful act."[1] Imagine now a different, though relevantly similar, kind of case: x promises to repay a debt to y by a certain time, but fails to do so and has neither justification nor excuse for his failure; as a result, y cannot make his car payment and the car is repossessed. Again, x owes y compensation for any loss y suffers (the equity in his car, let us say); and while in this case the loss is not *directly* inflicted by x on y as it is in the former, the duty of compensation is nevertheless a duty of reparation arising from x's previous wrongful act.

This essay originally appeared in *Philosophy & Public Affairs* 13:1 (Winter 1984): 79–88.

Now consider the following example, which is like the first of those discussed above in certain respects, but where the issues are far less clear:

> A becomes lost in the woods and desperately needs food and shelter. He stumbles upon a cabin owned by B which is secured for the winter, and which A can enter only by breaking in. He does so, and not only eats some food B has stored, but also burns some of his furniture to keep from freezing to death.

This kind of case is discussed by both Judith Thomson and Joel Feinberg, and it is clear from their discussions that they would regard A as having a duty to compensate B for his losses.[2] Moreover, on the Thomson-Feinberg account, compensation is owed in such cases because property rights are infringed. That is (in terms of the above example), A owes B compensation for destroying his furniture; and compensation is owed because A's destruction of B's furniture infringes a property right of B's. It is also part of the Thomson-Feinberg account that the rights in question here are Hohfeldian,[3] which implies that if A infringes a right of B's in destroying the latter's possessions, then he acts contrary to a duty or obligation in doing so. If we now say that one who acts contrary to a duty or obligation acts wrongly, then on the Thomson-Feinberg account, A owes B compensation as a duty of reparation in the sense described above.

There is a problem here, however. For as Thomson and Feinberg point out, it seems perfectly clear that one who acts as A does in our example acts permissibly.[4] Yet it is hard to see how A's destruction of B's property can be permissible if B has a right that A not do so, and if as a consequence A has a duty to forbear. It is probably also worth mentioning that if A's destructive act is indeed permissible, then any duty he might have to compensate B can hardly be viewed as a duty of *reparation,* which requires the duty to arise from some *wrongful* act.

Neither Thomson nor Feinberg provides anything like a satisfactory account of how A can be permitted to burn B's furniture if his doing so infringes a (Hohfeldian) right held by B. Thomson, for example, simply insists that A owes B compensation for his property losses even though A acts permissibly in causing those losses; and claims that A's action *must* infringe a right of B's because A owes B compensation. Regarding the apparent inconsistency in this conjunction of claims, she says only that, in the circumstances, it is "morally permissible, not bad, not wrong" for A to destroy B's furniture, but that even though A acts permissibly, he acts unjustly.[5] Perhaps these claims are true; but they either leave untouched or beg questions that are at the very center of Thomson's discussion. There is, moreover, not much room for maneuvering on Thomson's part. She might withdraw her contention that she is concerned with Hohfeldian rights, and deny that B's right against A implies a duty on A's part. But then we will be hard pressed to understand what kind of right B does have, and why its infringement generates a duty of compensation. Or she might deny that being permitted to act is incompatible with having a duty to forbear. But this would be to contradict what appears to be a necessary (and perhaps analytic) truth, namely that if x is permitted to do y, then x has no duty to refrain from doing y. *Perhaps* this problem can be solved by driving a wedge between acting contrary to a duty and acting wrongly (so that one is permitted to act contrary to a duty but not to act wrongly), but I doubt it. In any case, some sort of explanation of Thomson's position concerning these matters is sorely needed.

The positions of Thomson and Feinberg regarding the issues being raised here are sufficiently similar to justify treating them as a single account, but Feinberg's discussion contains an element that is absent from Thomson's. This is the idea that in cases of the sort we are considering here, "one owes compensation . . . for the same reason one must repay a debt or return what one has borrowed."[6] The common reason to which Feinberg refers here is presumably given by his claim that "if the other had no right that was infringed in the first place, one could hardly have a duty to compensate him."[7] Taken together, however, these two statements are puzzling at the very least. For they strongly suggest that, like duties of compensation, duties to repay debts and return borrowed articles arise from infringements of rights—which they clearly do not.

Thus, even if one has rights against his debtors and against those to whom he lends things, so that failing to pay a debt or return what is borrowed infringes a right; and even if compensation is owed a creditor or lender for any *additional* losses he suffers if not repaid or if what he lends is not returned, the duties to repay debts or return borrowed articles are not themselves duties of compensation, and do not arise when rights are infringed. This point can be made in terms of an example cited earlier, where one person's duty to compensate another for the loss of equity in his car arises from the former's failure to repay a debt on time. This failure on the debtor's part may infringe some right of the individual to whom he owes the debt, but surely the duty to repay this debt does not itself arise from any such infringement.

The difficulties which underlie the Thomson-Feinberg account of duties of compensation are independent of this last issue, however, and are related instead to the claim that A is permitted to burn B's furniture even though he infringes a (Hohfeldian) right of B's in doing so. If these claims are logically incompatible (as they certainly seem to be), then the Thomson-Feinberg account is inconsistent.

II

One way which suggests itself immediately for dealing with the problem here is by adopting a kind of modified Hohfeldian interpretation of rights according to which they entail something like prima facie duties (or obligations) rather than what might be called duties (or obligations) "on balance." On this interpretation, the proposition that A infringes a right of B's in destroying the latter's furniture implies only that A acts contrary to a *prima facie* duty; and there is no inconsistency in maintaining that A acts permissibly even though contrary to a prima facie duty (given any normal explanation of prima facie duties). It would therefore be possible by this maneuver to avoid what appears to be an inconsistency in the Thomson-Feinberg account.

I am unsure whether Thomson would find this modified Hohfeldian view congenial, but it is clearly incompatible with Feinberg's position regarding the nature of rights. For he accepts a strong version of the "correlativity doctrine," according to which rights and duties, when correlated at all, are simply two sides of the same coin.[8] On this view, B's right to not have his furniture destroyed by A is nothing more than A's duty to not destroy B's furniture; and hence B's right entails a *duty* on A's part—rather than merely a prima facie duty.[9]

I think it is clear, then, that Feinberg cannot accept the Thomson-Feinberg account if he accepts the correlativity doctrine and at the same time maintains that "A is permitted to burn B's furniture and has a duty to not do so" is inconsistent.[10] Of course, it would be possible to claim that the latter statement is *consistent,* but one who did so would certainly bear a heavy and cumbersome burden of proof. Moreover, this much is certain: if we say that A has a duty *on balance* (that is, all things considered) not to burn B's furniture, then we cannot consistently maintain that A is permitted *on balance* to do so. For whether x is permitted to do y depends on just those considerations which determine whether x has a duty to not do y; and one cannot be permitted to act and have a duty to not act relative to the same moral considerations.[11] Thus, someone who maintains that A has a duty to forbear even though permitted to act must deny either that A has a duty *on balance* to refrain from acting, or that he is permitted *on balance* to act. Since it is clear enough that, relative to the moral considerations mentioned in our example, A is permitted to burn B's furniture, it follows that A does not have a duty relative to those considerations to refrain from doing so. And since the idea that A has a duty to not destroy B's property is derived from the proposition that B has a right to not have his property destroyed, a significant qualification of A's duty will have implications for how B's right should be interpreted—or for whether B has a right at all. In particular, it may be necessary to maintain that if B does have a right then it is not straightforwardly Hohfeldian.

What then prevents us from avoiding what appears to be an inconsistency in our original premises by simply denying that B has a (Hohfeldian) right to not have his property destroyed by A? The answer contained in the Thomson-Feinberg account is that A owes B compensation for burning his furniture, and the only (or perhaps the best) explanation of A's duty of compensation is that he infringes a right of B's by his destructive act. But even though it is probably true that if A *did* owe B compensation, this would be in virtue of having infringed a right of B's, I would like to suggest that if A does in fact act permissibly in burning B's furniture, then he does not owe B compensation for the loss. My reasons for saying this refer back to the beginning of this discussion, when it was pointed out that someone who simply *vandalizes* another's property does owe compensation for whatever he destroys or damages. It strikes me as extremely implausible to regard both the vandal and A in our example as owing compensation, as we deny (even more implausibly) that their duties of compensation depend on their destructive acts. Of course, it might be *desirable* for A to compensate B, but this is not to suggest that he has a duty to do so. The point is that an act of vandalism is morally different from A's destructive action; and this difference is manifested primarily in the fact that acts of vandalism generate duties of compensation while acts like A's do not.

All this is not to say that every duty of compensation arises from a previous wrongful act—that is, that compensation must always be viewed as reparation. Such duties might also arise, for example, from agreements such as those which exist between employers and employees. There may even be duties of compensation that are duties of gratitude, such as when one person suffers a loss while doing a favor for another. Indeed, some might be tempted to view A in our example as owing B compensation out of gratitude for a kind of implicit service done A by B. Of course, this would be to assume at the very least that if given the chance B would willingly sacrifice his furniture to help A, and nothing like this is being assumed either here or in Thomson's and Feinberg's discussions.

Whether we simply deny that A has a duty to compensate B for the loss of his possessions, or maintain that A owes B compensation out of gratitude to B for (implicitly) allowing his possessions to be destroyed by A, we lose what is on the Thomson-Feinberg account a crucial reason for thinking that A infringes a right of B's when he burns the latter's possessions. Nevertheless, there remains the nagging idea that despite its permissibility, A's action is morally flawed, and that whatever is wrong with A's action has something to do with B's rights.

III

I have claimed here that A cannot possibly have a duty on balance to not burn B's furniture if A's burning the furniture is permissible on balance. If this is true, and if the correlativity doctrine is acceptable—or if rights at least imply duties on balance—then B does not have a right to not have his furniture burned by A. This last conclusion is even more credible if A does not owe B compensation for the property he destroyed as was claimed above.

It does seem reasonable to maintain, however, that rights imply at least prima facie duties, and that A has a prima facie duty to not destroy B's possessions arising from B's right against A. Suppose we agree that this is the case, and assume that A has *only* a prima facie duty to not burn B's possessions. This implies that there are considerations relevant to whether A has a duty *on balance* to not burn B's furniture that have no bearing on whether B has a right against A. In particular, the fact that burning B's possessions is necessary for A's survival is relevant to whether A has a duty on balance to not destroy the furniture, but is completely irrelevant to whether B has a right against A.

This last result strikes me as extremely odd. Indeed, it seems to me plain that the kinds of considerations appropriately taken into account when attempting to determine whether some x has a duty on balance to not impose treatment y on z are just the considerations that should be taken into account when attempting to determine whether z has a right to not receive treatment y from x. For this reason, I find it quite plausible to maintain that rights imply duties on balance.[12] But as has already been noted, if rights do indeed imply duties on balance (and whether or not the entire correlativity doctrine is accepted), then if A has *only* a prima facie duty to not burn B's furniture, then A infringes no right of B's when he burns the furniture.

IV

Here is a proposal for dealing with the cluster of issues that have been raised here:

Let us first of all take duties on balance as primitive, and define specific and general prima facie duties respectively as follows:

> x has a prima facie duty to (not) do y if and only if x's doing y is of a kind K such that there is a prima facie duty to (not) perform acts of kind K.[13] There is a prima facie duty to (not) perform acts of kind K if and only if, if x's doing y is K and other things are equal, then x has a duty on balance to (not) do y.[14]

Taking rights on balance as our second primitive notion, and focusing on what will be referred to here as "treatment rights," we can define specific and general prima facie rights in this way:

> x has a prima facie right to (not) receive treatment y from z if and only if x's receiving treatment y from z is of a kind K such that there is a prima facie right to (not) receive treatment of kind K.
>
> There is a prima facie right to (not) receive treatment of kind K if and only if, if x's receiving treatment y from z is K and if other things are equal, then x has a right on balance to not receive treatment y from z.

Treatment rights are related to duties in this way:

> x has a right on balance to (not) receive treatment y from z only if z has a duty on balance to (not) accord x treatment y.
>
> x has a prima facie right to (not) receive treatment y from z only if z has a prima facie duty to (not) accord x treatment y.
>
> There is a prima facie right to (not) receive treatment of kind K only if there is a prima facie duty to (not) accord others treatment of kind K.

The following propositions will also be useful here:

> x's doing y is permissible on balance if and only if it is not the case that x has a duty on balance to refrain from doing y.

If x has a prima facie duty to not do y, then x's doing y is justified if and only if x's doing y is permissible on balance.

If there is a right to not have one's property destroyed by others, then this is a treatment right. And if we say (as I think we should) that all general treatment rights are prima facie rights, then we can infer that B has a *right* (that is, a right on balance) to not have his furniture burned by A only if other things are equal—which they are not in our example. We can infer, however, that B has a prima facie right against A, and hence that A has a prima facie duty to not destroy B's possessions. This conclusion is compatible with the idea that A is permitted on balance to burn B's furniture, and hence is justified in doing so.

I suspect that proponents of the Thomson-Feinberg account would object to this explanation of our example by claiming that it provides no real basis for regarding A's action as morally flawed, and as some sort of wrong (or even an injustice) to B. While I probably cannot provide a completely satisfactory response to this objection, let me say some things which may diminish its force somewhat.

Consider first what might follow from the claim that A's action is morally flawed and involves some sort of wrong to B. There is, of course, the idea (rejected earlier) that A owes B compensation for his losses; and some writers would doubtless maintain that even if A owes no compensation to B for having destroyed the latter's possessions, it would be appropriate for A to feel guilt or remorse for his action.[15]

But if A acted *permissibly*—if his action is *morally justified*—then for what should he feel guilt or remorse? Granted, if A had no compunctions regarding the destruction of B's furniture prior to his action, and if (given the opportunity) A expresses no regrets to B for his losses, then this might reflect badly on A's character. But even if A is morally flawed, this in no way implies that his action is.

It seems to me that the only remotely negative judgments that can be made about A's *action* are these: that prior to acting A had good (but far from conclusive) reasons for not doing so; and that A would have had a duty on balance to not act had the circumstances been different in certain morally relevant respects. Both of these judgments can be accommodated quite comfortably by the definitions given above. And while they may also fit into the Thomson-Feinberg account, there are too many gaps in the latter to determine whether this is so.

CHAPTER 7

Gerald F. Gaus

DOES COMPENSATION RESTORE EQUALITY?

What does compensatory justice seek to accomplish? A formal answer, of course, is that, like all justice, it seeks to assure each his due. Aristotle's analysis of "corrective" or "rectificatory" justice, however, proffers a more specific answer:

> What the judge aims at doing is to make the parts equal by the penalty he imposes, whereby he takes from the aggressor any gain he may have secured. The equal, then is a mean between the more and the less. But gain and loss are each of them more or less in opposite ways, more good and less evil being gains, the more evil and the less good being loss. The equal, which we hold to be just, is now seen to be intermediate between them. Hence we conclude that corrective justice must be the mean between loss and gain. This explains why the disputants have recourse to a judge; for to go to a judge is to go to justice. . . . What the judge does is to restore equality.[1]

In this chapter I consider whether compensatory justice can be understood in this Aristotelian fashion as somehow restoring equality between parties. In contemporary ethics and political philosophy this notion of compensation as a return to equality has had two very different manifestations. The first is "the principle of redress," according to which the fundamental aim of social justice is to redress undeserved inequalities. Section 2 argues that this principle is based on a strongly egalitarian ethic hostile to the fundamental claim of liberalism. I then turn in sections 3 and 4 to a more modest understanding of the "return to equality." It is sometimes argued that a rights violator who fully compensates a victim for her

This essay originally appeared in *NOMOS XXXIII: Compensatory Justice*, John W. Chapman, ed., New York: New York University Press, 1991, pp. 45–81. Reprinted by permission of New York University Press. The heading "1. INTRODUCTORY" has been omitted from the beginning of the essay.

losses thereby restores his condition of moral equality with the victim. Here also, I shall argue, the Aristotelian account fails. However, I contend in section 5 that in one case compensatory justice does restore equality: justified rights violations.

Restoring Equality (I): The Principle of Redress

Social Justice and Moral Balance

Compensatory justice seems necessarily a second-level principle of justice insofar as it operates on other, more basic principles. Compensatory justice apparently tells us what to do when people do not live up to their first-level duties or when they fail to respect first-level rights. So understood, it is a part of what Rawls calls "nonideal" theory, that is, "principles for meeting injustice."[2] But Rawls seeks to assign an altogether more basic role to compensatory justice: he seems attracted to the view that it forms the foundation for much of ideal theory. Rawls explains the egalitarian character of the difference principle by saying that it achieves "some of the intent" of the principle of redress. "This is the principle that undeserved inequalities call for redress; and since inequalities of birth and natural endowment are undeserved, these inequalities are somewhat to be compensated for."[3] My point here is not simply that Rawls's theory of social justice is built upon a commitment to compensatory justice. As John Passmore points out, "From a certain point of view, facilitatory social justice can be thought of as reparative."[4] But to conceive of social justice as reparative is typically still to view it as a response to past injustices: social justice as compensatory justice would still be a nonideal, second-level principle. But if we take the principle of redress as the foundation of social justice—or as one of the foundational principles[5]—the very notion of ideal social justice becomes essentially compensatory.

Rawls is more than a little reluctant fully to commit himself to the principle of redress; the "difference principle," we are told, is "not the same as that of redress," although "it does achieve some of the intent of the latter principle."[6] However, Rawls's discussion draws on an essay by Herbert Spiegelberg that provides an unabashed defense of the principle of redress. Writes Spiegelberg:

> The argument for the demand of universal equality . . . rests on two premises: (1) *undeserved discriminations call for redress* (2) *all inequalities of birth constitute undeserved discriminations.* I shall conclude that (3) *all inequalities of birth call for redress.* Such redress implies, at least in principle, the cancellation of all inequalities of birth by equalization. In this sense it follows, that (4) *equality is a fundamental ethical demand.*[7]

In defense of (1) Spiegelberg refers to the legal notion of "unjust enrichment"; any special benefit that cannot be justified, it seems, constitutes an unjust enrichment. And in accord with Aristotle's analysis, Spiegelberg holds that this enrichment brings about a "moral disequilibrium"; compensatory justice calls for reestablishing the moral balance by equalization.[8] And since natural talents are undeserved discriminations, redress is called for.

David Gauthier has pointed out a fatal flaw in the case for the principle of redress. If we take seriously Spiegelberg's reference to unjust enrichment, the argument is that since the discriminations are undeserved, that is, they are contrary to desert, being enriched by them is unjust. But this does not provide the foundation for step (2). For "it is surely mistaken to hold that natural inequalities are undeserved. They are not deserved, they do not accord with desert, but equally they are not undeserved, they are not contrary to desert."[9] If (1) means that all discriminations contrary to desert require redress, it seems that nothing follows regarding discriminations based on natural talents. As Gauthier points out, though these inequalities are not sanctioned by desert, neither are they contrary to it. Indeed, as Rawls himself acknowledges, the upshot is that "The notion of desert does not apply to such cases."[10] At this point it seems that the argument for the principle of redress depends on an equivocation between "not deserved" (not sanctioned by desert) and "undeserved" (violating the principle of desert).[11]

A Reformulated Argument for Redress

We can reformulate the argument for the principle of redress in a way that saves it from equivocation by substituting for step (1), principle *E:*

> E: Any discriminatory act—any action that provides differential advantages or burdens—stands in need of justification; any unjustified discriminatory act calls for redress.

Spiegelberg actually seems to have something akin to principle *E* in mind. "The premise that undeserved discriminations call for redress," he affirms, "thus implies that only morally deserved inequalities justify unequal lots: *without such special justification all persons, whether equal or unequal, ought to have equal shares*."[12] The crucial claim here is not that these advantages are undeserved, but that they are unjustified (say, by the claim that they are deserved), and in the absence of such a justification they are unjust. For *E* it is enough that natural talents are not deserved (that is, not sanctioned by desert); there is no need to make the (false) claim that they are undeserved (that is, contrary to desert).

Building upon *E*, one could argue:

1. Any discriminatory act—any action that provides differential advantages or burdens—stands in need of justification; any unjustified discriminatory act calls for redress.
2. All social and economic inequalities are based on discriminatory acts—differential benefits and burdens are generated by social systems and institutions.
3. These inequalities thus demand justification.
4. They cannot be justified on the grounds that people deserve their differential

talents and, so, deserve the differential benefits or burdens that flow from them.

5. Consequently, in lieu of some other justification for these social and economic inequalities, redress is called for.

Two comments are required here. First, I have framed the revised argument for redress not in terms of the unjustness of nature—for example, what natural endowments a person has received in the lottery of birth—but rather in terms of actions that are based on these. As Rawls says, "The natural distribution is neither just nor unjust; nor is it unjust that persons are born into society at some particular position. These are simply natural facts. What is just and unjust is the way that institutions deal with these facts."[13] Secondly, the revised argument provides only a presumption in favor of redress. As step 5 explicitly allows, there may be some other justification for these inequalities. All the revised argument maintains is that unjustified discriminations call for redress, and that desert is not available as a justification.

The Principle of Redress as Antiliberal

E is an egalitarian principle. It asserts a blanket moral presumption in favor of equality; it is incumbent on he who is talented to show that his talents are justified or, I suppose, to show that any advantages that accrue to him (say, the admiration of his fellows) can be justified. If he cannot provide a justification, his advantages have upset the moral balance and require redress. And, presumably, because Spiegelberg does not think one can justify such talents and advantages, we are led to a notion of social justice that seeks to restore the moral balance by somehow compensating for their unequalizing effects.

Principles that place the onus of justification on one party rather than another are substantive moral principles: they state that some condition is the moral status quo in the sense that it requires no further justification whereas departures from it do."[14] They present us with a moral asymmetry. Now liberal political philosophy typically offers a competing presumptive principle:

> *L:* interference with another's activity requires justification; unjustified interference is unjust.

Certainly this is fundamental to liberal political and legal theory. As Joel Feinberg says, "most writers . . . have endorsed a kind of 'presumption in favor of liberty' requiring that whenever a legislator is faced with a choice between imposing a legal duty on citizens or leaving them at liberty, other things being equal, he should leave individuals free to make their own choices. Liberty should be the norm; coercion always requires some special justification."[15] Extending this presumption from liberal legal theory to liberal ethics seems straightforward.[16]

Now *L* and *E* are competing principles. If *L* holds, then Alf is free to praise Betty for her wonderful talents, and to shower gifts upon her, unless Charlie can justify interfering with Alf. Perhaps Charlie can provide some justification: all that the Liberal Principle says is that Alf is free to do as he wishes until Charlie can produce a justification for interfering with Alf by making him refrain from rewarding Betty as he sees fit, with his praise or his goods. But *E* holds that Alf or Betty must justify Alf's actions. According to the Egalitarian Principle Charlie need not say anything: unless Alf and/or Betty can justify their actions, they have upset the moral balance and so redress is in order.

Let me put my point in a less formal way. It is often argued that liberals suppose that each person is free to do as he wishes until some justification is presented for limiting his liberty. As Locke said, all men are naturally in "a *State of perfect Freedom* to order their actions . . . as they see fit . . . without asking leave, or depending upon the Will of any other Man."[17] To these liberals, the right to natural liberty determines the point of departure for all subsequent ethical and political justifications: all henceforth are concerned with liberty-limiting principles. Now the Egalitarian Principle postulates a very different starting point for normative theory: all successful justificatory argument establishes permissible inequalities. And in the absence of successful arguments, the fallback position is always a moral demand for equality. The formulated case for the principle of redress supposes precisely this: in the absence of some good reason, morality demands equality. And when we have departed from equality without justification, restoring equality is morally required. Hence the fundamental role of the principle of redress.

Liberalism and Formal Equality

Principle *E*, I have argued, is illiberally egalitarian. It may seem that this must be wrong. Many philosophers—indeed liberal philosophers—see *L*'s presumption in favor of equality as a demand of reason itself. Benn and Peters, for instance, defend the principle that "*none shall be held to have a claim to better treatment than another, in advance of good grounds being produced*."[18] They continue:

> Understood in this way, the principle of equality does not prescribe positively that all humans be treated alike; it is a presumption against treating them differently, in any respect, until grounds for distinction have been shown. It does not assume, therefore, a quality which all men have to the same degree, which is the ground of the presumption, for to say that there is a presumption means that no grounds need be shown. The onus of justification rests on whoever would make distinctions. . . . Presume equality until there is a reason to presume otherwise.[19]

This is an immensely popular position; Richard Flathman, Isaiah Berlin and William Frankena, to name just a few, endorse it.[20] The consensus is that so understood the presumption in favor of equality is (1) a demand of reason or logic and (2) only weakly egalitarian in its implications. Both, I think, are wrong.

Consider first the claim that the presumption in favor of equality is a demand of rationality or nonarbitrariness. According to J. R. Lucas—certainly no radical egalitarian—"formal equality" is simply a statement of the universality of reason. "It requires that if two people are being treated, or are treated, differently, there should be some relevant difference between them."[21] So if Alf gives a present to Betty but not to Doris then nonarbitrariness demands that Alf have some reason that differentiates Betty from Doris. If he does not, if, as far as he is concerned, Betty and Doris are equally deserving of his attention and affections, then he is being arbitrary, illogical or irrational to shower gifts on Betty. This example already shows that the principle is not as intuitively obvious as some of its exponents would have us believe. Some philosophers insist that in this sort of case Alf's action simply resists any universalization: even if Betty and Doris are *exactly alike,* it has been argued, it is perfectly understandable, and not at all crazy, for Alf to love Betty and not Doris.[22] But suppose (as I think is correct)[23] we take a more traditional view, and hold that even here Alf is committed to some conception of universalizable reasons. If he is rational, something about Betty attracts him to her rather than to Doris (perhaps simply their shared history—Alf saw Betty first). If Betty and Doris were really exactly alike in every way, Alf's preference really would be irrational. But surely, even granting this, Alf need not *justify* his preference to Doris or anyone else. It is one thing to acknowledge that a rational Alf will have his reasons (though he may not be cognizant of them); it is quite another to say that he must justify his preference. Yet advocates of presumptions of equality typically assert, as do Benn and Peters, an "onus of justification." As Benn claims in a later essay, "discrimination in treatment between persons requires *moral* justification: it is not enough simply to *prefer* one to another since that involves regarding another person from the point of view of one's own satisfaction; respect for a person involves a right to be considered from his *own* standpoint."[24]

As Benn recognizes, a justification must provide others with what are reasons from their perspectives.[25] Principle *E,* Benn and Peters's egalitarianism, as well as Benn's later principle, places on each of us a moral requirement to provide reasons to others—justifications—whenever our actions lead to differential treatment. So far from being a simple and uncontroversial demand of reason, this principle would wreak havoc on our lives. One would need to justify to potential spouses whom one did not choose—provide reasons from their perspectives—why one didn't choose them. If one chose to buy a house in one neighborhood rather than another, and both need new residents, one would have to justify one's choice to those disadvantaged by it. But why must I justify to others my choice to live in East rather than West Duluth? It hardly is a demand of rationality itself that I do so. Indeed, such a pervasive requirement to justify oneself is terribly intrusive, and quite at odds with the liberal presumption in favor of noninterference.[26]

To be sure, in political, legal and administrative contexts the presumption in favor of equal treatment is explicable and important.[27] In these contexts officials are properly required to justify their differential treatment of citizens. In the absence of justification we certainly are apt to conclude that an injustice has been committed. But two features of these settings render them unhelpful in showing that *E* is a basic principle of morality.[28] First, citizens come before judges and administrators with rights and duties. The egalitarian principle is thereby transformed into the requirement that those with equal legal rights and duties be treated alike. This is clearly neither foundational, because it supposes an independently defined set of rights and duties, nor is it strongly egalitarian. Second, public officials differ from private citizens in a crucial respect. Whereas we suppose that private individuals are free to act as they see fit, until, as it were, they run into the rights of others or some duty, *this* presumption does not hold for public officials. We presume that what one does in an official capacity always stands in need of justification, say, to a superior. If Alf is acting in his private capacity, it is entirely reasonable for him to respond to a request to justify his discriminatory actions with the retort that it is his own business why he acts as he does. Admittedly, if Alf has violated the rights of another we will insist on justification, but he is under no standing obligation to justify his actions to others. Public officials are. They must be able to provide publicly accessible reasons justifying what they do in their official capacity.[29] But we ask much less of private agents. And that is why the principle of formal equality before the law—so central to liberal political and legal theory—becomes illiberal when transplanted into ethical theory.

Restoring Equality (II): The Debt Model

What Is a Return to Equality?

So far I have argued that compensatory justice *qua* the principle of redress cannot provide the foundation for social justice in liberal theory. The principle of redress is most plausibly interpreted as relying on the presumption in favor of equality (*E*); and this presumption is inconsistent with the liberal presumption of noninterference (*L*). Now if we reject principle *E,* if equality is not the moral baseline, it follows that not every deequalizing act must be either justified or redressed. We have now two types of actions that produce inequalities: those that call for either justification or redress and those that do not. What distinguishes them? The most obvious answer is that the former are *wrongful,* or *rights-violating,* deequalizing acts while the latter are not. It thus might seem that we are led to something like the following principle:

> Any discriminatory action that provides differential benefits to Betty, or burdens on Alf, when Alf has a right to equality, must be either justified or compensated.

But now that we have rejected the strongly egalitarian notion of compensatory justice articulated in the principle of redress, this revision of the egalitarian conception looks manifestly strange. It cannot be only rights to equality that ground compensation. Consider the following possibility: Alf has lots of property, Betty very little. Betty violates Alf's property rights by stealing. Would the above principle require compensation be paid to Alf? Not obviously. Perhaps it could be argued that although Alf and Betty have unequal *property,* they have equal property *rights,* and that is the condition of equality, to which we seek a return. But that will not do. Say Betty promises to buy Alf lunch: he has a right against her, but she has no corresponding right against him. Now suppose she breaks her promise. If Alf is entitled to some form of compensation the aim cannot be to restore an equality of rights.

What, then, is meant when it is said that compensatory justice restores equality? William Blackstone provides the following interpretation of Aristotelian corrective justice:

> Corrective justice . . . involves a rectifying or reparatory transaction between one person or party and another. Here there is an attempt to restore the equality which existed prior to the injury of one party by the other. The penalty imposed on the party who inflicted the injury and the corresponding benefit bestowed on the injured party should be proportional to the difference created by the injury.[30]

Unfortunately, this explication is not pellucid. But the account seems to involve two elements: (1) redistribution that allows for (2) a return to moral equality.

The Redistributive Claim

A claim of an unjust distribution of resources is fundamental to compensatory justice. Some wrongful action by Betty against Alf leads to an unjust distribution of resources between them.[31] The most obvious case is where Betty steals some of Alf's property, and quite literally transfers resources. Unlike penal sanctions, which follow from the mere act of wrongdoing, compensatory justice focuses on wrongdoing with redistributional consequences.[32] Compensatory justice, then, is premised on some just distribution, and seeks to return to that distribution after unjustified departures from it.[33] Compensation thus aims at the "elimination of unjustifiable *gains and losses* owing to human action."[34] To be sure, sometimes questions of compensatory justice do not appear to involve distributive issues. If Betty attacks Alf, he may reasonably claim compensation for his pain. But, of course, here too we confront a distributive issue: Betty's unjust action inflicts costs on Alf, and he seeks to recover these costs.

Compensation is usefully seen as a repayment.[35] This is the basis for the familiar notion that compensation is a sort of *debt*. Judith Thomson, for instance, says that the notion of a debt of compensation is familiar: "if we have wronged A, we owe him something; we should make amends, we should compensate him for the wrong done."[36] A special moral relation exists, then, between victim and aggressor: the aggressor is indebted to the victim, she owes him something because of what she has done.[37] The idea of a debt points to a distribution of resources to which we have a moral reason to return: until a transfer is made from aggressor to victim, the victim does not have that to which he is entitled while the aggressor has more than she is entitled to.

The notion of debt indicates that some amount, or some particular thing, is owed by the aggressor to the victim.[38] Let us, then, say that the debt has been completely repaid if the victim receives *full compensation*. According to Robert Nozick, "[s]omething fully compensates a person for a loss if and only if it makes him no worse off than he would otherwise have been; it compensates person *X* for person *Y*'s action *A* if *X* is no worse off receiving it, *Y* having done *A*, than *X* would have been without receiving it if *Y* had not done *A*."[39] So we can say that by one's wrongful act one inflicts costs on another. Fully to compensate a person is to redistribute resources to him so that all these costs are, in a sense, repaid.

Blackstone points to a more modest notion of compensation. To determine the amount of compensation to repay a wronged party fully, Blackstone says, would require something like omniscience. His Aristotelian conception calls only for "proportional" compensation: "equal claims be given equal compensation."[40] However, for now let us pursue the demands of compensation as full repayment. Let us say, following Nozick and Gauthier, that full compensation demands that a victim receives the same utility from the two sets of actions: {being wronged, being compensated}, {not being wronged, not being compensated}.[41]

A Challenge to the Debt Model

The debt repayment model suggests a transaction between the victim and aggressor. And it does seem intuitively right that the aggressor owes the victim compensation. That is, the debt model suggests that if Betty has wronged Alf in a way that causes him loss, then (1) Alf has a claim to be compensated and (2) Betty has an obligation to repay. Jules Coleman, however, has repeatedly argued against this fairly standard view. He writes:

> If there is wrongful loss, it ought to be annulled; the same goes for wrongful or unwarranted gains. Nevertheless, the principle of corrective justice which enables us to identify compensable losses and unjust enrichments does not commit us to adopting any particular mode of rectification. The principle that determines which gains and losses are to be eliminated does not by itself specify a means for doing so. Presumably there is more than one way of rectifying undeserved gains and losses.[42]

At this point two aspects of compensatory justice to which I have pointed diverge. If compensatory justice is taken as concerned with protecting a certain distribution of resources, then what is essential is that wrongful losses and wrongful gains are eliminated, and the just pattern restored. It does not greatly matter who compensates the victim and how wrongful gains are annulled: what matters is that somehow this is done in a way that restores the just pattern.[43] But this proposal undermines the debt model. For the debt model *adds* to the redistributional requirement a moral relation between aggressor and victim: the aggressor *owes* the victim. And until compensation occurs the victim has a complaint *against the aggressor*. Not against others, or society at large, but against the aggressor.

Coleman's proposal can be interpreted in both a radical and a moderate sense. The radical interpretation is that the question (1) "who has aggressed against Alf?" is entirely independent of (2) "who has an obligation to compensate Alf?" Now on the face of it, Coleman misses a crucial moral fact: the victim's complaint is against the aggressor, and not against society at large. If he is not compensated, it is the aggressor who has not repaid her debt. It is hard to believe that our two questions are really independent. Coleman, however, would insist that they are—at least in the case where, although the victim has incurred wrongful losses, the aggressor has not accrued wrongful gains. He writes:

> So when I claim that if an injurer who through his fault imposes a wrongful loss on another but who does not thereby gain has an obligation to repair, his obligation cannot derive directly from the principle of corrective justice, I mean only to be emphasizing the obvious fact that he has secured no gain which would be the concern of corrective justice to rectify. His victim's claim to recompense is on the other hand a matter of corrective justice. And if we feel that the injurer should rectify his victim's loss, it must be for reasons other than the fact that so doing is required to annul his gain.[44]

This is not quite so obvious. The victim, as Coleman says, has incurred a wrongful loss—the aggressor has brought about a maldistribution of holdings. Resources, then, must be redistributed to return to a just pattern. Coleman's claim, then, is that compensatory justice does not tell us where these resources are to come from. But this seems mistaken. From the perspective of distributive justice, it can hardly be irrelevant who pays. Unless the transfer of resources to victims comes from aggressors, new injustices will have replaced the old. This is a real enough problem. Consider, for example, Judith Thomson's justification of preferential hiring:

> Lastly, it should be stressed that to opt for such a policy is not to make the young white male applicants themselves make amends for any wrongs done to blacks and women. Under such a policy, no one is asked to give up a job which is already his; the job for which the white male competes isn't his, *but is the community's,* and it is the hiring officer who gives it to the black or woman in the community's name. Of course the white male is asked to give up his equal chance at the job. But that is not something he pays to the black or women by way of making amends; it is something that the community takes away from him in order that it may makes amends.
>
> Still, the community does impose a burden on him: it is able to make amends for its wrongs only by taking away from him, something which, after all, we are supposing he has a right to. And why should he pay the costs of the community's making amends?[45]

Thomson clearly wants to avoid arguing that white males owe blacks and women some of their ill-gained opportunities. Instead of telling us that opportunities are to be transferred from the aggressors, that is, white males, to women and blacks, she argues the community is giving some of its opportunities to those who have been the victims of injustice. This is the crux of Coleman's simple redistributive theory: the important thing is that wrongful losses are annulled, and "the community" does this. So the aim is to annul wrongful losses. But eventually Thomson is forced to confront the fact that these opportunities will come from somewhere; and they will, in effect, be transferred from the white males, who (in the first, quoted paragraph) did not seem to owe women and blacks anything. In the end, despite all she says here, Thomson is forced back into the position that many of the opportunities and advantages of white males have been the result of prior wrongs, and therefore constitute a sort of wrongful gain.[46]

My point, then, is that the aim of returning to a just distribution cannot totally separate the questions (1) who is the aggressor? and (2) who is going to pay? Resources to pay victims have to come from somewhere, and simply to transfer them from the innocent is not, prima facie, just.[47]

This, however, brings us to the moderate interpretation of Coleman's proposal. Admit that the aggressors owe victims something; but let us also acknowledge that discovering who is an aggressor against what victim may be costly, perhaps impossible. Consider the case of compensation for road injury. Many aggressors, that is, those who drive dangerously, do not cause actual physical harm. They expose others to risk of injury, a cost on others, and the aggressor gets where she wants to go faster. But only sometimes does this aggression result in an accident. And, as Coleman points out, although the accident imposes additional costs on the victim, the aggressor does not accrue additional wrongful gains.[48] Now who is to pay? Just those who have caused the accident? But if so, the aim cannot be to transfer wrongful gains to compensate for wrongful losses. For the accident-causing aggressor has accrued no more benefits than the lucky aggressor, who has exposed others to risk without causing an accident.

Certainly we can see here good reasons for treating all aggressors as collectively owing all victims compensation. If some aggressors are simply lucky they did not cause accidents, it is reasonable enough to say that they should not be able to gain from their dangerous activity. So a policy that creates a pool contributed to by all aggressors—and perhaps all drivers are aggressors sometimes—to compensate victims of accidents would be justified. No doubt better proposals can be formulated. But for now, I wish only to stress that insofar as we are concerned with compensatory justice (as opposed to some utilitarian scheme to maximize total happiness by paying accident victims) we cannot totally separate the issue of who is an aggressor from who is to pay. But that does not mean that we must adopt a simplistic model of aggressor and victim—say, the layman's model of tort law. The debt model of compensatory justice has room for cost and risk-spreading schemes.

The Return to Moral Equality

Up to this point I have been concerned with explicating, and defending, the first element of Blackstone's proposal: the idea that compensatory justice is essentially redistributive. The debt model, I have argued, captures a good deal of our thinking about compensatory justice.

Blackstone's second claim is fundamental to his neo-Aristotelianism: once the debt has been paid, victim and aggressor have returned to a sort of moral equality. Compensatory justice, he says, "is an attempt to restore the equality which existed prior to the injury of one party by the other." Once the debt is paid, moral parity between debtor and creditor is restored. The moral slate, as it were, is wiped clean. This is the sense in which, according to the debt model, compensatory justice restores equality.

Here, I think, the debt model fails as an account of compensation for wrongful violation of rights. No redistribution of *resources* can by itself restore moral parity between victim and aggressor.[49] Full compensation, in the sense I define it above, does not achieve so grand a result.

Two Models of Rights and Wrongs

The Purely Instrumental Theory of Rights

To see why this is so, compare two models of rights. I shall call the first the purely instrumental theory of rights. The best examples of this instrumental theory are neo-Hobbesian accounts of rights. According to neo-Hobbesians, it is in the self-interest of everyone alike to accept a system of morality that restrains pursuit of self-interest. As Kurt Baier concludes, the "Hobbesian argument is sound. Moralities are systems of principles whose acceptance by everyone as overruling the dictates of self-interest is in the interest of everyone alike."[50] In this sort of theory, to justify some claim right *R* to *X* is just to show that each gains more through having her claim right to *X* respected than it costs her in having to acknowledge and respect others' claim rights to *X*.[51] To call such rights "instrumental" is just to emphasize that they are purely instruments for advancing one's interests. Rational utility maximizers would see that each can best achieve his goals if everyone acknowledges certain claims of others to act and to control resources. These rights have no point other than as instruments that further the goals of individuals. The system of rights is a *modus vivendi* among individuals devoted to their own ends: for each best to promote his ends, each agrees to honor limits on what may be done.

I take it that nothing is mysterious about an instrumental conception of rights in one form or another it is probably the most popular understanding of rights. Now violation of instrumental rights can be compensated in a way that *does* return victim and aggressor to a condition of moral equality. Say that Betty wrongfully appropriates Alf's property, *X*. In order to remedy the resulting unjust distribution, Betty must, according to the debt model, compensate Alf. And I have said that full compensation would be paid if Alf received the same utility from, or his interests were equally well served by, the two sets of actions: {not have *X* stolen, not have compensation paid}, {have *X* stolen, have compensation paid}. Full compensation, of course, is apt to require much more than just the market value of X.[52] Betty will need to make a payment that takes into account Alf's pain at having his property taken, his fear that the social order is breaking down, and so forth. But let us say that, whatever the necessary payment is, Betty has made it. Alf now is just as well off as before Betty invaded his rights. He has no further complaint against her. His rights are tools to advance his interests, and Betty has acted so that his interests are not in any way harmed by her violations. So on what basis could Alf still feel aggrieved? To keep complaining seems peevish.

But something seems amiss with this analysis (and so, I will argue, with the instrumental conception of rights). We do, I think, have reason to doubt that full compensation returns Alf and Betty to moral equality. If this account of rights and compensation holds, Betty can always convert any property right of Alf's into a liability right by paying full compensation. A property right, let us say, gives Alf a claim to *X* that excludes Betty from using it without his consent, unless she buys it from him; in contrast, a liability rule precludes Betty from using Alf's *X* unless she renders him compensation, after the fact, for using it. The crucial difference is that under property rules Betty must secure Alf's consent prior to her use of his *X* but she does not under liability rules.[53] Now the account I have given of Betty's compensating Alf shows that his property right was transformed into a liability right. Given adequate compensation made *after the fact,* Betty wipes clean the moral slate, and has rightful possession of *X*.

However, it might be said that even if Betty fully compensates Alf, she still has not restored her moral status with the community:

> The thief not only harms the victim, he undermines rules and distinctions beyond the specific case. . . . [W]e must add to each case an undefinable kicker which represents society's need to keep all property rules from being changed at will into liability rules.[54]

I shall not deal with the debate between proponents of the economic theory of the law and their critics as to whether this "kicker" explains why Betty, despite her compensation to Alf, remains open to criticism.[55] I wish to focus on a different question: putting aside the social kicker, is it true that Alf no longer has any complaint against Betty? If he does not have any remaining complaint, it follows that a significantly rich Betty can declare to anyone: "I can take whatever I want of yours—for a high enough price. Admittedly, I will have to pay you for your aggravation, perhaps rather extravagantly. But if I offer you enough, I can take it. And you will have no reason to complain." Betty may have trouble with the rest of society—she may have to pay out mountains in compensation to the rest—but at least she is squared away with the victim. Is she? It seems quite clear to me that she is not, and that the instrumental account of rights is unable to explain why she is not.

Lomasky's Instrumentalism

Loren Lomasky, an advocate of the instrumental view of rights, seeks to explain why Betty is not squared away with Alf. In reference to Nozick's compensation argument, Lomasky writes:

> It assumes that an infringement of a right can be made good through compensation, the moral balance restored to what it was *ex ante*. No such general assumption is justifiable. Compensation is inevitably a second-best response that comes into play when full rectification is impossible.[56]

Lomasky depends here on a distinction between rectification and compensation. "'Compensation' carries with it the connotation of providing something *equivalent* in value to that which has been lost, while 'rectification' has the sense of *restoring precisely* that which has been removed."[57] This distinction is important for Lomasky because he advances a strong *incommensurability* thesis that makes five claims.[58]

1. First, Lomasky affirms that any individual has certain ends or projects. Commitment to these projects or ends is the source of their value for an agent. Value is thus *personal* in the sense that what a person values depends on his ends; someone with different ends may quite properly value very different things.[59]
2. On this basis, Lomasky says that "individuals assign personal value to their own projects and not to a welfare measure consequent upon their acting in pursuit of particular projects. What A[lf] wishes to realize is specifically E1, not the attainment of whatever level of utility is associated with the realization of E1."
3. "A[lf] will therefore not be rationally indifferent between the necessary means to go about the pursuit of his project E1 and having the necessary means to pursue E2, even if it were somehow demonstrable that the attainment of E2 by A[lf] would have the same welfare measure as does the attainment of E1 by A[lf]."
4. And this is so, according to Lomasky, because Alf is not obligated to accept some impersonal standard of value that renders E1 and E2 commensurable. E1 and E2 need not be commensurable; indeed, it seems typically they will not be.
5. Lomasky concludes compensation is a second-best response to rights violations. Compensation depends upon providing the victim with something of equivalent value. But if values are not commensurable, this is not possible. In contrast, rectification aims to give back the specific thing that was lost and so is not undermined by the incommensurability of values.[60]

Lomasky, then, sides with philosophers such as Isaiah Berlin, Stuart Hampshire and Bernard Williams in holding that values are often incommensurable. Claims about incommensurability are often puzzling. But one thing is certain: it cannot generally be the case that Alf sees his own values as incommensurable. To see why, suppose that Alf really has no way to trade off his values against each other. When confronted with a choice between, say, advancing his project of securing Betty's love and working to compete for tenure, Alf is unable to choose. Fundamental to our conception of a rational valuer-agent is that one can decide which values to promote in particular choice situations. Alf may rationally forgo an opportunity to secure Betty's affections in order to work on his book; if so he has selected between his values. They are commensurable. If they were not, Alf would be at a loss when, as is always the case, he is confronted with decisions about which to promote.

So Lomasky certainly would not want to claim that, as a matter of course, Alf is unable to tell us whether advancing his end E1 to a certain degree is to be preferred to advancing E2 to some extent.[61] It cannot be the case that in Alf's valuational economy there are no trade-off rates between ends. That would lead to practical paralysis. What, then, do proponents of incommensurability such as Lomasky have in mind? They seem to have at least two worries. The first is real enough, but it is a special case rather than the general rule. Sometimes one's values have been harmed in such a way that one simply cannot be fully compensated. "No satisfactory rectification or compensation can be made to the athlete who becomes a paraplegic as the result of an automobile accident."[62] This is true and important. In this person's valuational economy he has no end he would ever choose to promote at such a cost.[63] So we must admit that sometimes a person suffers a loss for which full compensation is impossible. But that is a long way from saying that as a rule full compensation is not possible. Say we put the following proposal to Alf the athlete: agree to laboratory tests that will leave his athletic ability impaired for one month (but he will recover thereafter) and we will pay one hundred thousand dollars. Alf may find it easy to weigh the two conflicting goals. And of course we don't need fantastic stories to make the point. Real athletes do it all the time: some even decide to pursue academic courses at some cost to their training. Only a monomaniac would never trade off any opportunity to pursue some end for opportunities greatly to advance other ends.

What, then, is the other worry? Here I think Lomasky's concerns are much like those of Bernard Williams and Stuart Hampshire: commensurability, they believe, supposes the existence of some third value in terms of which the two conflicting values are appraised.[64] In this vein Bernard Williams proffers three incommensurability claims:

(1). No currency exists in terms of which each conflict of values can be resolved.

(2). It is not true that for each conflict of values some value, independent of any of the conflicting values, can be appealed to in order to resolve that conflict.

(3). It is not true that for each conflict of values some value can be appealed to (independent or not) in order to resolve that conflict rationally.[65]

Claims (2) and (3) are very much akin to Lomasky's assertion that what Alf "wishes to realize is specifically E1, not the attainment of whatever level of utility is associated with the realization of E1." It is, I think, quite right to deny that some third value is always employed to adjudicate the competing claims of E1 and E2. Lomasky, Williams and Hampshire are right to reject claims (2) and (3). Should we reject claim (1) too? Much depends here on just what we mean by a common currency. Writes Stanley Benn:

> To trade one value against another one must see them as in a sense substitutable—more of one *compensating* for less of another. The options open to us meet our competing commitments in varying degrees, and to reach a rational decision—to do the best we can in difficult circumstances—we have to be able to set a rate of substitution between them over the relevant range. Unlike a market price, which is also a rate of substitution, this is, in one sense, a subjective rate, the rate at which I am prepared to trade off commitments of one kind against commitments of another. That can be done without having to express the force of each in some common currency, such as utility or money; there can be a foreign exchange market without a gold standard.[66]

We need an exchange rate between ends and commitments; without it, action is impossible. It must be the case that Alf is able to decide whether advancing E1 to degree *x* compensates him for the loss of an opportunity to advance E2 to degree *y*. But if Alf can make that judgment, Betty can learn about Alf's character and conclude that he has a stable disposition to make this choice.[67] So she can compensate him according to his own subjective exchange rate. But, perhaps, Alf does not simply value that E1 be advanced to degree *x*, but that *he advances* it to that degree. But this would only seem to increase the costs of compensation to Betty: now she must compensate him for two losses: (i) that E1 was not advanced and (ii) that he was not able to act to advance his ends, but rather someone did it for him. Lomasky sometimes suggests that it is (ii) that is beyond compensation. So perhaps the problem isn't simply that one's ends are set back: perhaps the problem with a rights violation, as Lomasky suggests, is that one's ability to pursue projects is undermined.[68] But if, like Lomasky, we see this in terms of what a person values, compensation will still usually be possible. People certainly are willing to impair their ability to pursue projects—say, by endangering their health or even their lives—to attain some important goals. So even if, for example, when Betty steals Alf's car she impairs his ability to pursue projects, she probably will be able to compensate him. Suppose Betty says: "How about a hundred thousand dollars, that will allow you to achieve your dream of going to college? Will that compensate you for what I did yesterday, that is, stole your 1978 Pinto?" It probably will. To be sure, if Alf was interfered with so regularly that he never got a chance to act for himself, the loss would become so grave that compensation would become impossible (we are thus back to the first worry discussed above). But, putting aside this sort of massive interference, I see no reason why the loss of (ii) cannot also be compensated for.

Respect-Based Theories of Rights

I have examined Lomasky's instrumentalism in some detail as he is alive to the challenge full compensation poses to a theory of rights. If rights are simply a means to secure our values, and if (as we must) we have a trade-off rate between values,[69] then full compensation for rights violations restores moral equality between victim and aggressor—it wipes the moral slate clean. As long as they are willing to pay the appropriate "fee" (that is, compensation) instrumentalism gives a license to aggressors to override the rights of victims. But the instrumentalist must be wrong about this: it permits aggressors to turn our property rights into liability rights when they so choose (at least to the extent that they are squared away with the victim). And, of course, the problem does not simply concern property rights in the narrow sense of "property" as control over external things. All rights—except perhaps the right to life and some rights to bodily integrity—are subject to being bought out in this way. The instrumental theory of rights is unable to explain just why the aggressor wrongs the victim when he overrides rights but compensates afterwards (remember, I am leaving aside here the "social kicker"). The problem I want to suggest, is that the aggressor not only causes the victim a loss of *value;* in addition, he has acted in a way that is *unjustifiable* and so shows a lack of respect.

It may help to focus on a case in which violation of your rights is a boon to your values. Suppose that a colleague is known for not respecting your privacy. You have let it be known that you do not welcome visitors at night to your house. Indeed, you have made something of a point of it. Unfortunately, your colleague walks by your house on her way home from work, and often—all too often—she knocks on the door, looks through the window, you answer the door (it is hard to leave her outside knocking, especially tonight as it is twenty-five degrees below zero and she is obviously getting frostbite). When that happens it is almost impossible to keep her out; she stays for ten minutes, like clockwork. As usual, this all occurs one night; but tonight you have an appointment to tutor a really bad student. You promised his father (an old friend of yours) to tutor him in philosophy, so you are obligated to help. This, I should stress, really is a pretty awful student: he is the sort who, after two hours of discussing Kant, asks whether Kant was the same person as Hegel. It is all very trying. Now your colleague makes her nightly appearance at your window, and she barges in once again. Not even this student can withstand her, and this burdensome discussion ends. You feel a distinct relief; no, it is more than that—you are happy.

Does your colleague owe you compensation for violating your privacy?[70] It seems hard to see why: she has advanced your values. (Maybe you should pay her?) But, one may say, because of her you have failed to fulfill your obligation. Well, you have tried your best, and she is, after all, the one who ended the torture session, so you are blameless. So, then, should you thank her? Hardly. Indeed, you still have a complaint against her: she violated your rights (and so benefited you) by wrongfully interfering with your activity. Is, then, the complaint that she has set back your interest by undermining your ability to pursue projects? Surely not: you are now much freer than ten minutes ago to pursue projects (your colleague, after all, only stays for ten minutes or so.)

A defender of the instrumental interpretation may try to account for this by appealing to an act/rule distinction.[71] The *rules* that justify rights are instrumentally justified as a way for an agent to advance his values; but not every action that accords with rights advances interests, and not all rights violations set back interests. True enough. But the question remains: do you still have a complaint against your colleague who violated the rule and so benefited you? Aren't you lucky she didn't let the rule guide her? As Mill said, it is the pedant "who goes by rules rather than their reasons."[72] If in this case your rights are respected "we should employ the means and the end will not follow."[73] Consequently, Mill cautions against relying on "even the most plausible . . . absolute maxims of right and wrong" in such a way that one loses sight of the "paramount good they are intended to promote."[74] For you now to complain because your rights were violated (and, so, your interests were advanced) seems to be just the sort of rule worship Mill criticized.[75]

Perhaps *society* has an interest that the rule be kept; but we are now back to the social kicker. One might say: your colleague has shown once again that she does not respect your rights, and that is what you are complaining about. Your complaint is directed at her continuing disposition to violate your rights. But, surely, if she is moving to Australia tomorrow, wouldn't that make it all the better? In that case (i) she has benefited you and (ii) you don't have to worry that her disposition will ever lead to her violating your rights again.

I want to suggest that your complaint has nothing whatsoever to do with your values being set back, your projects being thwarted or your ends being hurt. Rather, the complaint is that whatever good consequences that came from the intervention, your colleague acted in a way that could not be justified to you. According to the Liberal Principle (*L*), interference with another's action requires justification; unjustified interference is unjust. Your colleague violated this principle: as always, she interfered with your activity in a way that could not be justified to you. And I take it that her violation was indeed unjustified. Despite its irksome character, you would have carried on with your tutorial duties—not because you wanted to, or because your interests were advanced, but because you understood it to be your duty. The fact that you were relieved that you were unable to fulfill that duty does not show you would have agreed to her interference. This does not seem mere rule worship. By interfering with your liberty in a way that was not justified, your colleague supplanted *you* as the source of decisions about what *you* should do. To an agent who conceives himself as self-directing, any attempt to subvert the natural tie between *his* practical decisions and *his* activity will be seen as a threat to his status as a person. That is why one has a residue complaint even when one has not been harmed, or even when the harm has been undone. In our example you have not been harmed, but you have been wronged. Consequently, you can still properly *resent,* or be indignant about, your colleague's interference;

the moral emotions of resentment and indignation,[76] as distinguished from simple anger, are responses to wrongs. As J. R. Lucas writes:

> We are angry when we are hurt, but indignant when we are treated unjustly. . . . Indignation, which is the conceptually appropriate response to injustice, expresses, as its etymology shows, a sense of not being regarded as worthy of consideration. Injustice betokens a lack of respect, and manifests a lack of concern.[77]

You can quite properly be resentful and indignant at your colleague's interventions; but, because you have not been in any way harmed, no compensation is owed. Nevertheless, you and your colleague are by no means on a moral par.

Property Rights and Respect

This account—I shall not say more here in defense of it[78]—provides the basis for a noninstrumental conception of the right to liberty, that is, the right that flows from Principle *L*. The claim, then, is that the Liberal Principle of noninterference is more than just valuable for promoting our aims. Often it is—although sometimes paternalist interference will promote our aims even better.[79] Rather, the idea is that the Liberal Principle articulates a basic demand of a self-directing person; by ignoring that demand your colleague did not respect your status as a self-directing agent. Wrongful violation of the Liberal Principle is always a sign of disrespect.

Charles Fried argues that this respect-based analysis carries over to property rights. The right to be free from violent intervention, he says, "is firmly rooted in moral notions of respect for persons and the physical basis of personality." This respect, according to Fried, extends also to a person's right to control the disposal of his labor and talents. "To deny him the right to dispose of his labor and talent is to assert that . . . [others] have rights to them also. . . . But a person's right to his own person is a fundamental tenet of liberal individualism."[80] Property rights, Fried maintains, extend this relation. "By casting the relation between a person and a thing in this form of a right, we withdraw it *pro tanto* from the domain of collective imposition. To say that the collector's 'penny Black' is *his* assimilates that relation to the relation between a man and what is quintessentialiy his, namely, his person, his effort, his talents."[81] The core idea is that property extends one's person: and so one who ignores property rights shows disrespect for personality.[82]

We need not, however, embrace Fried's extension thesis. The crucial point is that property rights are not rights simply to some flow of benefits; they give the owner control.[83] Like other liberal rights, property rights provide a morally protected sphere in which a person may act according to his own values and aims as he understands them.[84] Consequently the agent must have discretion over how these rights are to be employed. Now if these are the sorts of rights that are justified in a community of self-directing agents, aggressors act unjustifiably when they seek to convert property rights to liability rights. The aggressor endeavors to supplant

Betty as the source of decisions about the disposition of her resources: this usurpation betokens a lack of respect. In this manner, violation of any of one's rights constitutes an unwarranted interference with one's activity, and so runs afoul of the Liberal Principle.

A word of caution, however, is in order. Although, like all rights property rights give scope to the agency of the right holder, it must also be kept in mind that much of our practical interest in property is precisely in the benefits—especially the income—that flow to us from property rights. We readily trade property if doing so increases our benefits. Consequently, we should expect that a justified system of holdings will have a place for "takings" or liability rights—cases in which property can be taken without prior consent provided compensation is paid.[85]

We all might benefit in some cases from decreasing certain transaction costs, from public goods, or from the liberty to use another's property in cases of dire need (see section 5). Given these practical interests, we all may concur full compensation for taking one's property will, in some sorts of cases, wipe clean the moral slate.

What Can and What Cannot Be Compensated

Say Alf steals a "penny Black" from Betty. Lomasky is right that the best remedy would be rectification: for Alf to return it. If it has been lost, however, compensation in some other form is due. So let us suppose that in some way, Alf redistributes: he transfers resources to Betty such that, all things considered, her values and projects are at least as well off as before. But even if he returned the stolen property he has not wiped clean the moral slate: it remains the case that he acted without justification. Can he, then, increase the payment to make up for that too? Well, he can make up for the pain of being affronted. But repayment can only give back what was lost, the value the victim lost through the aggression. But I have tried to show that wronging is not simply harming; consequently, undoing the harm does not undo the wrong. One cannot undo wrongs in the way one can repay debts.[86]

Is poor Alf doomed forever, and can he never return to moral equality with Betty? At this point we come to questions of penal justice, and the place for mercy and forgiveness. All I wish to insist upon is that redistribution of resources does not allow Alf to recover his moral equality.[87] For in addition to the maldistribution he has brought about (which does require compensation), Alf has also wronged Betty by unjustifiably interfering with her. If Betty has a property right to *X,* Alf is not justified in expropriating it subject to compensation: if that was justified, Betty would have only a liability right. So when Alf unilaterally seeks to transform Betty's rights in this way, he is interfering without justification, and so, according to Principle *L,* wrongs Betty.

The Aristotelian model does not capture this continuing inequality. But some argue that this is misleading, because compensatory justice, properly understood, includes penal justice: a transfer of resources to the victim and the punishment of the aggressor would then both be parts of compensatory justice.[88] Understood in this sense we can say that compensatory justice entails a return to equality (although we may want to say in some cases that even after punishment the aggressor is not fully squared away with the victim). But if so, compensatory justice only restores equality because we include in it penal justice. I think it doubtful that punishment is usefully understood as annulling wrongful gains, and in this way part of compensatory justice.[89] The important point, however, is not how we use the term "compensatory justice." What is crucial is that no mere redistribution of resources, no matter how generous, can restore moral equality between victim and aggressor.

Justified Rights Violations and Paying Debts

The debt model misdescribes the aim of compensation for unjustified violations of rights. In contrast to Coleman I do not reject the debt model because it links the questions of who has aggressed and who is obligated to pay; rather, I object to the claim that payment of compensation restores moral equality between victim and aggressor. Once a debtor transfers the resources back to the owner, the debt is paid. Not so with unjustified rights violations. But the debt model does seem to capture at least some *justified rights violations*. Consider an example introduced by Joel Feinberg, and since the subject of extensive discussion:

> Suppose that you are on a backpacking trip in the high mountain country when an unanticipated blizzard strikes the area with such ferocity that your life is imperiled. Fortunately, you stumble onto an unoccupied cabin, locked and boarded up for the winter, clearly someone's private property. You smash the window, enter, and huddle in a corner for three days until the storm abates. During this period you help yourself to your unknown benefactor's food supply and burn his wooden furniture in the fireplace to keep warm.[90]

Feinberg holds that you would surely be justified to infringe the person's property rights in this way. However, "almost everyone would agree that you owe *compensation* to the homeowner for the depletion of his larder, the breaking of his window, and the destruction of his furniture."[91] Most philosophers have indeed agreed that what you did was justified, but you still owe compensation.[92] Yet some have questioned this: if you were actually justified in burning the furniture, Philip Montague holds, then you owe no compensation. If, says Montague, you were a vandal, simply destroying a person's property for the fun of it, you certainly would owe compensation. To say that the backpacker owes compensation too is to treat the backpacker as morally on par with the vandal and that, maintains Montague, is "extremely implausible."[93]

A respect-based account of rights provides a rationale for Feinberg's position and a reply to Montague. Here, the debt model really does apply. The backpacker owes the owner for what has been destroyed and used: until resources are redistributed back to the owner the backpacker is, quite literally, in the owner's debt. But once the debt has been paid, moral equality has been restored. Why?

Presumably because this infringment of one's property rights can be *justified* to the owner. A justified system of property rights will presumably allow for others in dire and unexpected need sometimes to treat your property right as a liability right. Even the owner can see the point of allowing such action in special cases. So when the backpacker breaks the windows, she displays no disrespect. But the vandal does: his violation of the property right cannot be justified to the owner. Consequently, even if the vandal should compensate the owner, the moral slate is not wiped clean, equality is not restored. Hence, *pace* Montague, to follow Feinberg does not require treating the backpacker and the vandal as moral equals.

Conclusion: A Liberal Theory of Compensatory Justice

In this chapter I have sketched some of the main elements of a liberal theory of compensatory justice. First, we have seen that such a theory will not include the principle of redress, which is based upon an egalitarian presumption that conflicts with the Liberal Principle of noninterference. If we understand the Liberal Principle as the fundamental requirement of respect among self-directing moral agents, we reach a somewhat surprising conclusion: compensatory justice, understood as transfer of resources, cannot fully compensate for wrongdoing in the sense of returning aggressor and victim to moral equality. In cases of wrongful violations of rights, compensatory justice has a more modest, albeit important, task: to rectify the maldistribution of resources that results from wrongdoing. Although this may be a surprising conclusion, it nevertheless is attractive, for it shows why our rights so stubbornly resist being bought out, regardless of the size of the payment. Purely instrumental accounts of rights permit a complete return to equality after wrongful violation. And for that reason they are objectionable.

A "return to equality" is possible only when rights have been justifiably infringed. Although aggressors can repay victims for the harm done, transfer of resources cannot right a wrong.

CHAPTER 8

Louis F. Kort

WHAT IS AN APOLOGY?

The act of apologizing is of interest both in ethics and in the theory of speech acts. Writers in the latter field, most notably Austin,[1] have often cited it as a paradigm of performative utterance. But so far as I know, no analysis of apologizing has so far appeared in the philosophical literature. It is my aim here to offer one. An instructive characterization of the apology has recently been produced by Erving Goffman, a social psychologist, in his book, *Relations in Public*[2]; and I shall take certain of his remarks about apologizing as my point of departure. In the first section of this chapter, I shall argue that Goffman's characterization of apologizing, however true it is, and however suitable for his theoretical purposes, is too general to distinguish the apology from many other speech acts which are characteristically performed for the same social purpose. In the second section, I shall try to bring the specific conceptual features of apologizing into focus by setting out my analysis of it.

I

According to Goffman, an apology is a piece of what he calls "remedial work." Remedial work is a sort of social activity occasioned by a real or apparent violation of a social rule. Its function is "to change the meaning that might otherwise be given to an act, transforming what could be seen as offensive to what can be seen as acceptable."[3]

On Goffman's view, the apology is one of three basic ritual devices by which we effect such a transformation. The other two are the "account" and the "request."[4]

To give an account is to represent oneself as not responsible, or not entirely responsible, for an offense of which one is, or is liable to be, thought guilty. As Goffman points out, this can be done in a variety of ways. Suppose, as an illustration,

This essay originally appeared in *Philosophy Research Archives* 1 (1975): 80–87. Reprinted by permission of the Philosophy Documentation Center.

that Y is walking through a hall and thinks that X has bumped into him. Several defenses may be open to X. He may deny, for example, that any collision in fact occurred, that anyone really bumped into Y. Or he may acknowledge that *someone* bumped into Y, but deny having done so himself. Or again, he may admit that it was he who bumped into Y but argue that he did so in special exculpatory, or at least mitigating, circumstances, that, for instance, he was pushed in Y's direction by a third party. Any of these defenses would be an account.

The second of Goffman's remedial rituals, the request, "consists of asking license of a potentially offended person to engage in what could be considered a violation of his rights."[5] Thus, for example, I am making a request if I ask your leave to smoke while we are traveling in the same automobile or if I ask your permission to use your telephone before proceeding to make a call on it.

Accounts and requests both serve to keep one's actions from being construed as offensive. Thus, for some actions they are not suitable remedies. In particular, if one has done something which plainly *is* offensive, and can plead no mitigating circumstances, the most one may be able to do is to show by what one says and does that it does not reflect one's present attitude, that one presently takes seriously one's obligations and the rights of the offended party under the rule one has infringed. As Goffman puts it, "after an offense has occurred, the job of the offender is to show that it was not a fair expression of his attitude, or, when it evidently was, to show that he has changed his attitude to the rule that was violated. In the latter case, his job is to show that whatever happened before, he now has a right relationship—a pious attitude—to the rule in question. . . ."[6]

The ritual device we use for this task is the apology, which, according to Goffman, is "a gesture through which an individual splits himself into two parts, the part that is guilty of an offense and the part that dissociates itself from the delict and affirms a belief in the offended rule."[7]

Now the conception of an individual as capable of splitting into two social selves is of central importance in Goffman's theory of remedial interchanges; and it may prove to be a useful one in understanding the *general* sort of remedial ritual an apology is. However, Goffman's characterization of apologies seems to apply not *just* to them, but also to many other speech acts which are on many occasions performed as "splitting gestures" of the same kind and which then serve to remedy offenses in the same general way.

Consider again X's bumping into Y in the hall and suppose that X can give no satisfactory account of the incident, that, let us say, it is obviously the result of X's culpable negligence. X may here owe it to Y to say something to him as a gesture of the general sort Goffman describes. But this is not to say that he owes Y an *apology* specifically. There seem to be a considerable variety of things X can say to dissociate his present self from his offense, among them:

1) "My fault entirely."
2) "I beg your pardon."

3) "Forgive me."
4) "How negligent of me."
5) "Sorry."

What these various utterances have in common, I submit, is not that they are all apologies. It is rather that they all serve to remedy X's offense in the same general way apologies do. Any of them will suffice to show Y the seriousness with which X takes his offense and the respect he presently has both for Y's right to walk through the hall without risk of collision and for his own correlative obligation to watch where he is going. But although all these utterances frequently serve the same remedial purpose as an apology, I think they constitute distinguishable speech acts (e.g. admitting fault, asking forgiveness, etc.)[8] and that it would be a conflation to assimilate all of them to the specific act of apologizing. Only the last of them, I think, would count as an apology, in the ordinary sense of the term.

II

But what, in the ordinary sense of the term, *is* an apology? What must an utterance be like if it is to count as one? I shall try to answer this question by setting out an analysis of apologizing, the analysis consisting of a set of five conditions which are separately necessary and conjointly sufficient for the performance of an apology. Statements of the conditions are interspersed with argumentative and explanatory comments. Let X and Y be people, and U be an utterance. Then, *in saying U to Y, X apologizes to Y for something, A,* if and only if the following conditions obtain.

1) *In saying U to Y, X expresses regret about A.*

I think this condition distinguishes apologies from most other speech acts which are often performed in lieu of them to remedy offenses. Thus, for example, to admit being at fault or to ask forgiveness is not *ipso facto* to express regret. (It would be a possible, even if insolent, way of asking a person's forgiveness to say, "I do not in the least regret having done it, but I would like and ask your forgiveness if you think I have mistreated you.")

In claiming that to apologize for something, one must, *inter alia,* express regret about it, I do not, of course, mean to imply that one must *actually* regret it. As the term "express" is used here, and as it seems often to be used colloquially, it is possible to express an attitude, sentiment, opinion, or what not without having it. This is indeed precisely what a person does when he expresses an attitude or feeling insincerely. Thus, in particular, people can, and frequently do, apologize, and so express regret, with no genuine regret about whatever they are apologizing for. Such apologies are insincere, but they are full-fledged apologies nonetheless.

Now although every apology is an expression of regret, clearly not every expression of regret is an apology. For one thing, we do not ordinarily apologize for matters which are beyond our control, however much we may feel and express regret about them. If, for instance, X says to Y that he is sorry that the weather is dismal, that the economy is in a slump, or that a mutual friend is in poor health, he is thereby expressing regret about these things; but he is not likely to be apologizing for them. One reason he is not, I think, is that an apology for these things, as opposed to a mere expression of regret about them, would involve accepting responsibility for them. Thus, unless X somehow *feels* responsible for the state of the weather, the economy, or his friend's health, or wishes to give Y the impression that he does, he will not ordinarily apologize for these things. This consideration suggests that a second necessary condition for X's performance of an apology is this:

2) *In saying U to Y, X accepts responsibility for A.*

Note that this condition does not imply that X must *expressly* accept responsibility for A. In many, perhaps most, ordinary cases a person who apologizes for something accepts responsibility for it *tacitly* or *implicitly* in saying whatever he does to express regret about it.

It is worth noting here how various are the sorts of things over which the variable A can range; its scope is much wider than just acts. In addition to them, people can apologize for habits, events, states of affairs—any kind of thing, in fact, for which they can intelligibly accept responsibility.

Now it seems clear that if an expression of regret about something is to count as an apology, more is necessary than merely that one accept responsibility for it. We do, after all, express regret and take responsibility for many matters which are no one's business but our own and for which, therefore, we should not ordinarily apologize. X is unlikely to be apologizing to Y, for example, if he expresses regret about having spent last summer working instead of vacationing or about having purchased his present car. I think the reason X would not be apologizing to Y in expressing regret about such things is simply that, in doing so, X would not be acknowledging that he has treated Y in any way which constitutes an offense to him. And it is partly definitive of an apology, surely, that it is a way of acknowledging that one has offended one's hearer. A third condition is thus required.

3) *In saying U to Y, X acknowledges that by virtue of his having been responsible for A, he has treated Y in a way which constitutes an offense to him.*

A further condition must now be added to those on hand to take proper account of the intentionality of the concept of "regret," in particular, of the fact that it is possible to regret something under one description while not regretting it under another.

To see the necessity of this, consider the following case. Suppose X has swindled Y by charging him twice as much money for some item as it is worth. Now if X is hard-boiled enough, he may later brazenly say to Y, "You know, I'm awfully sorry about that swindle. You were so gullible I could easily have got away with charging you twice as much as I did."

This utterance would, of course, be no apology, though it would satisfy the three conditions so far given. X is not apologizing here, I think, because he is expressing regret about the swindle, *not as an offense to Y*, but only as a less grand feat of larceny than he might have pulled off. To rule out counter-instances of this sort, we need the following as a fourth necessary condition:

4) *In saying U to Y, X expresses regret about A as something, being responsible for which, he has offended Y.*

So far, the analysis has focused primarily on the attitude which the speaker, X, must express about his *offense* in order to apologize to Y. He must express *regret* about it, it has been argued, *as* an offense to Y. A final necessary condition is now required to specify a second attitude X must express, one toward Y himself, for it seems that in certain social contexts, a speaker can say something to his hearer in such a way as to satisfy the four conditions so far considered and yet fail to apologize precisely because in doing so he does not express an appropriate attitude toward his hearer.

Here is such a context. Suppose that X offends Y in some way and later comes to regret it. Suppose, further that several years afterward Y is employed as a journalist and is commissioned to write a biographical article about X, his erstwhile malefactor. In the course of interviewing X about his life, Y asks him if he has any regrets. X says that he does and goes on, at tedious length, to express regret about his many misdeeds and mistakes. Now suppose that as Y is recording these various expressions of regret, X expresses regret about the very wrong he earlier did Y. Is X, in doing so, apologizing to Y?

The possibility seems undeniable that he is not. And this possibility cannot be accounted for in terms of the necessary conditions for apologizing so far adduced, for all of them are satisfied here. X is expressing regret about his misconduct toward Y, accepting responsibility for it, and so on. How, then, is it possible that he is nevertheless not apologizing to Y?

The answer, I think, is that X may here be saying to Y what he does only to show Y the way in which he regards his offense, and not, in addition, the way in which he regards Y himself. I suggest that in order for X to be apologizing and not merely expressing regret about his offense, he must, in saying what he does, be making a *gesture* to Y, one by which he presents himself as taking seriously Y's right not to be treated as he is acknowledging having treated him. In a word, in saying what he does, X must be making a gesture of *respect* to Y as a person with such a right. In this situation it seems likely that however profusely X is expressing regret about his offense, he is not thereby making a gesture of respect to Y, and hence that he is not apologizing to him. To take this aspect of apologizing into account, a fifth necessary condition must be added to the others.

> *5) In saying U to Y, X makes a gesture of respect for Y as a person having a right not to be treated as X is acknowledging having treated him.*

The analysis now seems to be complete. To sum it up roughly, I have argued that a speaker is apologizing to his hearer for something, if and only if in saying what he does, he is 1) expressing regret about it, 2) accepting responsibility for it, 3) acknowledging it to constitute an offense to his hearer, 4) expressing regret about it as such, and 5) making a gesture of respect to his hearer as a person with a right to be spared such mistreatment.

I think that this analysis is compatible with Goffman's characterization of the apology, and indeed that it complements it. It may, in addition, suggest certain refinements which ought to be made in his explanation of the function of the apology in social life. But that is another matter.

CHAPTER 9

Kathleen A. Gill

THE MORAL FUNCTIONS OF AN APOLOGY

Apologizing is a common social practice that has received a considerable amount of attention from sociologists, psychologists, and linguists. Absent from such discussions is an analysis of the moral functions of an apology. In this chapter, I examine the moral aspects of apologizing, considering its impact on those who offer the apology, the recipient of the apology, and relevant communities.

I begin with an analysis of the concept of an apology, building on the work of various social scientists. Discussion is then limited to apologies offered in response to a violation of moral standards as I focus on three specific types of situation. Apologies offered in the context of the criminal justice system are interesting for several reasons. We find here, for instance, that the public has a strong interest in offender apologies. Furthermore, apologies offered in this context are related to issues of compensation and punishment, topics that have received quite a bit of attention from philosophers. Apologies offered by groups, and those which are offered to groups, are also given attention in this chapter. These are of particular philosophical interest insofar as they involve the ascription of actions, beliefs, etc., to groups. Those problems are merely mentioned, not resolved, in this chapter. What is of particular interest with regard to morality is the sheer size of apologies involving groups. The harm that governments are capable of inflicting, for example, is enormous with respect to both numbers of people involved and severity of harm. Yet the distant, impersonal nature of dealing with an agent which is "the government" makes dealing with moral wrongdoing especially difficult. Further complications arise as we try to grapple with historical acts of injustice, acts of destruction that were engaged in many years ago but have a lingering impact on society today.

This essay originally appeared in *The Philosophical Forum* 31:1 (Spring 2000): 11–27. Reprinted by permission of Blackwell Publishing Ltd.

This chapter only begins a discussion of the topic, citing a few of the more salient features of the moral functions of apologizing in these contexts. It is hoped that those who are interested in the way morality is played out at a social level will see that an analysis of the practice of apologizing may be an interesting and fruitful way of approaching that more general topic.

The Nature of Apologizing

Since little attention has been paid to apologies in the philosophical literature,[1] it is useful to begin by taking a look at work being done in the social sciences. In the early 1970s, the sociologist Erving Goffman published what has turned out to be a very influential analysis of the social dynamics of apologizing.[2] Goffman characterized the apology as a form of remedial interchange. According to Goffman, a person engages in remedial activity when "he has acted (or is about to act) so as to give the appearance of encroaching on another's various territories and preserves; or he finds himself about to give a bad impression of himself; or both. In these circumstances he is likely to engage in remedial activity in order to reinforce a definition of himself that is satisfactory to him."[3] Basic categories of remedial strategies include denials, excuses, justifications, and apologies.[4]

Excuses and justifications are sometimes referred to as accounts.[5] An account is "a statement made by a social actor to explain unanticipated or untoward behavior."[6] Excuses involve a denial of responsibility. The action, for instance, may have been performed unwittingly or unintentionally. The excuse is offered as an explanation for the action that frees the actor from blameworthiness. In giving a justification, the actor accepts responsibility but is not willing to characterize the act as inappropriate. Instead, an account is offered that explains why the act in question, along with whatever harm it may have caused, should be considered justified. In contrast to excuses and justifications, an apology involves both an acceptance of responsibility for the act and an acknowledgment of its wrongfulness.

Distinguishing among the various types of remedial tactics highlights the need to identify specific elements of the apology. An apology generally consists of a cluster of interrelated beliefs, attitudes, emotions, and intentions. In its fullest version, an apology includes the following elements:

(1) an acknowledgment that the incident in question did in fact occur;
(2) an acknowledgment that the incident was inappropriate in some way;
(3) an acknowledgment of responsibility for the act;
(4) the expression of an attitude of regret and a feeling of remorse; and
(5) the expression of an intention to refrain from similar acts in the future.

Of course, not all apologies explicitly contain each of these items. When the offense is minor, a simple "sorry" may be all that is stated. As offenses become more serious, apologizing may become more elaborate, making it more likely that explicit reference will be made to the various elements listed above.[7] But is the recipient of the apology justified in believing that each of these elements is being conveyed, even if only implicitly? Let's examine these elements and try to determine which ones are necessarily constituents of the apology.

For an act to count as an apology it must include (1). More specifically, the apology presupposes that at least one of the parties involved believes the incident actually occurred. Some version of the second element also seems to be necessary. It is not necessary that the person who offers the apology believes that her behavior was inappropriate. What is necessary is that the apologizer is willing to accept the legitimacy of the addressee having taken offense. Sarcastically stating something to the effect that "if anyone took offense at my comments, I'm very sorry" may be considered a classic non-apology. The message is that listeners are simply too sensitive, not that the speaker is offering an apology. On the other hand, it isn't necessary that the recipient of the apology has actually taken offense. But in this case it must be true that the apologizer believes the act was inappropriate. We may revise (1) and (2) as follows: (1') at least one of the parties involved believes the incident actually occurred; and (2') at least one of the parties believes the act was inappropriate. If the person offering the apology does not believe that the act was inappropriate, she must be willing to accept the legitimacy of the addressee having taken offense.

It is not necessary that the person offering the apology take direct responsibility for the offensive act. We accept, for instance, the fact that parents sometimes apologize for the behavior of their children. But there is an obvious link here; parents are generally considered responsible for their children. Suppose there is no connection at all between the behavior of the person apologizing and the offense. Suppose, for instance, that your neighbor's child develops leukemia. In this case, saying "I'm sorry" is an expression of sympathy, not an apology. The speaker is not responsible for the child's illness, and it may be that no one is responsible. For an act to count as an apology, it must be true that (3') someone is responsible for the offensive act, and either the person offering the apology takes responsibility for the act, or there is some relationship between the responsible actor and the apologizer that justifies her taking responsibility for offering an apology.

As will be discussed below, some apologies are offered by, or on behalf of, a group. In these cases (4), which involves an attitude of regret and a feeling of remorse, may not be operative in any straightforward way. But a statement that only satisfied conditions (1') (2'), and (3') would not be taken as an apology. Suppose I acknowledge that an incident occurred, that it was wrong, and that I'm the person who did it. Far from being sorry that it happened, I could be quite pleased with myself. What's missing is a belief that I should not have done the act or a wish that I had not—i.e., an attitude of regret. And there is no remorse; no empathy, no feeling of distress over the harm done to the victim, no sense of guilt. Some version of these seem to be essential to apologizing. So for an act to count as an apology (4') the apologizer must have an attitude of regret with respect to the offensive behavior, and a feeling of remorse in response to the suffering of the victim.

And what about (5)? Does every act of apologizing necessarily involve an intention to refrain from similar acts in the future? When someone utters the simple phrase "I'm sorry," are we justified in believing that such an intention has been implicitly conveyed? Surely the speaker need not consciously be thinking, or have thought, such a thing. Nonetheless, we commonly use post-apology behavior as a test of sincerity. We accept that a person may struggle to control certain offensive behaviors, and that even a heartfelt apology doesn't guarantee those behaviors won't be repeated. But if a person carelessly continues to offend in the same way, apparently not even trying to stop, we have reason to believe the apology was not sincere. In the absence of some explanation to the contrary, we have reason to believe that the offender had not actually experienced remorse or regret at the time the apology was offered. That's because of an apparent inconsistency; believing that a certain act is wrong, experiencing regret and remorse for having done it, is inconsistent with a carefree repetition of similar acts. We can say, therefore, that (5') the person to whom the apology is offered is justified in believing that the offender will try to refrain from similar offenses in the future.

Gathering together our modified list of elements, we have the following as necessary conditions for apologizing:

(1') At least one of the parties involved believes that the incident actually occurred.

(2') At least one of the parties involved believes that the act was inappropriate. If the person offering the apology does not believe the act inappropriate, she must be willing to accept the legitimacy of the addressee having taken offense.

(3') Someone is responsible for the offensive act. And either the party offering the apology takes responsibility for the act, or there is some relationship between the responsible actor and the apologizer such that her taking responsibility for offering the apology is justifiable.

(4') The apologizer must have an attitude of regret with respect to the offensive behavior and a feeling of remorse in response to the suffering of the victim.

(5') The person to whom the apology is offered is justified in believing that the offender will try to refrain from similar offenses in the future.

Social scientists commonly emphasize the way remedial tactics are used to address negative perceptions created by the offense. They speak in terms of "impression management" and "face-saving" strategies. Janet Holmes, for instance, suggests that "the remedial exchange may incorporate an attempt to simultaneously redress the speaker's positive face needs as well as the victim's face needs." The victim may "need that others recognize her or his achievements and respect them."[8] The offender has "face needs" resulting from the "unfavorable evaluations or emotions" that may have been provoked by her actions.[9]

In order to create more favorable perceptions, the offender must present herself to others in a certain way. Goffman describes this as "splitting the self in two." The offender distances herself from the earlier, blameworthy self by joining in the community's disparagement of the act. As a "new" person, the offender makes a commitment to abide by the norms shared by the community. Acceptance of the apology indicates that the offender has been reestablished as a member of the community.[10]

What I would like to do in this chapter is further enrich our understanding of apologies by identifying several functions that are pertinent to morality, and that seem to be absent from the discussions of social scientists. This short chapter does not represent an exhaustive analysis of the moral dimensions of apologizing. But it does bring to the foreground a number of salient features that could serve as a starting point for further discussion. In what follows, I will focus attention on apologies that are offered in response to violations of moral norms. Discussion will be limited to a few specific contexts, but these are contexts in which the harm caused by violations may be quite severe.

Compensation and Punishment

Given that apologizing is one of a variety of possible responses to the violation of a norm, it seems reasonable to consider in what ways it might be related to the issues of compensation and punishment. Those who violate moral standards, as well as legal and social norms, are generally subject to some sort of sanction. And people who are harmed by others, especially when the harm is severe, are generally thought of as deserving compensation. An examination of apologies in the context of the criminal justice system, where issues of compensation and punishment are central, should help to further illuminate the nature of apologizing.

As a matter of fact, apologizing seems to have a prominent place in the criminal justice system. A show of remorse by a defendant, for instance, routinely has an impact on sentencing and parole. The power and resources of the system, it is said, are reserved for the unapologetic.[11] Apologizing is also prominent in the restitution process and in the settlement of lawsuits. Finally, defamation law encourages apologizing by reducing damages when one is offered, or when the offending statement is publicly retracted.[12]

Compensation is commonly characterized as aiming at either returning victims to the state they were in before the harm occurred, or putting them in a position they would have been in had the harm not occurred. Both of these goals are frequently associated with monetary compensation, something the apology does not accomplish. But, as will be further described below, apologies do seem to have the potential for facilitating certain changes in the victim. And those changes are restorative in nature. In some sense, therefore, apologies do help return victims to a pre-offense state.

Is this reason enough to consider apologies a form of compensation? I think not. Compensation aims, as do apologies, at the restoration of the victim. But compensation seems necessarily to involve the giving of something that offsets losses suffered by the victim. The apology is not a thing; it is an act that displays a certain set of beliefs, attitudes, etc., experienced by the offender. More importantly, an apology is not a mechanism for offsetting losses. The apology does not compensate for loss; it is instead a way to acknowledge the value of what was lost. Let's look more closely at what an apology means to a victim.

As Louis Kort has pointed out, the apology is a gesture of respect recognizing the victim's right not to be treated as he or she has been.[13] When the offender apologizes, it verifies this right. It makes clear, in a public forum, that even the offender knows the victim was harmed unjustly. Extreme cases of violence, such as murders and assaults, indicate extraordinary levels of disrespect for human life. The importance of having an offender explicitly recognize the value of what he has destroyed is perhaps most evident in its absence; it is as though the refusal to recognize the harm done, the value of what was taken, is a continuing devaluation of the moral worth of the victim. Public recognition, voiced by the offender, of that moral worth may help restore the victim's sense of his or her own value, and provide confidence that he or she will be treated with respect in the future. In other words, the apology has a psychological impact on the victim related to moral status; the moral value of the victim is not in fact diminished by the act of the offender, but perceptions of that value may have been altered. The apology reshapes those perceptions, helping to restore a sense of self-worth and confidence on the part of the victim.

It is not only the victim who has an interest in whether or not an offender apologizes. The general public has an interest as well. A person who is incapable of recognizing the value of human life, of empathizing with the pain of others, is a danger to society. Being able to apologize, even if the apology is not especially heartfelt, at least indicates that the offender has some of the basic moral capacities necessary for social life.

The interests of the community can be seen as represented in the way apologizing functions in sentencing and parole hearings. In these situations, the expression of an apology is sometimes used as a basis for the reduction of punishment. There are several ways to understand this practice. For one thing, the judge is given a certain amount of discretion in sentencing and is expected to take mitigating circumstances into account. Genuinely apologetic behavior on the part of the offender may be indicative of such circumstances. The reduction in sentencing might also be justified in terms of theories of punishment. If a judge considers rehabilitation to be a goal of punishment, apologetic behavior may indicate that less punishment is necessary to achieve that goal. Of course, in practice the courts may be driven largely by the demands of "judicial economy."[14] The costs of imprisonment put pressure on judges to minimize sentences when possible. A refusal to be apologetic may provide a rough but ready indication of where maximum levels of punishment are most necessary to protect the public from further injury.

At any rate, both the victim and the public have an interest in apologies being offered by an offender. The victim's interest is backward-looking, requiring the offender to recognize the value of that which his act destroyed. The public's concern is more forward-looking, having a strong interest in the future behavior of the offender. Taking a cue from Goffman, we should also note that the practice of having offenders publicly express apologies helps to maintain a general attitude of respect for the law; the legitimacy of the law is reaffirmed as those who violate it acknowledge that they were wrong.

Besides looking at the interests of the victim and the community, we need to consider what functions the apology may play with respect to the offender. In some reported descriptions of apologies, the offender does seem to feel a strong and genuine sense of remorse and shame. Some offenders, at any rate, seem capable of empathizing with the victims of their actions. In these cases, being able to address the victim, to make a "gesture of respect" acknowledging the wrongfulness of the act, may be an end in itself for the offender. Furthermore, the public nature of the apology provides the offender with an opportunity to reestablish his own moral integrity. The offender is able to show others that he isn't the monster he may seem to be, that he does have those moral capacities which are the mark of being human. But the level of pressure placed on offenders to apologize seems to be enormous, which raises important questions about what an apology expressed in this context really means. At its best, the expression of an apology enables the offender to salvage a bit of moral integrity, confirms the injustice of the harm done to the victim, gives some assurance of safety to the public, and engenders an attitude of respect for the law. But of course things aren't always at their best. There is definitely potential for abuse here.

The language of morality is often very effective, both as an emotive force and as language that "trumps" other sorts of appeals. The danger is that the moral language of an apology will be used merely to manipulate others' perceptions for one's own goals. It is possible for an offender to be an excellent con artist, to express an apology that convinces others that he feels genuine remorse when in fact he feels none. He may be entirely motivated by the hope of a reduction in punishment.

And it is not just the offender who may be using the apology merely to advance his own interests. The various agents of the criminal justice system collectively have an enormous amount of power over the offender, which may be used in a careless or self-serving manner. Nor are victims exempt; it is not very difficult to find examples of a victim using an apology as a tool with which to manipulate public perceptions. In 1995, for instance, ABC News agreed to express a public apology as part of the settlement of a defamation suit brought by the Philip Morris Companies.[15] Philip Morris does not appear to have put much effort into making their success sound like a moral victory. Instead, the gleeful "we win!" ad in which they dramatically accepted the apology made the episode look like a blatant struggle for power.

We can't expect the various parties to the apology to be motivated simply by the demands of morality. But expressing apologies in the absence of any genuine remorse is deceptive, and so is morally suspect. Using coercion to elicit apologies from others as a way of establishing dominance is also a morally suspect practice. Suspicion of motives leads to cynicism, and as we shall continue to find in our investigation, countering cynicism is a major challenge to those trying to use apologies in a public forum.

When the Offender Is a Group

The legal system consists of a set of public institutions that serve as an enforcement mechanism. The offender is held accountable to both the victim and the general public; apologies may well be directed toward both. Even though in many cases the victim and the offender are individuals, it is clear that apologies of this sort are not simply a private matter. An even more dramatic shift away from the private, interpersonal apology occurs when the offender is a group. Public apologies of this sort have been very common in the past few years, frequently being offered on behalf of governments, businesses, and religious organizations.

Looking once more at the list of elements identified as constituting the act of apologizing, we find that the very possibility of a group apology seems problematic. Items (1') through (3') require that the offender hold certain beliefs. Item (4') requires the offender to adopt an attitude of regret and experience feelings of remorse. Are groups actually capable of entertaining beliefs, having attitudes, and experiencing emotions? These capabilities are most comfortably ascribed to individuals, not groups. One way of developing an account of the group apology, therefore, would be to construe (1')-(4') in terms of group members.

To begin, suppose that every group member has the appropriate beliefs, attitudes, and emotions. In this case, it seems clear that an apology on behalf of the group is warranted; conditions for expressing an apology are satisfied. It doesn't seem necessary, however, that every member of the group experience each element of the apology. In some situations that would be an impossibly high standard to meet. Holding groups to such a standard would, for instance, have prohibited the German government from offering an apology to surviving victims of the Holocaust. And the opposite extreme seems just as unreasonable; if only a small minority of members has accepted the appropriate beliefs, etc., the group has no business offering the apology. It is not obvious where, between these two extremes, a reasonable standard lies. Perhaps this could only be determined on a case-by-case basis, since there might well be a shifting set of factors to consider as contexts change.

The issuing of an apology by a group also presupposes that the group is capable of performing actions and being held responsible for actions that are considered morally wrong. Quite a bit of philosophical attention has been paid to the nature of collective action and responsibility, and it seems that the practice of offering group apologies is consistent with some positions on those issues. In particular, groups that have a high level of organization, including a certain sort of decision-making process, can most reasonably be considered capable of acting as a group and being held morally responsible for those actions.[16] In fact, the groups whose apologies receive public attention do seem to be just such highly organized entities. Without having fully described the structural mechanisms at work in group apologies, let's move on to consider the moral aspects of how they function.

The actions of large organizations can affect a lot of people. And those organizations may have the resources to inflict severe levels of harm. It is especially important, therefore, that governments, businesses, and religious organizations act in accordance with norms of morality. It is perhaps a cliche to say that, in order to promote such conduct, those organizations must be held accountable for their actions. Actually holding them accountable can, of course, be quite difficult. But it is not impossible, and even large organizations sometimes respond to charges of improper conduct. The full range of options identified as "remedial tactics" is open to them; they may offer a denial, an excuse, or a justification rather than an apology.

The moral functions of an apology expressed by a large organization are similar in some ways to the functions identified in our examination of the criminal justice system. For instance, apologies issued publicly by large organizations give some assurance that an effort will be made to refrain from similar behavior in the future. Roy L. Brooks points out that an "undercurrent of fear" exists among survivors that the atrocities they have suffered will be repeated. Apologies directly address that fear; "heartfelt contrition just might signify a nation's capacity to suppress its next impulse to harm others." Apologies do not guarantee safety, but without them "there would be greater concern, perhaps not just among the survivors, that those shameful acts might be repeated."[17]

And just as apologies offered within the criminal justice system help engender respect for the law, apologies issued by large organizations help reinforce acceptance of the violated standards, and perhaps moral standards generally, within the society. As Brooks puts it, this type of apology helps to "raise the moral threshold" of a society.[18]

We can also see a parallel in the impact the apology has on the offending organization. Governments cannot function without some level of trust among the citizenry. A government that routinely violates commonly accepted moral standards undermines its own political authority. Businesses too need to maintain trust, in this case on the part of consumers, in order to survive. Religious organizations especially have an important social role with respect to morality, often functioning as a source of moral authority. In order to maintain that role, the organization must be perceived as a model moral agent. But of course no human, and no humanly constructed organization, is a perfect moral agent. And so there is a role for apologizing. The apology provides a mechanism for reestablishing the moral credibility of large organizations, which in turn provides a basis for the trust that is necessary for them to function. This is not only good for the organization itself; as society is now structured, the general public has a strong interest in the effective functioning of these institutions.

One feature prominent in group apologies that did not emerge in our discussion of the criminal justice system is the way in which these apologies provide a mechanism for social change. In particular, apologizing enables long-lived institutions to adapt to shifting moral standards.[19] In 1995, for instance, Southern Baptists apologized to African Americans for supporting the practice of slavery and later opposing the civil rights movement. That act of apologizing sent a signal to members of the church, to African Americans outside the church, to the general public, and to future generations of all these groups that a new standard of moral behavior had officially been adopted.[20]

The question of mixed motives, of interplay between morality and manipulation, seems to be even more on the surface here than it is in the criminal justice system. There are probably many reasons for this, but the impersonal nature of many large organizations makes it that much more difficult to assess sincerity. As a member of the general public, I have no idea who within the organization of Southern Baptists initially decided that it was a good idea to issue an apology to African Americans, or why they decided to do it at this time. Was it done in response to a demand from African Americans? Did leaders within the organization just recently come to realize the immorality of the church's past behavior? Or is the apology a response to falling membership, part of a new recruitment drive?[21]

When we turn from religious organizations to governments and businesses, reasons for cynicism are even easier to find. After all, politicians must be able to manipulate public perceptions in order to get into office. And manipulation of the public, in the form of advertising, is part of routine business practice. As a citizen and as a consumer, my distrust runs deep, and I'm not alone in having that reaction.[22]

When Victims Are Groups

In many cases, apologies issued by organizations are offered to groups rather than individuals. During the past few decades a surprisingly large number of groups have demanded apologies for wrongs done to them in the past. As an example, let's consider claims made by two indigenous groups, the Maori in New Zealand and native Hawaiians. Both have requested apologies for actions taken in the second half of the nineteenth century.[23]

Conceptual difficulties similar to those which arose when considering the notion of a group apology are found here as well. Requesting and accepting an apology as a group, for instance, would seem to take a level of organization on par with that found in groups issuing apologies. Yet that is not what we find in either of these cases, group membership is not a straightforward matter, and group agency is complicated. After decades of interethnic marriage and the various processes of cultural alienation, determining who is and who is not native Hawaiian or Maori is not a simple task. And, apparently, in neither case is there a single organization that has a highly structured decision-making process and the authority to represent all members of the group.[24]

Furthermore, in cases of historical injustice the issue of responsibility is especially problematic. No current group members on either side were actually involved in the disputed event. Even with a very robust view as to the identity of groups over time, which would allow us to assume that the groups at the time of the event and at the time of the apology are the same, it surely matters that their membership is entirely different. The idea that contemporary group members are responsible for the actions of past members does not seem to have widespread popular support. And similar resistance is found to the idea that the descendants of group members who were harmed have a right to compensation.[25]

Having acknowledged such difficulties, however, I will move on to consider the potential moral significance of these apologies for victim groups.

In some cases, official recognition from the government that a certain event actually occurred may be extremely important. The sociologist Nicholas Tavuchis has suggested that, while expressions of remorse and regret are appropriate in the formulation of apologies offered on behalf of groups, they are less central than in interpersonal apologies. Instead, it is the creation of a public record that "takes us to the heart of the collective apology."[26] In general, historical apologies have a role to play in the struggle to create history, to establish a certain version of events as the "official story." Examples of governmental denial of wrong-doing, even in the face of common knowledge to the contrary, are not difficult to find. Denials by the former Soviet Union of the atrocities of Stalinism and the refusal by Turkey to recognize the extermination of Armenians are extreme versions of this practice.[27] A dramatic example of how suddenly an official story can be changed was seen in the shift, within the span of a few days, from denial of U.S. involvement in the Guatemalan civil war to expressions of regret for its role.[28] Though difficult and often unsatisfying, the strategy taken in South Africa, where revealing the truth was given a higher priority than punishing those responsible, gives some indication of just how important it is to have a public record of injustice.[29]

For the Maori and native Hawaiians, however, a simple denial of the occurrence of events is not really the issue. Soon after the 1893 takeover of the Kingdom of Hawai'i by U.S. forces, the Senate sent a former Congressman, James Blount, to investigate. Blount's report remains an important official document of events. In it he concludes that the change in government did not reflect the will of the people, especially native Hawaiians, but was instead the result of an abuse of power by U.S. diplomats and military men stationed in Hawai'i. Furthermore, the morality of U.S. actions was publicly debated at the time. U.S. citizens and lawmakers of the 1890s found it somewhat difficult to justify the takeover of the Kingdom of Hawai'i because it conflicted with accepted principles of political sovereignty. But the belief that the takeover was morally justified seems to have won the day. It was justified by an appeal to arguments in favor of U.S. imperialism. Among those was the claim that native Hawaiians would benefit from having their own, intellectually and morally inferior culture displaced by Westem culture.[30]

As Will Kymlicka points out, the ideology of Western cultural superiority has been dominant (among Westerners) until fairly recently, and it was used by many powerful organizations to justify their behavior towards non-Western ethnic groups.[31] But now things have changed. Such a strong and simple belief in the superiority of Western culture is no longer widely held even within its own ranks. What once were widely accepted as legitimate reasons to engage in extremely destructive behavior now come across as transparently self-serving rationalizations. Now that the justifications have crumbled, the demands for apologies begin to flow. Perhaps with a certain "critical mass" of apologies from various Western institutions, the new valuations will become firmly entrenched and help us as a society to set a new moral course.

Just as the apology plays a role in both marking and promoting changes in the moral beliefs of descendants of the offender groups, so does it signal changes, and promote further changes, among descendants of the victim groups. It is uncontroversial, I think, that the badge of inferiority placed on so many groups in the ideological framework of Western culture has had an enormous negative impact on many people over the years. And that impact continues today. The apology not only acknowledges the moral worth of the group at this time, but it makes clear that past treatment of the group never was morally justified. In an official apology, the highest political authorities acknowledge that the culture of the victim group is not now, and never was, morally inferior to that of the offender group. The very identity of the victim group may be reshaped in this process.[32]

Another important aspect of these cases is the relationship between the apology and compensation. An apology, it seems, is not a form of compensation, and it should certainly not be used as a substitute for compensation or as part of an attempt to avoid compensating victims. At the same time, it is important to recognize that avoiding an apology by offering monetary compensation is also reprehensible. Note, for instance, the demand made by Asian "comfort women" to receive both an apology and compensation from the Japanese government. When compensation without an apology was offered it was characterized as hush money, a way to buy their silence while allowing the Japanese government to avoid taking responsibility.[33] In an analysis of the destruction of an Iranian passenger plane in 1988 by a U.S. warship, which killed the 290 civilians on board, Lisa Portmess lays out the moral shortcomings of offering compensation without acknowledging guilt.[34] Apologies offered in place of compensation may well be empty, cynical gestures, but compensation alone cannot perform the functions of an apology.

Furthermore, since it incorporates an acknowledgment that an unjustified harm has been done to the victim group, the apology may provide moral grounds for making compensation claims. For example, the apology expressed by President Clinton to native Hawaiians took the form of a resolution passed by Congress; it is not only a public apology, it is an "official" apology. The result is a document that has legal as well as moral force. Native Hawaiians seem to be taking advantage of this fact, using the official apology as a basis for claims to land and autonomy.[35]

Here again we find symptoms of the power struggle that seems to be the constant companion of the moral dimension of apologizing. Many indigenous groups, as well as other groups historically oppressed in Western societies, are using gains made in the past few decades to challenge the status quo. At a broad social level, this conflict is described as "the culture wars," and exemplifies the intense controversies that arise in the telling of history.[36]

Conclusion

In this brief examination of the moral dimension of apologizing, several points have emerged that seem significant. First, it is important to recognize that apologies commonly involve more than two parties. The public may have a variety of interests at stake; apologies are a mechanism for holding offenders accountable to the community, and apologies give some assurance that the offender will refrain from violations in the future. Furthermore, the community itself may be strengthened, as the norms that bind it together are either reaffirmed or adjusted.

It seems evident that in some ways the significance of an apology depends upon the situation. Context and circumstances determine which elements are most important and so will shape the form the apology takes and the impact it has on those involved. But generally it is extremely important that the apology provides a mechanism by means of which the offender reaches out to the victim in a gesture of respect. More specifically, the apology involves a recognition of the injustice of the harm done to the victim, a confirmation of the moral worth of the victim and the value of what has been lost. In offering the apology, the offender exercises the moral capacities that seem to have failed in committing the offense. After such a display, the offender may be reestablished as a more trustworthy and respectable member of the community. The moral domain is an uncertain and challenging landscape. As offenders, we need ways to recover from our moral failings and to reconfirm our commitment to moral ideals. As victims, we need ways to confirm the injustice of the harm we have suffered and to regain confidence that others will treat us with respect. The act of apologizing may not always be sufficient to "restore social harmony"[37] but it does play a significant role in enabling us to respond to moral failure and to keep traveling through this difficult territory more or less together with others.

CHAPTER 10

Bernard R. Boxill

THE MORALITY OF REPARATION

In "Black Reparations—Two Views,"[1] Michael Harrington rejected and Arnold Kaufman endorsed James Forman's demand for $500 million in reparation from Christian churches and Jewish synagogues for their part in the exploitation of black people. Harrington's position involves two different points; he argues that reparation is irrelevant and unwarranted because even if it were made, it would do little to "even up incomes"; and he maintains that the *demand* for reparation will be counterproductive, since it will "divert precious political energies from the actual struggle" to even up incomes. Now, though Kaufman seemed to show good reason that, contra Harrington, the demand for reparation could be productive, I shall in the ensuing, completely disregard that issue. Whether the demand for reparation is counterproductive or not is a question the answer to which depends on the assessment of a large number of consequences which cannot be answered by philosophy alone.

In this chapter I shall take issue with what I have distinguished as the first of Harrington's points, viz. that reparation is unwarranted and irrelevant because it would do little to even up incomes. I assume that, by implication, Harrington is not averse to special compensatory programs which will effectively raise the incomes of the poor; what he specifically opposes is reparation. By a discussion of the justification and aims of reparation and compensation, I shall now try to show that, though both are parts of justice, they have different aims, and hence compensation cannot replace reparation.

Let me begin with a discussion of how compensation may be justified. Because of the scarcity of positions and resources relative to aspiring individuals, every society that refuses to resort to paternalism or a strict regimentation of aspirations must incorporate competition among its members for scarce positions and resources. Given that freedom of choice necessitates at least the possibility of competition, I

This essay originally appeared in *Social Theory and Practice* 2:1 (Spring 1972): 113–123. Reprinted by permission of Social Theory and Practice.

believe that justice requires that appropriate compensatory programs be instituted both to ensure that the competition is fair, and that the losers be protected.

If the minimum formal requirement of justice is that persons be given equal consideration, then it is clear that justice requires that compensatory programs be implemented in order to ensure that none of the participants suffers from a removable handicap. The same reasoning supports the contention that the losers in the competition be given, if necessary, sufficient compensation to enable them to reenter the competition on equal terms with the others. In other words, the losers can demand equal opportunity as well as can the beginners.

In addition to providing compensation in the above cases, the community has the duty to provide compensation to the victims of accident where no one was in the wrong, and to the victims of "acts of God" such as floods, hurricanes, and earthquakes. Here again, the justification is that such compensation is required if it is necessary to ensure equality of opportunity.

Now, it should be noted that, in all the cases I have stated as requiring compensation, no prior injustice need have occurred. This is clear, of course, in the case of accidents and "acts of God"; but it is also the case that in a competition, even if everyone abides by the rules and acts fairly and justly, some will necessarily be losers. In such a case, I maintain, if the losers are rendered so destitute as to be unable to compete equally, they can demand compensation from the community. Such a right to compensation does not render the competition nugatory; the losers cannot demand success—they can demand only the minimum necessary to reenter the competition. Neither is it the case that every failure has rights of compensation against the community. As we shall see, the right to compensation depends partly on the conviction that every individual has an equal right to pursue what he considers valuable; the wastrel or indolent man has signified what he values by what he has freely chosen to be. Thus, even if he seems a failure and considers himself a failure, he does not need or have a right of compensation. Finally, the case for compensation sketched is not necessarily paternalistic. It is not argued that society or government can decide what valuable things individuals should have and implement programs to see to it that they have them. Society must see to it that its members can pursue those things they consider valuable.

The justification of compensation rests on two premises: first, each individual is equal in dignity and worth to every other individual, and hence has a right, equal to that of any other, to arrange his life as he sees fit, and to pursue and acquire what he considers valuable; and second, the individuals involved must be members of a community. Both premises are necessary in order to show that compensation is both good and, in addition, mandatory or required by justice. One may, for example, concede that a man who is handicapped by some infirmity should receive compensation; but if the man is a member of no community, and if his infirmity is due to no injustice, then one would be hard put to find the party who could be legitimately forced to bear the cost of such compensation. Since persons can be legitimately compelled to do what justice dictates, then it would seem that in the absence of a community, and if the individual has suffered his handicap because of no injustice, that compensation cannot be part of justice. But given that the individual is a member of a community, then I maintain that he can legitimately demand compensation from that community. The members of a community are, in essential respects, members of a joint undertaking; the activities of the members of a community are interdependent and the community benefits from the efforts of its members even when such efforts do not bring the members what they individually aim at. It is legitimate to expect persons to follow the spirit and letter of rules and regulations, to work hard and honestly, to take calculated risks with their lives and fortunes, all of which helps society generally, only if such persons can demand compensation from society as a whole when necessary.

The case for rights of compensation depends, as I have argued above, on the fact that the individuals involved are members of a single community the very existence of which should imply a tacit agreement on the part of the whole to bear the costs of compensation. The case for reparation I shall try to show is more primitive in the sense that it depends only on the premise that every person has an equal right to pursue and acquire what he values. Recall that the crucial difference between compensation and reparation is that whereas the latter is due only after injustice, the former may be due when no one has acted unjustly to anyone else. It is this relative innocence of all the parties concerned which made it illegitimate, in the absence of prior commitments, to compel anyone to bear the cost of compensation.

In the case of reparation, however, this difficulty does not exist. When reparation is due, it is not the case that no one is at fault, or that everyone is innocent; in such a case, necessarily, someone has infringed unjustly on another's right to pursue what he values. This could happen in several different ways, dispossession being perhaps the most obvious. When someone possesses something, he has signified by his choice that he values it. By taking it away from him one infringes on his equal right to pursue and possess what he values. On the other hand, if I thwart, unfairly, another's legitimate attempt to do or possess something, I have also acted unjustly; finally, an injustice has occurred when someone makes it impossible for others to pursue a legitimate goal, even if these others never actually attempt to achieve that goal. These examples of injustice differ in detail, but what they all have in common is that no supposition of prior commitment is necessary in order to be able to identify the parties who must bear the cost of reparation; it is simply and clearly the party who has acted unjustly.

The argument may, perhaps, be clarified by the ideas of a state of nature and a social contract. In the state of nature, as John Locke remarks, every man has the right to claim reparation from his injurer because of his right of self-preservation; if each man has a duty not to interfere in the rights of others, he has a duty to repair the results of his interference.[2] No social contract is required to legitimize compelling him to do so. But when compensation is due, i.e. when everyone has acted justly, and has done his duty, then a social contract or a prior agreement to help must be appealed to in order to legitimately compel an individual to help another.

The case for reparation thus requires for its justification less in the way of assumptions than in the case for compensation. Examination of the justifications of reparation and compensation also reveals the difference in their aims.

The characteristic of compensatory programs is that they are essentially "forward looking"; by that I mean that such programs are intended to alleviate disabilities which stand in the way of some *future* good, *however* these disabilities may have come about. Thus, the history of injustices suffered by black and colonial people is quite irrelevant to their right to compensatory treatment. What is strictly relevant to this is that such compensatory treatment is necessary if some future goods such as increased happiness, equality of incomes, and so on, are to be secured. To put it another way, given the contingency of causal connections, the present condition of black and colonial people could have been produced in any one of a very large set of different causal sequences. Compensation is concerned with the remedying of the present situation however it may have been produced; and to know the present situation, and how to remedy it, it is not, strictly speaking, necessary to know just how it was brought about, or whether it was brought about by injustice.

On the other hand, the justification of reparation is essentially "backward looking"; the reparation is due only when a breach of justice *has* occurred. Thus, as opposed to the case of compensation, the case for reparation to black and colonial people depends precisely on the fact that such people have been reduced to their present condition by a history of injustice. In sum, while the aim of compensation is to procure some future good, that of reparation is to rectify past injustices; and rectifying past injustices may not insure equality of opportunity.

The fact that reparation aims precisely at correcting a prior injustice suggests one further important difference between reparation and compensation. Part of what is involved in rectifying an injustice is an acknowledgment on the part of the transgressor that what he is doing is required of him because of his prior error. This concession of error seems required by the premise that every person is equal in worth and dignity. Without the acknowledgment of error, the injurer implies that the injured has been treated in a manner that befits him; hence, he cannot feel that the injured party is his equal. In such a case, even if the unjust party repairs the damage he has caused, justice does not yet obtain between himself and his victim. For, if it is true that when someone has done his duty nothing can be demanded of him, it follows that if, in my estimation, I have acted dutifully even when someone is injured as a result, then I must feel that nothing can be demanded of me and that any repairs I may make are gratuitous. If justice can be demanded, it follows that I cannot think that what I am doing is part of justice.

It will be objected, of course, that I have not shown in this situation that, justice cannot obtain between injurer and victim, but only that the injurer does not *feel* that justice can hold between himself and the one he injures. The objection depends on the distinction between the objective transactions between the individuals and their subjective attitudes, and assumes that justice requires only the objective transactions. The model of justice presupposed by this objection is, no doubt, that justice requires equal treatment of equals, whereas the view I take is that justice requires equal consideration between equals; that is to say, justice requires not only that we *treat* people in a certain way, for whatever reason we please, but that we treat them as equals precisely because we believe they are our equals. In particular, justice requires that we acknowledge that our treatment of others can be required of us; thus, where an unjust injury has occurred, the injurer reaffirms his belief in the other's equality by conceding that repair can be demanded of him, and the injured rejects the allegation of his inferiority contained in the other's behavior by demanding reparation.

Consequently, when injustice has reduced a people to indigency, compensatory programs alone cannot be all that justice requires. Since the avowed aim of compensatory programs is forward looking, such programs *necessarily* cannot affirm that the help they give is required because of a prior injustice. This must be the case even if it is the unjustly injuring party who makes compensation. Thus, since the acknowledgment of error is required by justice as part of what it means to give equal consideration, compensatory programs cannot take the place of reparation.

In sum, *compensation* cannot be substituted for *reparation* where reparation is due, because they satisfy two differing requirements of justice. In addition, practically speaking, since it is by demanding and giving justice where it is due that the members of a community continually reaffirm their belief in each other's equality, a stable and equitable society is not possible without reparation being given and demanded when it is due.

Consider now the assertion that the present generation of white Americans owe the present generation of black Americans reparation for the injustices of slavery inflicted on the ancestors of the black population by the ancestors of the white population. To begin, consider the very simplest instance of a case where reparation may be said to be due: Tom has an indisputable moral right to possession of a certain item, say a bicycle, and Dick steals the bicycle from Tom. Here, clearly, Dick owes Tom, at least the bicycle and a concession of error, in reparation. Now complicate the case slightly; Dick steals the bicycle from Tom and "gives" it to Harry. Here again, even if he is innocent of complicity in the theft, and does not know that his "gift" was stolen, Harry must return the bicycle to Tom with the acknowledgement that, though innocent or blameless, he did not rightfully possess the bicycle. Consider a final complication; Dick steals the bicycle from Tom and gives it to Harry; in the meantime Tom dies, but leaves a will clearly conferring his right to ownership of the bicycle to his son, Jim. Here again we should have little hesitation in saying that Harry must return the bicycle to Jim.

Now, though it involves complications, the case for reparation under consideration is essentially the same as the one last mentioned: the slaves had an indisputable moral right to the products of their labour; these products were stolen from them by the slave masters who ultimately passed them on to their descendants; the slaves presumably have conferred their rights of ownership to the products of their labour to their descendants; thus, the descendants of slave masters are in possession of wealth to which the descendants of slaves have rights; hence, the descendants of slave masters must return this wealth to the descendants of slaves with a concession that they were not rightfully in possession of it.

It is not being claimed that the descendants of slaves must seek reparation from those among the white population who happen to be descendants of slave owners. This perhaps would be the case if slavery had produced for the slave owners merely specific hoards of gold, silver or diamonds, which could be passed on in a very concrete way from father to son. As a matter of fact, slavery produced not merely specific hoards, but wealth which has been passed down mainly to descendants of the white community to the relative exclusion of the descendants of slaves. Thus, it is the white community as a whole that prevents the descendants of slaves from exercising their rights of ownership, and the white community as a whole that must bear the cost of reparation.

The above statement contains two distinguishable arguments. In the first argument the assertion is that each white person, individually, owes reparation to the black community because membership in the white community serves to identify an individual as a recipient of benefits to which the black community has a rightful claim. In the second argument, the conclusion is that the white community as a whole, considered as a kind of corporation or company, owes reparation to the black community.

In the first of the arguments sketched above, individuals are held liable to make reparation even if they have been merely passive recipients of benefits; that is, even if they have not deliberately chosen to accept the benefits in question. This argument invites the objection that, for the most part, white people are simply not in a position to choose to receive or refuse benefits belonging to the descendants of slaves and are, therefore, not culpable or blameable and hence not liable to make reparation. But this objection misses the point. The argument under consideration simply does not depend on or imply the claim that white people are culpable or blameable; the argument is that merely by being white, an individual receives benefits to which others have at least partial rights. In such cases, whatever one's choice or moral culpability, reparation must be made. Consider an extreme case: Harry has an unexpected heart attack and is taken unconscious to the hospital. In the same hospital Dick has recently died. A heart surgeon transplants the heart from Dick's dead body to Harry without permission from Dick's family. If Harry recovers, he must make suitable reparation to Dick's family, conceding that he is not in rightful possession of Dick's heart even if he had no part in choosing to receive it.

The second of the arguments distinguished above concluded that for the purpose in question, the white community can be regarded as a corporation or company which, as a whole, owes reparation to the sons of slaves. Certainly the white community resembles a corporation or company which, as a whole, owes reparation to the sons of slaves. Certainly the white community resembles a corporation or company in some striking ways; like such companies, the white community has interests distinct from, and opposed to, other groups in the same society, and joint action is often taken by the members of the white community to protect and enhance their interests. Of course, there are differences; people are generally born into the white community and do not deliberately choose their membership in it; on the other hand, deliberate choice is often the standard procedure for gaining membership in a company. But this difference is unimportant; European immigrants often deliberately choose to become part of the white community in the United States for the obvious benefits this brings, and people often inherit shares and so, without deliberate choice, become members of a company. What is important here is not how deliberately one chooses to become part of a community or a company; what is relevant is that one chooses to continue to accept the benefits which circulate exclusively within the community, sees such benefits as belonging exclusively to the members of the community, identifies one's interests with those of the community, viewing them as opposed to those of others outside the community, and finally, takes joint action with other members of the community to protect such interests. In such a case, it seems not unfair to consider the present white population as members of a company that incurred debts before they were members of the company, and thus to ask them justly to bear the cost of such debts.

It may be objected that the case for reparation depends on the validity of inheritance; for, only if the sons of slaves inherit the rights of their ancestors can it be asserted that they have rights against the present white community. If the validity of inheritance is rejected, a somewhat different, but perhaps even stronger, argument for reparation can still be formulated. For if inheritance is rejected with the stipulation that the wealth of individuals be returned to the whole society at their deaths, then it is even clearer that the white community owes reparation to the black community. For the whole white community has appropriated, almost exclusively, the wealth from slavery in addition to the wealth from other sources; but such wealth belongs jointly to all members of the society, white as well as black; hence, it owes them reparation. The above formulation of the argument is entirely independent of the fact of slavery and extends the rights of the black community to its just portion of the total wealth of the society.

Hugo Adam Bedau

COMPENSATORY JUSTICE AND THE BLACK MANIFESTO

In May 1969, James Foreman interrupted a religious service at Riverside Church in New York to deliver "The Black Manifesto," which included a stunning "demand of $500 million in "reparations" for black Americans from the white religious establishment. In the period since that date, The Manifesto has aroused rather less serious discussion than one might have thought it would.[1] No doubt, the burden of The Manifesto has struck many whites and some blacks as so outrageous in its morality, so unrealistic in its politics, so unfeasible in its economics, that intellectuals may have done a public service by consigning The Manifesto to relative neglect.[2] Not that The Manifesto has had only unfavorable publicity, nor that the churches have ignored it; quite the contrary. What remains true, however, is that the crucial burden of The Manifesto, indeed, the precise *argument* it advances for reparations and compensatory justice, has not so far as I can tell received the thoughtful attention it deserves. Until it does, and is appraised with care and fairness, it is impossible either to support or to reject The Manifesto's "demands." Let us try, then, however belatedly, to state and assess the argument of The Black Manifesto.

The full text of The Manifesto runs to less than three thousand words; its "Introduction" adds another two thousand words. What is needed, however, is neither quotation, excerpt, or summary of these texts but a reconstruction of the argument they contain, since it is the merits of that argument which demand scrutiny and appraisal. The problem immediately evident to any reader of The Manifesto is that its argument is elliptical and obscure. The rhetoric of revolution, plain indignation, threats, predictions, and the sketch of how the reparations are to be used once they are in hand—all these confuse and fail to advance

This essay originally appeared in *The Monist* 56:1 (January 1972): 20–42.

the argument implicit in The Manifesto and upon which whatever merit it has rests. My first task, therefore, is to take it as it is written and to reconstruct the argument it must contain if its central explicit and manifest assertions and accusations are meant seriously. As a first approximation to a complete reconstruction I offer the following sixteen-premise version. Premises not tagged with a page citation (only a minority are not so tagged) are my interpolations of what I take to be among the tacit assumptions relied upon by the explicit assertions to be gleaned from the published text of The Manifesto. Expanded though the argument in my reconstructed version is, I have not tried to make it formally valid; no doubt that could be done, but it is not essential to my purposes here to try to do so. All the really interesting tacit premises I have tried to state.

The Argument of The Black Manifesto[3]

(1) Blacks in the United States of America since 1619 have been "exploited and degraded, brutalized, killed and persecuted" by whites (p. 120).

(2) This has been the objective effect of the commitment to "racism, capitalism and imperialism" practiced by the white power structure (pp. 116–117, 118, 124).

(3) The historic white Christian and Jewish religious establishment is "part and parcel" of the white power structure, "another form of government in this country" (p. 125); it has actively supported and continues to support this systematic objective exploitation of blacks (pp. 119, 126).

(4) Corporate black America is the heir of the historic victims—and includes in its heritage the harm and injury suffered by the parents, grandparents, etc., of living blacks.

(5) The existing white religious establishment is liable to living blacks for whatever harm has been inflicted by its historic organizational forebears upon blacks.

(6) The chief purpose of slavery and its racist aftermath was to develop "the industrial base" of America (pp. 119, 123).

(7) The wealth exacted by this exploitation has been astronomical—in the thousands of billions.

(8) Much of this profit is owned or controlled or has otherwise been diverted to the benefit of the white religious establishment—"the white Christian churches and synagogues." (p. 120).

(9) Little if any of that profit has been returned over the centuries for the benefit of those who were exploited to earn it.

(10) This profit constitutes an unjust enrichment in the hands of white America, including the white religious establishment.

(11) Such unjust enrichment constitutes a basis for justifiable compensation (restitution being impossible in the nature of the case), or "reparations" (pp. 119, 120, 122, 123, 126).

(12) The compensation owed should be paid to and on behalf of "all black people" by the white religious establishment (p. 126).

(13) Just reparations are a sum which will fund the development of those institutions, skills, and services for living blacks and their heirs of which their heritage has deprived them and in virtue of which they can not compete today as the socio-economic equals of whites (pp. 120–122).

(14) $500,000,000 (or "$15 per nigger") is part of such a sum (pp. 119, 120, 122); but "it is only a beginning of the reparations due" (pp. 120, 126).

(15) The white religious establishment can afford to pay such a sum; it has "tremendous wealth" (p. 120).

(16) The white religious establishment in the United States of America must pay $500,000,000 indemnity to corporate black America.

There are, at the onset, three kinds of objections to the argument of The Manifesto which I wish to state here so as to be relieved of any need to discuss them later. Some will object, first, that The Manifesto advances a claim ostensibly for reparations based on past wrongs, when in fact this only disguises the real argument for *redistribution* of currently available social resources given the present unfair disadvantages of blacks. In other words, some will say that the argument for compensatory justice in The Manifesto is really a disguised argument for distributive justice.[4] Others will object, second, that the real argument is not one for reparations nor is it a disguised argument for distributive justice. They will argue that it is really a disguised argument of an entirely different sort, namely, for special benefits to blacks given their special needs, on the ground that the *net social welfare* is maximized by this treatment. These critics of The Manifesto think that the entire appeal to justice (compensatory or distributive) is a deception, because the point to be made really relies upon the utility of redistributed wealth. Still others will object, third, that the argument of The Manifesto is disguised *extortion,* a veiled threat of violence unless half a billion dollars is transferred from white control to black. Those who view the argument in this third way see nothing moral in it at all.

All of these objections, one must concede, have some force. No doubt the third has the least plausibility, certainly in retrospect. Yet even this notion is not wholly absurd; after all, people do sometimes threaten to harm those whom they believe owe them compensation, especially if the plea for compensation falls on deaf ears. Nevertheless, I urge that we put aside this third possibility, and also the first two as well, because in a certain sense they are neither controversial nor interesting (except among politicians, perhaps, and racists). Hardly anyone (else) denies or contests the claim on behalf of living black Americans to a larger share of the total wealth and power in the nation. Hardly anyone (else) denies it would do them good to have a larger share in the nation's affluence and in its control, quite apart from the debatable question of the advisability of accomplishing these results by granting the demands contained in The Manifesto. Nor is it doubtful that present injustices in the distribution of social wealth provide a sufficient justification for transfers of wealth from white hands to black on a scale even greater than that contemplated by The Manifesto. Indeed, it may even be that the redistributive or the utilitarian version of the argument of The Black Manifesto is really the best way to construe it, given the political and economic realities of the 1970's.[5] After all, one need not shut his eyes to the possibility that the point of a manifest argument for reparations is in fact contained in a coordinated but concealed argument for distributive justice or social welfare.

Nevertheless, all these possibilities should be put clearly off to one side, because they are all alike in being *reinterpretations* of the argument evidently being advanced, and to that extent at least, they are evasions or repudiations of The Manifesto. It is as an argument for reparations, for compensatory justice, that The Manifesto makes its plain claim upon our understanding, and it simply cannot be taken seriously unless its force (and limitations) as *this sort* of argument are granted at the onset and without reservation.

Let us turn, then, to those objections which take the argument of The Manifesto at face value. Fundamentally, of course, any such counter-argument is going to proceed by alleging either that the argument-form itself is invalid or that some explicit or implicit factual or moral premise is false. We know in advance, thanks to elementary logic, that only if at least one of these faults obtains can the argument be rejected. At the risk of being excessively contentious I propose to canvass possible objections and then rebut them as well as I can, and I shall begin with the least plausible objections and move to the more perplexing and complex ones. My survey will not be thorough, for I shall not try to dissect the reconstructed argument premise by premise, but I think the full range of possible obstacles to accepting the argument will at least be sketched and, I hope, the gravest objections directly stated and answered.

Objection (1). The figure of "$15 per nigger," mentioned in premise (14), is an arbitrary and really senseless sum because it bears no relation to any assessment of the injury suffered or the benefits exploited by whites from blacks.

This objection is partly wrong-headed. It regards the figure of $15 as a charge per head, whereas that figure is merely an arithmetic artifact produced by dividing $500 million by the number, roughly, of living black Americans. Besides, The Manifesto does not attempt to show that $15 per head is the upper limit, or anywhere near it, of the liability owed. It claims only that the lower limit of the liability is not below this sum. Whether that is so depends on certain calculations, and I return to this topic below in connection with Objection (10).

Objection (2). The Manifesto ignores the fact that the white religious establishment mentioned in premises (5) and (8), of which white churches are alleged to be a part, is not "lily white" at all. For some decades, black Americans have been part of the congregations and, increasingly, of the clergy in all major national Protestant denominations and in the Catholic church, too. If so, then part of the current wealth and power of these churches has been contributed to them by some of the very group on whose behalf the claim of exploitation is made. This is doubly paradoxical: First, because from this fact of black membership in allegedly white churches, the victim turns out to be at one, as a member in a common institution, with his oppressor; and second, because the wealth of the oppressor has been given to him and not extorted or exploited by him from his victims.

The way to dissolve these paradoxes is by insisting that in fact the numbers of black persons in white churches is insignificant (perhaps one in a hundred, or in a thousand); and consequently, that the portion of white church wealth today which has been obtained from the voluntary contributions of black church members and clergy is equally negligible. The objection, then, is sound in implicitly raising the point (*pace* Hobbes) that a person or a class cannot "injure" himself, and *a fortiori* cannot hope to obtain redress for that injury from himself. It is wrong, however, in that the facts in this case do not permit application of this point.

It may also be part of this objection that it is inconceivable that the churches, as institutions, should owe reparations to blacks. This is a complex question, and I shall deal with part of it in my reply to Objection (4) and with more of it in my reply to Objection (10). Here, I would point out that The Manifesto asserts racist bias in the historic white churches of America, it implies racist exploitation among the lay and clerical members of white churches, and I think it also assumes corporate continuity of today's predominantly white churches with the historic "lily white" churches. If so, the anti-racism of the contemporary white church will fail to be a barrier against the demand for reparations to the extent that today's churches cannot legitimately deny continuity with their racist predecessors nor point to prior acts of reparation of their own or of their predecessors.

Objection (3). The idea (introduced in premise (4)) of corporate black America being indemnified is absurd and unworkable. Blacks are no more a corporate body in America than are W.A.S.P.s. And the Black Economic Development Conference, which first formulated and publicised The Manifesto, cannot claim to speak for blacks; it has no authority to act as their representative or trustee. So, even if the argument were sound, there would be no legitimate body to receive and disburse the indemnification. (One might argue the other way, and claim that insofar as blacks can be thought of corporately or as a class, they can be so only as Jews or W.A.S.P.s are, viz., as a consequence of self-identification and group acceptance. But these two conditions are too imprecise and unpredictable in their actual operation to be sufficient for the purpose of granting the assumption of The Manifesto).

The reply, I believe, is that it is not impossibly difficult to think of ways in which all and only living black Americans might be convened so as to create a truly representative body, or anyway a body with genuine ethnic legitimacy and authority, to receive and administer these reparations. It is not necessary that blacks undertake to effect physical, economic, or legal separation from their white fellow citizens in America in order to be, for the purposes of these reparations, identifiable as a nation within a nation. Likewise, B.E.D.C. or its successor could be established as a trustee, holding the monies received in indemnity until such a legitimate representative of corporate black America emerged. As for criteria of membership in black America, a suitable "grandfather clause" in disjunction with a nativity clause could be used to supplement self-identification and group acceptance, so as to exclude non-American blacks, e.g., Jamaican Negroes, and new black Americans, e.g., Ghanian immigrants—provided it was in fact thought necessary or desirable to limit eligibility in corporate black America in such ways.

Objection (4). The argument of The Manifesto, in being addressed to the churches, is arbitrary and unfair. The churches as corporate bodies are, if anything, less guilty of racist exploitation than other white institutions.

We may concede that The Manifesto does not make clear whether the churches are the only or simply the first white institution to be subjected to demands for reparations. In theory, The Manifesto might well be reformulated and addressed to tax-exempt foundations (typically created by the surplus profits of American commercial and industrial enterprise), institutions of higher learning (endowed from the same sources), and other non-profit organizations (such as hospitals, theatres, galleries, museums, libraries). The Manifesto explicitly does allude to demands for reparations from "private business and the United States government."[6] However, most of these other white institutions have already been asked to make quasi-restitutionary compensation, rather than monetary reparation. They have been asked to extend their services and open their jobs to blacks. It is an ironic commentary on the state of religious life in America that the chief contribution by way of compensation it is thought white churches can make to black Americans is—merely money. Whether other institutions which have more to offer could wholly discharge their debt to black America through compensatory jobs and services, however, is very doubtful, if the argument of The Manifesto is sound.

As for the complaint that among white institutions the churches are not the most guilty of racist practices, this is irrelevant in two respects. First, it remains true that the guilt of the churches would not vanish before the fact that other white institutions share or even exceed that guilt. But the truth is, the question of *guilt* is not properly at issue. Guilt carries with it the atmosphere of punitive sanctions, whereas reparations is not a punitive remedy at all. Instead, what is at issue here is corporate *liability;*[7] like guilt, liability admits of degrees and is such that the greater liability does not erase the lesser.

Second, the objection overlooks an important consideration. Churches, more than any other white institution, are specially vulnerable to a demand for reparations because such a demand can be understood perhaps best within the ancient pattern of sinfulness, contrition and penance which is inseparable from the entire historical theology of the Judeo-Christian religion. This religion, in every version and throughout history, teaches that it costs a sinner something to put himself into a right relationship with his God and his fellow-man. Surely, it is this consideration which makes the professedly religious bodies of America the very best place to begin a campaign for reparations.[8] For what other institution is equally susceptible to the demand to confess and make amends? If anything, the difficulty raised by Objection (4) lies in quite the reverse direction. If the importance of the pattern of sinfulness, confession and penance—true repentance—is stressed as central to the setting in which this demand for reparations is made, then it will entail that the argument of The Manifesto has little or no application to any other white institution! Certainly, no secular corporation, whether it makes a profit or not, will be or will think of itself as susceptible to a demand for reparations cast in this form. Nor is this an idle and inconsequential consideration. If white America owes reparations to black America, then the vast non-church-going bulk of the white population today in this country will evade paying its share of the corporate indemnity, simply by virtue of confining the argument of The Black Manifesto exclusively to white churches. Obviously, this was not the intent of The Manifesto's authors and supporters.

There remains, then, a certain tension in the fact that it is the churches to whom The Manifesto is officially and initially addressed. If the aptness of addressing the churches is stressed, then no other institutions will be subject to reparations, at least, by the terms of this argument. This is a considerable price to have to pay in order to avoid the charge of unfair and arbitrary selection of the churches as the sole target of The Manifesto, when one considers the relatively small percentage of the nation's total wealth in church control.

Since, however, the argument of The Manifesto relies upon the idea of corporate black America, and since according to the argument every white American is in some way and to some degree accountable for historic harms visited upon blacks, why doesn't The Manifesto ignore all white institutions, such as the churches, and address itself directly to corporate white America? If corporate black America can be viewed as the injured party and the party deserving reparations, why not serve the demand for reparations against corporate white America?

The answer, I think, is twofold. Corporate white America is too unrepresented, too disorganized, too diffuse to be effectively approached by anybody for anything, much less by black spokesmen for something as disturbing as reparations. The churches, by contrast, are well organized and like other voluntary organizations are accessible to black leaders; they meet weekly to transact their spiritual business behind open doors. The Black Manifesto is obviously already symbolic enough without being reduced to pure gesture, as it would be if it were addressed to corporate white America as such. Thus, while from a logical point of view, the ideas of corporate black and corporate white America are on precisely equal footing, from a practical point of view as regards the motive for organizing under such a rubric, they could not be farther apart. Moreover, since the churches might be said to be the functional conscience of the nation, addressing The Manifesto to them might be viewed legalistically as placing the churches in subrogation for corporate white America: the white churches are made to answer for the liability of all white Americans. (Once again, however, if we accept this latter interpretation, only the churches can ever be made liable for reparations.)

Objection (5). The argument, if not strictly inconsistent, at least poses a dilemma for its advocates. It begins with a radical Marxist critique in its complaint of "exploitation," in premises (1)–(3), and (6)–(7). But before it ends, in premises (10)–(12), it shifts into a conventional Liberal demand for "justifiable compensation." Now, the argument cannot be both Marxist and Liberal. If it is the former then it should demand expropriation of the exploiters, a revolutionary redistribution of the product of the worker's labor to all the people, public ownership of the means of production and distribution, etc.[9] For this version of the argument to be sound, it is essential to establish that current wealth in white institutions is the causal product of historic capitalist exploitation. But if the argument is merely Liberal and reformist, as it seems in the end to be, then the initial complaint of exploitation (like the alleged surplus profits) is irrelevant. It is sufficient on this version of the argument to establish only that blacks still suffer from uncompensated wrongs while others (whites) still enjoy the undeserved benefits of those historic wrongs.

The reply to this alleged dilemma is two-fold. There is nothing wrong, in Marxist theory, with arguing for half a loaf rather than all. In a pre- or non-revolutionary situation, there is no reason why a sincere and consistent Marxist should not appeal to reparations, redistribution, or to any other familiar Liberal principle of social justice provided it will succeed in persuading a nominally Liberal (and unquestionably anti-Marxist) society to shift the current allocation of its resources away from protecting the propertied class to assisting the workers. In any case, Liberals have ample reason to press the purely Liberal version of the argument to its conclusion, quite apart from the evident Marxist overtones in the argument as it stands. For others, who are sympathetic to if not imbued with Marxist theory, one might insist that the notion of exploitation used in The Manifesto's argument is truly equivocal. The labor of generations of blacks has created surplus profits of slight or no benefit to them, and this labor was originally stolen and thenceforth made captive under conditions of structured injustice which a Hume, a Mill, or a Rawls would be able to recognize as such. The slave and Jim Crow heritage, therefore, constitutes both a moral and an economic exploitation. Blacks in America have been doubly exploited, so their argument for compensation is entitled to take this into account and it does. To put it another way, we might view The Black Manifesto as attempting to invoke not merely one or another version of conventional Liberal principles of justice, nor of Marxist justice—if there is such a thing[10]—but what might be called *socialist justice* (the full outline of which, I would concede, is nowhere as yet stated).

Objection (6). The Manifesto's argument rests on racist (i.e., immoral racial) assumptions. It concedes that the claimant is not the party directly injured, and that the party liable to pay up is not the party who directly inflicted the injury. Yet it argues that it is just to make the heirs of the former pay the heirs of the latter because the one continues to profit from the injury as the latter continues to suffer from it. But to do this the argument must imply that blacks as a class or a race have been injured; how can this be true unless every black has been injured? Likewise, if whites as a class have inflicted the injury, is not every white responsible? But these implications are very probably false and certainly not proved. True, The Manifesto's argument does not impute fault to every white distributively, any more than it imputes benefits to every white distributively from the slavery of blacks and its aftermath. But it does allege that whites as such have benefitted and blacks as such have suffered at their hands. This pattern of reasoning does, therefore, rely upon the idea of liability or responsibility (if not guilt) by mere racial association, as well as the suffering of injury by mere racial association. Any argument relying upon such concepts is morally unsound. Moreover, the nature of the argument is such that no evidence of good faith, either individually or collectively, by whites or white institutions towards blacks prior to the levy of the demand for reparations in The Manifesto would seem to exempt such whites from its thrust.

The basis of the rebuttal must lie in the incontestable fact that blacks in America have been regarded as a class historically by slave and post-slavery segregation legislation and coordinate social practices. However difficult it may be, according to anthropologists, to develop an adequate empirical basis for a sound theory of races, this difficulty has not stood in the way of a practical development of the concept of a *black* as distinct from a *white* race in this country. Consequently, it is possible that various other practical relations, including injury, liability, benefit, and redress should obtain between the parties so defined, despite spatial, temporal, and hereditary dispersals among the members of the two classes (races). There is, in short, no purely logical or conceptual reason why there should not be liability and the rest by virtue of merely racial association or membership in a racially defined class. Whether there is any factual basis for such a doctrine is a separate question.

As for guilt by association, where criminal guilt before a court of law is the question, it is perfectly fitting that such guilt should be attacked and repudiated. Criminal guilt and individual fault, however, are not in question here. Therefore, any criticism of The Manifesto based on complaint against the immorality of guilt by association is simply beside the point. The appeal to corporate or institutional liability is legitimate just in case the facts show participation in and profit from racial slavery and segregation by the institution in question. The record is far from complete, but in so far as the liability of the white churches of America is in question, it would appear—even without the exhaustive researches scholars have yet to provide—that it ill-behooves contemporary defenders of the major American religious denominations to repudiate the moral legitimacy of the notion that their churches as institutions are liable for claims of reparations based on the fact that they are beneficiaries and preservers of racist practices against blacks.[11]

Objection (7). The argument of The Manifesto relies upon tacit analogy either with reparations exchanged between sovereign nations (as in German war reparations under the Versailles Treaty) or with indemnities granted by a sovereign nation to one of its dependent or custodial peoples (as in our government's indemnities to certain American Indian tribes). Neither analogy is plausible. In the latter class of cases, there is always some specific treaty violation which serves as the basis of the claim for reparations; but no such treaty exists between black and white America. In the former class of cases, we have a very dangerous analogy because only the defeated ever pay war reparations and they look upon them not as just compensation owed to the victims of their unjust aggressive war, but rather as the tribute exacted from the loser under the time-honored doctrine that to the victor belongs the spoils.

First, while it is of course true that no legal treaty binds black and white Americans together, the federal Constitution and the host of federal "Civil Rights" legislation and decisional law do testify to a kind of implicit social contract among racial equals. Black Americans are entitled to argue that individually they are parties to this implicit contract but that as a class they have yet to receive their full and fair share under its terms. Second, the parallel with war reparations only points to the truth that it is unreasonable to demand reparations from a party who has made no concession of liability, and today it is doubtful whether white America has conceded its liability for wrongs visited upon black America. Yet one can make too much of this. It is true that it is unreasonable, in the face of white intransigence and the absence of overwhelming black power, to *demand* reparations, just as it is futile to threaten to *take* property or services valued in the amount of the reparations demanded unless they are paid promptly and in full. Some may have found such intentions in The Manifesto, because near its end we read: ". . . we are not opposed to force and we are not opposed to violence."[12] However, it is not necessary to construe this remark as a genuine threat. For those without any access to an appropriate court room, part of an effective strategy to get someone who is liable for reparations to accept that liability is to press upon him a well-reasoned argument imputing liability and demanding compensation. This is what (with perhaps less than perfect success) The Black Manifesto attempts to do.[13]

A better rebuttal to the complaint based on the weakness of the analogy proceeds by denying that the argument relies on any such analogy at all. The argument of The Manifesto, as I have reconstructed it, relies not on analogy with treaty violations or war reparations, but upon the common legal notion of *unjust enrichment* (see premises (6)–(12)). Arnold Kaufman has correctly emphasized this idea, though without using the term, when he asserted:

> The sons of privilege are being asked to compensate the sons of slaves whether or not the former are responsible for the disabilities of the latter. . . . The sons of slave masters continue to profit, the sons of slaves to suffer the disabilities of the original iniquity. Under these conditions the sons of slaves have rights of compensation against the sons of slave masters.[14]

In this, there is no argument by analogy at all. Instead, there is a straightforward appeal to the fundamental principles of compensatory justice on the assumption that the facts of the situation of black Americans today vis-a-vis white Americans (or, at least, the white churches of America) satisfy those principles.[15] Moreover, there is reason to see some disanalogy between compensation for black Americans and the German war reparations, because the latter case does not rely upon the notion of unjust enrichment. It relies upon the idea of criminal harm, or at least tortious injury: the deliberate waging of aggressive and unprovoked warfare with peaceful neighbors. But an analogous complaint against the churches is at most obliquely asserted in The Manifesto.

Objection (8). The argument of The Manifesto is sufficiently legalistic that it invites criticism on at least two legalistic grounds. (a) the defense of belatedness of claim, and (b) the defense of unsought benefits. (a) Claims of compensatory desert based on harms that occurred decades, generations, even centuries ago are not payable because civilized society cannot be expected to entertain such claims on grounds of justice over an indefinitely long period. The parties who were originally liable are not now around to pay up, and it is unfair to expect their unknowing and innocent heirs to pay in their stead. Blacks as a class have no right today to ask the white churches or any other white institutions for reparations for ancient wrongs. (b) "A person is not ordinarily required to pay for benefits which were thrust upon him with no opportunity to refuse them. The fact that he is enriched is not enough, if he cannot avoid the enrichment."[16] But if The Manifesto's assumptions about racism in America are correct, this is precisely the predicament of most whites, including white institutions, in this society. The wealth which the churches have is obtained entirely through their member's voluntary contributions and the subsequent profitable investment of the unspent portions. This wealth derives from persons all of whom possess the unsought advantages of color and race, advantages of which they cannot divest themselves. There is a certain tragedy and pathos in this for blacks, but no occasion for reparations from whites.

The objection in (b) is easily met. The defense of unsought benefits in law is clearly designed to protect the recipient of a gift forced upon him from having to make restitution to the donor upon demand at a later date. The donor is entitled to restitution only when he affords the donee an opportunity to decline the benefit or else has a reasonable excuse for failure to do so.[17] But the special advantages accruing to whites in virtue of their race and color are not benefits given to or conferred upon whites by blacks. Historically, they have been exacted from blacks by whites only by the utmost use of terror and violence. So, while it may be true that many whites have enjoyed unsought advantages deriving from their race and color, it is false that these advantages were somehow inherent in race and color themselves, just as it is false that these advantages were thrust upon whites by blacks choosing to disadvantage themselves.

The objection in (a) is based on what might be called a moral statute of limitation or a moral analogy to the legal bar of laches. Equity, we are told in an old maxim, aids only the vigilant; and a victim of another's injustice who is negligent in the assertion of his right to compensation may discover that his negligence bars him from remedy. The passage of time may result in unfair hardship for the defendant, or for third parties, or increase the likelihood of substantial change or error regarding the relevant facts.[18] It is for these reasons that statutes of limitation and the equitable defense of laches are available to protect defendants. No doubt they have comparable force in the forum of conscience as well. Whether they should work to defeat the claim for reparations advanced in The Black Manifesto is doubtful. One might argue persuasively that it is only in recent years that black spokesmen have been in a position to advance and press a claim for reparations, and thus that their failure to do so in earlier decades is not evidence of black negligence so much as it is a measure of the severity of black disabilities. In addition, the churches cannot plead that they are unable to pay the compensation demanded or that it would bankrupt them to do so. But only this kind of severe hardship enables a defendant to successfully invoke laches. Whether, however, the enormous passage of time—more than three centuries, over which the injury to blacks was inflicted and the unjust enrichment by whites was reaped—is so great as to make incalculable the injury and the benefit, and for this reason something like laches should enter, this is a difficulty to which I will turn in Objection (10).

Objection (9). Although The Manifesto claims that "black people are the most oppressed group of people inside the United States,"[19] its authors do not and could not claim that blacks alone have been exploited by others to create profits in which they have not shared, because the same is true of most white and other nonwhite immigrants throughout the history of the nation. This creates the possibility of destroying the argument of The Manifesto by reducing it to absurdity through constructing parallel arguments for compensatory reparations on behalf of other exploited and disadvantaged groups. The aboriginal American Indians are survived by tribes whose title to such reparations is every bit as good as that of erstwhile African blacks; the same is true of Mexican Americans in the Southwest and of Puerto Ricans on the eastern seaboard. But then the same is also true of the East Boston Irish, the North End Italians, the West End Jews, etc., etc. Every minority has been exploited by the established society of its day, so the heirs of every exploited minority have a right to file a claim comparable to that levied in The Manifesto. Now, since each such argument is valid only if all are valid, none is valid—because it is absurd for all to be valid. It is simply preposterous to imagine seriously working out the details of the cross-claims for class-indemnities which would be established by this multitude of valid claims for reparations.

Again, there are two replies to this objection, one of which concedes the assumption in question and the other of which denies it. It is true that the spectacle of a whole series of claims and cross-claims for compensation by each American ethnic group against all others boggles the mind. But this is not a theoretical objection to entertaining such a complex set of intertwined claims. Lawyers are paid every day to work on cases nearly as complex. Practically, of course, it would be extremely difficult to work out a suitable scale of historic injury and to parcel out the relative degrees of liability among the various groups in question. One might hypothesize, on behalf of The Manifesto's authors, that if such cross-claims in indemnity were worked out, we would discover that they would cancel out so far as all the claims among white ethnic groups are concerned, leaving only the massive claim of blacks against whites, one portion of which is the explicit preoccupation of The Manifesto.

However, I think it is more likely to suppose that the authors of The Manifesto did not anticipate this kind of objection, because it seems in fact to be frivolous. It may be that The Manifesto's claim of compensation rests upon the assumption that blacks are historically only the nation's most exploited and least rewarded ethnic group, and that for this reason only their claim for compensation goes to the head of the list. Certainly, nothing in The Manifesto as such implies that no other ethnic group in America also deserves reparations from whites. But the economic, psychological, and other societal facts have convinced most observers that the unique history of forced immigration (in contrast to free immigration) and chattel slavery (in contrast to indentured servitude and "wage slavery") has left a heritage of defeat among blacks incomparably more devastating than that suffered by any other initially disadvantaged immigrant minority group. Likewise, the evidence that blacks as a class, like Irish, Italian, Jewish, and other non-W.A.S.P. immigrants, can take the upwardly mobile route to its own economic prosperity and social diffusion throughout society at all levels without special compensatory efforts is doubtful at best.

There is, nevertheless, one other rival claimant to the unique status advanced by The Manifesto on behalf of blacks: the Indians. Only the American Indian as an ethnic minority has suffered what might be called (after British criminal law) 'constructive genocide', a fate even more brutal in its effects than forced immigration and chattel slavery. The legitimacy of the Indians' claim, on Liberal if not on Marxist assumptions, is if anything more valid and incontestable than the claim of blacks.[20] Without the mineral resources and real estate bargained, wrested and stolen from the Indians, white culture in this nation would lack the material base for the past century's agricultural and industrial growth and the ensuing wealth in its possession. One reply to this objection, therefore, is that,the Indians are entitled to make a claim against whites in terms no less stark than those used in The Manifesto. What we need alongside The Black Manifesto is a Red Manifesto; but this concession is not sufficient to establish a *reductio ad absurdum* at all.

Finally, we should not overlook a purely logical point. The argument of The Manifesto cannot be shown to be unsound merely by the possibility that if the form of argument it employs were valid, then infinitely many other versions of the same argument would also be valid. For this is uninteresting unless it is likely that because The Manifesto's argument is sound, so are all or many of these other compensatory arguments. However, that cannot happen so long as at least one premise is false in every other version of the argument. In my criticism above, I have relied on precisely this outcome, with the one notable exception already discussed.

Objection(10). In order to make out a claim for compensatory justice, one needs to know the value of the loss suffered, the benefit derived therefrom by another, the causal connection between the injured and injuring parties, and the acts committed by the latter upon the former for which reparations are sought. But in this case, we cannot (and The Manifesto does not) identify with sufficient precision the specific harm suffered by blacks as a class nor the specific benefits secured by and on behalf of the white churches, nor the causal relation between the two. The argument for recompense depends on some assessment of how blacks would be today as a class if they had not been exploited historically. Otherwise, their loss cannot be calculated; but there is no way to establish the value of this loss, nor the wealth unjustly in white hands. The result is that the demand of any given amount in reparations is hopelessly unmoored from the necessary factual base. It is hardly surprising that the militant authors of The Manifesto themselves are unable to settle upon a proper sum for reparations. Although they initially announced the sum as $500 million, within two months they had raised it by a factor of six.[21]

Many will think this is the most fundamental and unanswerable objection of them all, so it deserves careful consideration. To take the last point first, the fact that the authors of The Manifesto upped their claimed indemnity is perhaps owing as much to the rapid change in their knowledge of the assets controlled by white churches as it is either to greed or to the sobering costs of the programs to be financed with the reparation money. Quite apart from any other considerations, if reparations are owed blacks as a class by the white churches, it does not seem unreasonable that they should amount to a sum equivalent to (what has been reasonably estimated as) 3% of the total real estate holdings of the churches,[22] or perhaps one year's worth of Sunday morning church offerings.

The Manifesto is not clear as to the precise mechanisms of white enrichment at the expense of black slavery and discrimination, and a certain sympathetic inventiveness on behalf of the authors of The Manifesto is required if we hope to do justice to their argument. I suggest that we view the wealth of the churches as created by white membership and administered by white clergy on behalf of implicitly racist (or with indifference to anti-racist) policies, in which the actual creation and perpetuation of slavery itself played an important but not decisive part. Thus, whether black chattel slavery was or was not itself a profitable institution on these shores (a matter much debated by historians)[23] is not crucial to The Manifesto's complaint at all. We are to think of the wealth in the churches today as created bit by bit over the generations, and as representing in part the surplus profits available only to whites because of the racist character of the larger society. Presumably, if blacks had been paid their fair share (i.e., at the same rates as whites doing equivalent jobs) during these centuries for the services they rendered to white employers, there would have been proportionately less wealth now in the control of the white churches, and the position of blacks today would be more nearly that of whites as well.

Blacks, we know, arrived on these shores virtually penniless and with few exceptions remained that way generation after generation, thanks to the repressive forces harnessed in slavery. Economic research, theoretically at least, should be able to give us estimates at, say, fifty-year intervals throughout our entire history and at decennial intervals during the past century of the total wealth in the control of corporate black America and corporate white America, respectively. If we were to plot these data on a graph, so as to get a representation of the economic growth rate of blacks vs. whites in America since the earliest days, we know without any question both that (a) the rate of slope for black growth would be much shallower than for whites, and that (b) the growth curve for blacks would start at the point of origin on the graph and remain nearly there for decades, whereas the comparable curve for whites would begin above zero and without faltering would continue to rise. What we don't know and could not calculate is the shape the curve for blacks would have taken had they been free men from the start and had they suffered discriminations in degree and in kind no worse than the average of those discriminations imposed by the dominant white groups upon the immigrant white groups. We might get some idea of what that curve would look like by plotting, if we could, on our graph the economic growth rate for every other identifiable ethnic group which has landed on these shores. One can assert with fair confidence that (a) and (b) above will be true no matter what white ethnic group's growth rate curve is compared with the blacks!

Given, then, that The Manifesto's argument is entitled to rely upon proof of continuous severe racial discrimination by whites against blacks in this country, proof of continuous severe economic disadvantages for blacks as against whites, proof that the latter is in considerable part explained by the former, the only fundamental question which remains is whether $500 million (or $3 billion, or any given amount) can be said to be an adequate measure of the reparations owed, given the cost to blacks of their losses and the unjust wealth accrued by whites and transferred to their churches? The only honest thing one can say is that we do not know whether it is or whether it isn't.[24] Between ludicrous extremes (such as asking for $10,000 in reparation, or asking for black control of the total wealth and income of all the churches) there are many equally plausible sums to fix upon, because our economic knowledge about the matters discussed in this and the preceding paragraph is too vague for more precision. Both $500 million and $3 billion seem to me to be within that plausible range and not at all ludicrous. Beyond that I cannot venture. One sympathizes with the predicament of white church leaders and the black authors of The Manifesto, for none of them has knowledge on these economic questions adequate to being more confident and more precise than I have been.

Yet further difficulties beyond the ten objections I have discussed can be imagined. It might be argued that if whites as a class are liable to blacks as a class for reparations, then not even if all voluntary non-governmental white institutions make reparations will all whites have paid their fair share; only the government, through the use of its tax monies, can truly compensate blacks for centuries of slavery, injury, and degradation. Or, as another objection, one might urge that the entire argument of The Manifesto, resting as it does, upon the concept of desert, is anachronistic, because desert is a concept of declining relevance in the adjustment of social relations where inequalities suffered on the scale of those which burden American blacks are concerned.[25] Or one could argue that The Manifesto constitutes an example of what has elsewhere been called "inflated desert" claims; that is, The Manifesto commits the fallacy of inferring from the true conclusion that blacks as a class *deserve* reparations to the unproved further conclusion that blacks as a class *ought* to be paid $3 billion in reparations.[26] Or, to mention a fourth possibility, one might object that

> . . . the Negro's past suffering seems beyond the remedy of society to redeem. There is no payment that can supply its balance. It would be a sign of contempt for the

> Negro should the white community offer to compensate this debt, for there are trials of the spirit too large and awesome to stand comparison with any good that might be proposed as their measure. . . . The strictly compensatory act of payment for *past* suffering is impossible. . . .[27]

There is no end to the objections that might be raised.

Perhaps, however, it is enough to have come as far as we have. I hope I have shown what the basic structure of the argument of The Black Manifesto is, and that although it can be subjected to various criticisms, these in turn, with varying degrees of finality, can be rebutted. Little I could add now would make the argument significantly more persuasive for those to whom it is addressed. Nor do I wish to stand in impartial judgment on the demands of The Manifesto and deliver any final verdict. Once in a while, at least, it ought to be enough for philosophers to try to understand and not at the same time judge, much less to change, the world.[28]

CHAPTER 12

J. Angelo Corlett

WRONGDOING, REPARATIONS AND NATIVE AMERICANS

North American history is replete with accounts of atrocities being inflicted by members of one group on members of another. Some such examples include: the seizure by the French, the British, the Spanish, the Dutch (and later by the United States and Canadian governments, respectively) of millions of acres of land inhabited by Native (North) Americans; the genocide (or attempt therein) of various Native Americans[1] by the U.S. military at the order of, among others, former U.S. President Andrew Jackson; the enslavement of several Native Americans in the United States, etc.[2] These and other significant harms have found little justice in the form of reparations. This chapter seeks to clarify the nature of reparations and analyzes philosophically objections to policies of reparations to historically and seriously wronged groups with the primary focus being on the Native American experiences in the United States.[3]

It is an embarrassing fact that major Western political philosophies by and large ignore (or, at best, give short shrift to) the claims of Native Americans[4] to property.[5] And given the importance of the concept of private property rights in historic and contemporary Western political philosophy,[6] it is vital to delve into problems which, among other things, question who ought to be seen as having the overriding moral claim or right to, say, the lands on which entire countries and their respective citizens reside, such as with the United States. The moral legitimacy of a country, it is assumed, is contingent on at least the extent to which that country acquires *justly* the land on which it and its citizens reside. The problem of reparations to Native Americans raises queries concerning the fundamental moral legitimacy of the United States. For it challenges the moral basis of putative U.S.

This essay originally appeared in *War Crimes and Collective Wrongdoing: A Reader*, Aleksander Jokic, ed. (Blackwell, 2001) as "Reparations to Native Americans?". Reprinted by permission of Blackwell Publishing Ltd.

rights to lands which, it is assumed, are necessary for its economic and political survival.

Reparations, according to *Black's Law Dictionary,* involve "payment for an injury; redress for a wrong done." They are payments "made by one country to another for damages done during war." Reparations involve restitution, which is the "act of restoring . . . anything to its rightful owner; the act of making good or giving equivalent for any loss, damage or injury;[7] and indemnification. . . . A person who has been unjustly enriched at the expense of another is required to make restitution to the other."[8] Those receiving reparations are typically groups, though there seems to be no moral or logical preclusion to individuals receiving them. Often the evils perpetrated are such that there is no "just" or genuinely sufficient manner by which to rectify matters between the wrongdoer (or her descendants) and the party wronged (or her descendants). *Reparative compensation* is the main form of reparations. It seeks to rectify severe wrongs of the distant past by providing the wronged parties or their descendants a sum of money (often collected by general tax revenues),[9] property, etc. which might be (roughly) proportional to the harms experienced by them. Moreover, reparative compensation must always conform to the Principle of Proportional Compensation: *Compensation and/or punishment for significant wrongdoing is always to be meted out in (albeit rough) proportion to the wrongdoing(s) committed.*

Although reparations are for the most part a compensatory matter, they share much in common with some of the "expressive functions" of punishment articulated by Joel Feinberg.[10] Reparations share with punishment these expressive features. Like punishment, reparations disavow the wrong(s) committed, and charges that the wrongdoers had no right to perform such evil(s). Reparations, like punishment, say publicly that wrongdoings do not represent society's highest aims and aspirations. In democratic regimes, reparations speak in the name of the people against the wrongdoings in question, and they uphold the genuine standards of law in the face of past failures of the legal system to carry out true justice. In addition, reparations alienate a reasonably just society from its corrupt past, absolving society of its historic evils. These are some of the specific expressive functions of reparations.[11] Some of these expressive functions of reparations are articulated by Feinberg when he states that "Reparation can express sympathy, benevolence, and concern, but, in addition, it is always the acknowledgment of a past wrong, a 'repayment of a debt,' and hence, like an apology, the redressing of the moral balance or the restoring of the *status quo ante culpum*."[12] More generally, the expressive feature of reparations is to make public society's *own* liability concerning the wrongs *it* has wrought upon a group or individuals. It is to offer an unqualified and unambiguous *apology* to the wronged parties (or their successors) without presumption of forgiveness or mercy. Moreover, it is to acknowledge, in a public way, the moral wrongness of the act(s) in question, and to never forget the act(s). For as George Santayana encourages, those who do not remember the errors of the past are doomed to repeat them. The expressive feature of reparations is articulated by Jeremy Waldron when he writes: "Quite apart from any attempt genuinely to compensate victims or offset their losses, reparations may symbolize a society's understanding not to forget or deny that a particular injustice took place, and to respect and help sustain a dignified sense of identity-in-memory for the people affected."[13] Insofar as reparations have their expressive functions, they send messages to citizens (and to others, for that matter) which seek to build and strengthen social solidarity toward justice and fairness. In this way, the justification of reparations is forward-looking.

Moreover, there are at least two sorts of arguments that might be given for reparations: end-state arguments and historical ones. A. John Simmons clarifies the difference between these kinds of reparations arguments:

> Historical arguments maintain that whether or not a holding or set of holdings is just (that is, whether or not we are entitled to or have a moral right to our holdings) depends on the moral character of the history that produced the holdings. We must see how holdings actually came about in order to know who has a right to what. End-state arguments maintain that the justice of holdings (and our rights to them) depends not on how they came about, but rather on the moral character of the structure (or pattern) of the set of holdings of which they are a part.[14]

I provide the foundations of an historical argument for reparations to Native Americans, as well as an assessment of several objections to such an argument.

Briefly, reparations can be supported on the ground that they truly respect the actions (inactions, or even attempted action, as the case may be) of history in the sense that they try to correct significant imbalances of power or fortune which result from undue force or intrusion, fraud, or other gross forms of wrongdoing. Moreover, reparations disrespect as being morally arbitrary any statute of limitations pertaining to the kinds of cases in question.[15] This is especially true where the extent of the facts of guilt, fault, harm and identity of the perpetrators and victims are unambiguous. Whether it is a crime occurring 40 or 400 years ago, justice requires that significant wrongdoings are compensated in manners that would do justice to the idea of proportional compensation for damages in cases where the perpetrator(s), victim(s) and damages are provable by current legal standards (beyond reasonable doubt, for example, in criminal cases, and by the preponderance of evidence in tort cases). With reparations, then, both the balance of human reason and history must be our twin and primary guides to the truth of whom owes what to whom, and why. For purposes of this chapter, it is assumed that the law ought to follow these guides. The argument for reparations to Native Americans insists that reparations ought to be made when a right has been infringed by way of significant injustice[16] (In assessing the plausibility of precisely this sort of argument, David Lyons points out that it relies on the ideas of original acquisition and legitimate transfer of land).[17] Thus the justification for reparations is essentially backward-looking, though it might involve aspects of considerations that are forward-looking.

The foregoing suggests the following Reparations Argument: (1) As much as is humanly possible, instances of clear and substantial historic rights violations ought to be rectified by way of reparations; (2) The U.S. government has clearly committed substantial historic rights violations against millions of Native Americans;[18] therefore, the historic rights violations of the U.S. government against Native Americans ought to be rectified by way of reparations, as much as humanly possible. The basis for (1) might be a desert-based (retributivist) one which insists that there is either a perfect duty or an imperfect duty to rectify past injustices of a substantial nature. Or, to the extent that it is humanly possible to rectify substantial wrongs for which a wrongdoer is responsible, the wrongdoer ought to rectify the wrongdoing.

Objections to the Reparations Argument, and Replies

If the Reparations Argument is plausible, then wherever there is significant injustice there is at least a *prima facie* reason to believe that such injustice deserves compensation or rectification. Moreover, where the facts of the guilt, fault, harm and identity of the perpetrators and victims are clear, reparations ought to be pursued for the sake of corrective justice.[19] Hence, there is a presumptive case in favor of reparations to Native Americans by the U.S. government, given the substantial wrongs many Native Americans have experienced at the hands of the United States.

Precisely what is/was the harm perpetrated against Native Americans? At the very least, it is the following. To the extent that Will Kymlicka is correct when he argues that cultural membership is crucial for self-respect,[20] and to the extent that a Rawlsian liberalism is correct in arguing that cultural membership is a primary good,[21] the *particular* cultural membership which is crucial to *their* self-respect is/was undermined for Native Americans by force and fraud. The campaigns against various Native American nations by the United States military serve as examples here. One specific instance of United States crimes against the Lakota Sioux was the massacre at Wounded Knee, which in turn culminated in the retaliatory violence against the United States military at Little Big Horn. Examples of United States torts against Native Americans are the fraudulent takings of lands, often followed by the U.S. government's refusal to honor its treaties made with various Native American nations. Yet for all of the several instances of unjustified violence and other crimes, torts and contract violations committed by the United States against various Native Americans, few, if any, apologies or reparations have been issued by the U. S. government. These are some reasons that form the presumptive case for reparations to Native Americans.[22] But such a presumption can be overridden if it can be shown that considerations against such reparations outweigh the strength of the *prima facie* case for them where the instances in question are not "hard cases."[23] Hence it is important to consider the plausibility of various of the strongest objections to reparations to Native Americans: the Objection From Historical Complexity, the Objection to Collective Responsibility, the Objection From Social Utility, the Acquired Rights Trumping Original Land Rights

Objection, the Supersession of Historic Injustice Objection, and the Counterfactual Objection. To the extent that such objections are defeasible, the presumptive case for such reparations gains strength, and the Reparations Argument gains plausibility.

The Objection from Historical Complexity

Given the above understanding of the nature of reparations, are reparations to Native Americans by the U.S. government morally required? Ought the U.S. government to provide reparations to Native Americans? A number of arguments can be marshaled against the imposition of reparations, and they deserve close scrutiny. First, there is the *Objection From Historical Complexity*. This objection says that history contains far too many and complex situations of conflict such that it would be impossible to figure out all of the injustices that would putatively require reparations. Where the perpetrators of the evils are dead and cannot be punished for their horrors, it would be sheer dogmatic idealism to think that respecting rights requires or even permits the kind of complex legal casework that would rectify all past wrongs. To award reparations to the wronged party or her descendants would end up forcing innocent parties (perhaps the descendants of the wrongdoer(s)) to pay for what they themselves did not do.[24] Among other things, the Objection From Historical Complexity seems to assume that past injustices should not forever burden future putatively "innocent" generations.[25] The Objection From Historical Complexity challenges (1) of the Reparations Argument, suggesting that there are some instances of historic injustice that ought *not* to be rectified by way of reparations.

The Principle of Morally Just Acquisitions and Transfers. In response to this argument, it might be pointed out that the inability to figure out with precise accuracy *all there is to know* about a case which putatively involves reparations hardly prohibits a juridical system from awarding some measure of significant reparations where cases are clear (based on unambiguous historical records, for example). Even if it were true that a full-blown policy of reparations would involve reparations to Native Americans by not only the U.S. government, but by the governments of Spain, Portugal, England, France, the Netherlands, etc., and even if it proved overly difficult to figure out the extent to which each such government contributed to harms against Native Americans, this would hardly show that clear cases of U.S. harm to Native Americans ought not to be compensated by the United States. Moreover, though the parties to a putative case of reparations would involve those who themselves did no harm to the victims in question, such "innocent" parties who currently reside on or "own" lands that were once resided on by Native Americans are in violation of the *Principle of Morally Just Acquisitions and Transfers: Whatever is acquired or transferred by morally just means is itself morally just; whatever is acquired or transferred by morally unjust means is itself morally unjust.*[26]

Basically, the intended meaning of this principle is that to the extent that property is acquired or transferred in a morally justified way (i.e., without force, fraud, etc.), the acquisition or transfer of that property carries with it a genuine moral claim or entitlement to occupy it without interference from others. To the extent that the Principle of Morally Just Acquisitions and Transfers is violated, there is no legitimate claim or entitlement to occupy the property being acquired or transferred. Thus the principle need not specify ownership rights to property. In this way, then, it is neutral concerning the matter of property rights of ownership between liberals and Marxists. This point of clarification precludes a Marxist-style objection that reparations to Native Americans are not morally justified in that they are contingent on Native Americans having original land rights, which themselves are dubious on moral grounds. For the Principle of Morally Just Acquisitions and Transfers does not support reparations to Native Americans by the United States because Native Americans had property ownership rights to the lands, but because Native Americans had property *sovereignty* or *occupancy* rights therein. [27]

Although the locutions "morally just" and "morally unjust" are somewhat vague, relatively clear cases of unjust acquisition or transfer, for instance, exist: when such acquisitions or transfers occur as the result of significant nonvoluntariness (the violent use of force, for example) on the part of those relinquishing property,[28] when acquisitions or transfers involve fraud,[29] or severe misunderstanding between principal parties.[30] In the case of Native American lands (then a part of the United States) most of which were taken from them forcibly by the U.S. military at the direction of Jackson and other U.S. officials (many of which lands were encroached upon illegally by U.S. citizens or civilians), there is no question who the wrongdoer was (the U.S. government, along with its citizen trespassers) and who the harmed parties were (Native Americans of various nations). In other cases, Native Americans were believed to have "given away" their land to invaders, interpreted as such, presumably, because of the hospitality of the Native peoples toward the invaders. In such cases, the questions are not who is the guilty party and who was the victim, but precisely how ought the victims to be "reparated" for the wrongdoings. In still other instances, such as our own, U.S. citizens have purchased in good faith lands from other non-Native peoples to which the former may not in fact have an overriding moral right. That a person purchased in good faith a stolen item in no wise entitles him to that item, as even the law stipulates. She who is truly entitled to the item has a right to it, and that right must be respected by all who take seriously what morality requires. Note that this argument is *not* contingent on the status of well-being of either the perpetrators or the victims of the evils inflicted that might require reparations. For reparations are morally required even if, say, the United States and its citizens were not well-off and if Native Americans were indeed relatively better-off. Reparative justice does not depend on the ability of perpetrators of wrongdoing to enrich their lives by inflicting wrongdoings on others. It is concerned primarily with rectifying past injustices regardless of whether or not perpetrators have been enriched at all by their wrongdoings. Thus the attempt of the Objection From Historical Complexity to defeat (1) of the Reparations Argument fails.

The Objection to Collective Responsibility[31]

This raises the issue of collective moral retrospective liability responsibility of, say, the U.S. government for severe wrongs committed in *its* name or on *its* behalf against Native Americans. The *Objection to Collective Responsibility* challenges the morality of reparations to Native Americans on the grounds that it is problematic to hold the current U.S. government and its citizenry morally accountable for wrongs committed by previous generations of people who acted or failed to act, as the case may be, to harm Native Americans and on behalf of the U.S. government, its agencies, and/or on behalf of themselves as actual or putative U.S. citizens. Thus the Objection to Collective Responsibility challenges (2) of the Reparations Argument insofar as (2) seeks to hold the U.S. *government* responsible for certain substantial wrongs against Native Americans.

However, the Objection to Collective Responsibility falls prey to at least two weaknesses. First, the fundamental documents which form at least the basis of U.S. government are still those which govern the United States. Even though the atrocities committed against Native Americans generations ago were not the direct responsibility of today's U.S. citizens, the fact is that the U.S. government has persisted over time. Furthermore, it is plausible to think that when the U.S. Army and the U.S. government acted in committing genocidal acts of violence against various Native American nations that they did so in such ways that the United States was collectively guilty, at fault, acting knowingly, intentionally and voluntarily to such extents that *we are* justified in inferring that they were both causally responsible and morally liable (culpable) for those harms committed by them against the Native American nations.[32] Additionally, though legally speaking it is not required that a guilty party apologize to the victim(s) of its wrongdoing(s), the extent of the harms committed by the U.S. government against various Native American nations would seem to suggest one. If this is true, then it would appear that both U.S. governmental (collective) feelings and expressions of guilt and remorse are suggested. That is, we would expect that the U.S. government would, in some official manner, express its genuine feelings of guilt and remorse to Native Americans, publicly renouncing its history of racially motivated oppression and holocaust against Native Americans and vowing that it never occur again. Of course, a clear record of governmental policies should reflect a support for such genuine feelings of guilt and remorse.

It is reasonable, then, to hold *it* (the U.S. government) accountable for *its* past wrongdoings, pending some adequate argumentation in support of the morality of a statute of limitations on trying and punishing/compensating such crimes. If it was just "discovered" that a corporation committed a gross wrongdoing (including murders) in 1900, would not justice dictate that the courts seek rectification in such a case, especially if that corporation is still in operation? The reasoning behind this might be either that the putatively guilty corporation is simply deserving of being forced to compensate some parties for the wrongdoing in question (a retributivist rationale) and/or that the corporation has gained an unfair advantage in committing such acts (a non-retributivist rationale). In either case, where matters are clear, past wrongs of such magnitude as what happened to many Native Americans require that justice be realized and there appears to be no adequate reason why past wrongs against Native Americans by U.S. governmental representatives should not be treated in a similar manner as those in which we treat gross corporate wrongdoings that result from corporate representatives' actions or inactions.[33] As for the individuals or aggregate mobs who committed theft, violent crimes, etc. against Native Americans, in some cases some criminals' transfers of assets/fortunes can be traced to current U.S. citizens or institutions, thereby providing a source of reparations. Of course, one who inherits what has been acquired or transferred to her hardly deserves what she inherits if possession of it is in violation of the Principle of Morally Just Acquisitions and Transfers.

A second problem with the Argument Against Collective Responsibility is that the Principle of Morally Just Acquisitions and Transfers renders irrelevant the issue of whether or not the current U.S. government and its citizenry can legitimately be held accountable for the past injustices committed against Native Americans. And the principle does this in the following way: *If, say, most or all of the lands currently occupied by the U.S. government and its citizens are in fact occupied in violation of the principle, then it matters not whether current occupants of those lands are actually liable for the illegitimate transfer of the lands. What truly matters here is whether or not the lands in question have indeed been transferred legitimately. Since most or all of them have not been legitimately transferred to current occupants, then no such occupants can have a legitimate and overriding moral claim to the lands they occupy.* The problem of collective responsibility simply does not affect this fact. It is a red herring given the plausibility of the Principle of Morally Just Acquisitions and Transfers. This rebuttal to the Objection to Collective Responsibility relies on a "weak" form of compensation.[34]

The significance of these replies to the Objection to Collective Responsibility is that they provide a link between the U.S. government and many of the serious wrongs committed against Native Americans, satisfying the legal criteria of privity, standing and nexus, each of which is necessary to establish a legal case for reparations. Thus the Objection to Collective Responsibility fails to defeat (2) of the Reparations Argument.

The Objection from Social Utility

There is another objection to the argument for reparations to Native Americans, and it concerns whether or not the awarding of reparations to Native Americans by the United States would significantly decrease overall social utility. It would render the United States and its citizens—not to mention Native Americans themselves—worse-off. For, as John Locke argues, the European-based commercial system makes life far better-off for everyone than the primitive hunting and gathering ways of life enjoyed by the Native American nations.[35] I shall refer to this as the *Objection From Social Utility*. This utilitarian-based concern is that, strictly speaking, the awarding to Native Americans of the lands that were acquired from them in violation of the Principle of Morally Just Acquisitions and Transfers would surely mean the dissolution of the United States as we know it, as mostly each U.S. citizen resides on land which would, presumably, be relinquished to Native peoples should reparations be enforced. The economic, political, and social implications of this action would be unthinkable, even if the awarding of reparations in this fashion were required by the balance of human reason. So social utility requires that reparations not be awarded because of the undue disruption that would certainly be experienced by the majority of citizens of each of the countries in question. Where would such citizens go if forced by, say, international law, to vacate the premises? Which countries would be in economic and political positions to admit these newly homeless persons? Thus reparations to Native Americans are morally unjustified, it is argued, because they would violate some acceptable principle of social utility.

However, the Objection From Social Utility does not take seriously what people deserve and what retributive justice requires. For even if, strictly speaking, the balance of human reason permitted or required reparations which would then force U.S. citizens from the land on which they reside, this would not mean that the moral prerogative of the reparations in question would lead to the disbanding of the current citizens of the United States. For Native peoples might very well settle for sovereignty rights to the existing lands, yet lease such lands to the rest of the inhabitants. This mode of reparations would most likely dissolve the United States as we know it. But perhaps the United States, insofar as it was founded on the clear, repeated and intentional violation of the content of the Principle of Morally Just Acquisitions and Transfers, deserves to be dissolved in favor of taking seriously morality and justice. Nonetheless, the sovereignty over certain lands by Native Americans to others satisfies the concern for morality and justice in that it gives back to Native peoples the lands to which they had and have ultimate ("trumping") moral rights. But it also does not unduly affect those currently living on those lands in violation of the Principle of Morally Just Acquisitions and Transfers. For they are not left without a place of residence, evading the aforementioned concern. Thus the Objection From Social Utility does not pose an insoluble problem for reparations to Native Americans, though at least one strict form of reparations to Native Americans does imply the dissolution of the United States as we know it. The citizens of the United States would become highly dependent on the goodness of the Native tribes. Of course, history shows that most, if not all, Native peoples are not the kinds of people about whom one has to worry regarding good will and cooperation. A lengthy history of upheld treaties with the United States speaks loudly to this effect.

Furthermore, there is something misleading about the Objection From Social Utility as it applies to reparations to Native Americans. The objection is that the majority of persons now residing in the United States would be significantly and adversely effected by the awarding of such reparations to a minority of persons, all in the name of some "ideal" of retribution. Yet the argument fails to recall that upon the invasion of such lands centuries ago by Europeans, the clear majority of residents were Native Americans! The Objection From Social Utility seeks to argue that reparations to Native Americans would pose social utility problems for current U.S. citizens. This objection, at least in some contexts, represents a rather insensitive attitude toward the crimes committed by the U.S. military against various Native Americans. Moreover, if the informational content of the same argument is indexed to the times in which Native American lives and lands were improperly acquired by the U.S. government, then considerations of social utility might well favor a policy of reparations to Native Americans as a (then) numerical majority whose rights were violated by certain (then) numerical minority of invaders. Thus we cannot without independent and plausible argumentation simply assume that current U.S. citizens, say, count as the primary index of social utility maximization. For when social utility maximization is indexed to the times in which Native American lands and lives were lost to, say, Jackson's military campaign to fulfill manifest destiny, then Native Americans are the ones who (cumulatively speaking) count as the index of social utility maximization. After all, if the Objection From Social Utility works against the awarding of reparations to Native Americans by indexing what counts as social utility maximization to what maximizes happiness for today's residents of the lands in question, then by parity of reasoning it works against attempts to compensate U.S. citizens should, say, a more populous China succeed in conquering North America by way of genocide. After all, if what is most important is the maximization of social happiness or such for the greatest number of persons, then what truly maximizes a majority group of conquerors will always trump the rights of those of the conquered minority groups. The difference between this sort of "ethic" appears indistinguishable from a policy of "might makes right," hardly to be taken seriously by a moral philosopher. If it demonstrated anything at all, the Objection From Social Utility shows the futility of an act utilitarian standpoint in taking seriously the rights of minority members of society. This point about act utilitarianism is not novel.[36]

The Acquired Rights Trumping Original Land Rights Objection

Some would argue that certain rights can be acquired where previously there were no such rights. In particular, some would object to the moral requirement of reparations to Native Americans on the grounds that the U.S. descendants of the European invaders are not themselves morally accountable for the evils inflicted on earlier Native peoples in America, thus escaping the pale of moral retrospective liability responsibility on which such reparations are said to be based. Those who currently reside on putatively U.S. soil and who are not Native Americans did not secure the land illicitly. Furthermore, it is argued, recent generations of U.S. citizens have actually acquired moral rights to the lands on which they reside.[37] What grounds such rights? To be sure, many U.S. citizens have mixed their labor with the land in the forms of building/purchasing homes, working the land, etc.[38] This Lockean point regarding what one has a right to is said to ground the moral rights of contemporary U.S. citizens to "their" land. In addition, one might argue that what the supporters of reparations to Native Americans neglect to see is that there is more to this matter than mere original land acquisition rights. There are also the issues of merit and desert. Arguments for reparations to Native Americans based on original land acquisition are implausible given that they ignore the fact that current non-Native peoples have since acquired rights to the lands based on their acquiring such lands legitimately. Because property (including land) rights change over time, argues David Lyons, today's Native Americans would probably not have rights to their ancestors' lands even had they not been stolen from them by the U.S. government. Thus reparations to Native Americans by the U.S. government for the past injustices are unwarranted.[39] I shall refer to this as the *Acquired Rights Trumping Original Land Rights Objection.*

But the Acquired Rights Trumping Original Land Rights Objection is flawed, and for several reasons. First, reparations do *not* require that those who pay them are morally accountable for the wrongdoing that justifies—even requires—them. Secondly, a ruthless invader can steal land and then mix her labor with it and thereby, according to the argument, gain rights to the stolen land. Yet this is hardly morally justified. Furthermore, that invader may sell her ill-gotten land to an "innocent" party, yet this is a clear violation of the Principle of Morally Just Acquisitions and Transfers. In a similar way, then, the mixing of one's labor with the land is insufficient to ground a moral right had by U.S. citizens to the lands in question. Furthermore, as Waldron argues,

> the Lockean image of labor (whether it is individual or cooperative) being literally embedded or mixed in an object is incoherent. . . . For it would be impossible to explain how property rights thus acquired could be alienable—how they could be transferred, through sale or gift, from one person to another—without offense to the personality of the original acquirer.[40]

So something else must be true to make plausible the claim that current U.S. citizens have overriding moral rights to the lands on which they reside. But what would that be, except that one must inherit or acquire land *without* it being the case that the Principle of Morally Just Acquisitions and Transfers is violated? One cannot legitimately inherit or deserve what has been acquired or transferred by way of immorality or injustice. As Christine M. Korsgaard argues, ". . . if a theft or swindle succeeds, we do not take it that the new distribution of property is legitimate."[41] Finally, if some U.S. citizens have moral rights to "their" lands by "just" inheritance,[42] then why would we not think that original land rights of Native peoples in turn accrue to current Native Americans? This would mean that the real question of which set of rights "trumps" another's boils down to, among other things, whether or not there was a violation of the Principle of Morally Just Acquisitions and Transfers concerning what is now deemed by many to be U.S. territory.

It might be argued that there is a justified limitation of time placed on rights claims, and that the limitation on the claim of a right to reparations has expired for Native Americans to justly claim their rights to the lands. In U.S. law, this is referred to as the *Laches Doctrine:* If there is a significant amount of time that passes without a wronged party attempting to claim its right to something, then the claimant loses her right to that thing. Or, at the very least, the right "fades" over time.[43]

But this line of reasoning neglects the historical reality that at several points in time various Native American nations have publicly claimed their land rights—even to the U.S. government! That such claims were made repeatedly and not respected is a matter of historical fact, and that the claims of many Native Americans were not respected fails to count as evidence for the claim that the opportunity to claim the right to reparations has truly expired.[44] For many Native Americans satisfied the condition in question. But their pleas were simply ignored or turned away. We must bear in mind that an unjust legal system's failure to uphold Native American claims to lands (and compensation for crimes constituting violence to persons, among other things) hardly serves as a rational foundation for a statute of limitations on Native American claims concerning what they deserve as compensation for wrongdoings. Reparations to Native Americans in the United States are either morally required or they are not, regardless of the fact that morally corrupted legislative and judicial systems were put in place to (among other things) bias decisions against Native American claims, thus supporting the idea of the expiration of the statute of limitations on Native American land claims. Furthermore, that contemporary U.S. citizens are not causally responsible for the past wrongs committed against Native Americans in no way nullifies the fact that today's lands are, in the main, occupied by those who have acquired them through a chain of possessions which is in clear violation of the Principle of Morally Just Acquisitions and Transfers. For as was pointed out in the refutation of the Objection to Collective Responsibility, that one has not wronged Native Americans in some direct way hardly justifies one's being in the possession of stolen or ill-gotten property. Thus there needs to be a reason other than the one provided by the statute of limitations advocates that would ground the acquisition of moral rights to lands now occupied by U.S. citizens.

Some might argue that the Lockean Proviso grounds the rights of current U.S. citizens to the lands on which they reside in that Native Americans in the distant past had more land than they could use, and that the Native Americans had no right to deprive European "invaders" of their settlement of North American lands that were not in use by Native Americans.

However, this line of reasoning is problematic for the following reasons. First, most of the land acquired by the European invaders (including the U.S. government) was by way of force and fraud against Native Americans (not to mention, non-Native Americans!). So even if Native Americans had an obligation (based on the Lockean Proviso) to share some of the North American lands with others, it does not follow that the lands had to be shared with those who dealt Native Americans injustices of the harshest order. This holds whether the invaders were conquering "explorers" or "mere settlers." The possible difference between these two groups in terms of their putative collective moral liability for harms against Native Americans does not diminish the fact that each group played a crucial role in the unjust acquisitions and transfers of lands that were inhabited by Native Americans.

Secondly, the Lockean Proviso states that one has a right to *X* to the extent that there is enough and as good of *X* for others.[45] However, U.S. history is replete with examples of Native Americans *welcoming with open arms* European invaders, under the assumption, no doubt, that something like the Principle of Morally Just Acquisitions and Transfers would not be violated in the course of the latter groups' settling the lands. So Native Americans, by and large and from the outset of the invasion of the Americas, acted in congruence with the Lockean Proviso both in terms of their dealings with non-Native Americans and in terms of their dealings with most other Native Americans. Yet history tells the complicated and dismal stories of injustices Native Americans experienced in losing their lands to European invaders, hardly a moral foundation for current U.S. claims to North American lands.[46]

Furthermore, it is unclear whether the Lockean Proviso was violated by Native Americans as a whole. Considering that there were hundreds of such nations in North America, and that many of them were nomadic, it is not at all certain that there was sufficient land and resources for them to share with Europeans.[47] Thus it is difficult to see how original rights of Native Americans to the lands and resources in question are trumped by subsequent European putative rights to the same lands and resources for reasons of the Lockean Proviso.

The Supersession of Historic Injustice Objection

Furthermore, there is the *Supersession of Historic Injustice Objection* to reparations, articulated by Waldron. The basic idea here is that "changing circumstances can have an effect on ownership rights notwithstanding the moral legitimacy of original appropriation."[48] Applied to the Native American experience, the argument runs as follows. There have been historic injustices committed against Native Americans, as we all know. But historical circumstances have changed, and situations where resources are scarce, such as now, are those in which the future generations of those who themselves wronged Native Americans are morally *entitled* to share resources (including land) with Native Americans. Thus the initial injustices by past generations of European invaders and the U.S. military (among others) against Native Americans is superseded by changing circumstances. "Claims about justice and injustice must be responsive to changes in circumstances," as Waldron argues.[49] So the issue of historic injustice, though an important one, is superseded by the fact that inhabitants of lands are entitled to share it with others under conditions of scarcity of resources. After all, "the aboriginal inhabitants would have had to share their lands, whether the original injustice had taken place or not."[50] Waldron writes,

> If circumstances make a difference to what counts as a just acquisition, then they must make a difference also to what counts as an unjust incursion. And if they make a difference to that, then in principle we must concede that a change in circumstances can affect whether a particular continuation of adverse possession remains an injustice or not. . . . It may be that some of the historic injustices that concern us have not been superseded, and that, even under modern circumstances, the possession of certain aboriginal lands by the descendants of those who expropriated their original owners remains a crying injustice. My argument is not intended to rule that out. But there have been huge changes since North America and Australasia were settled by white colonists. . . . We cannot be sure that these changes in circumstances supersede the injustice of their continued possession of aboriginal lands, but it would not be surprising if they did.[51]

There are problems, however, with the Supersession of Historic Injustice Objection to reparations to Native Americans. Although the argument admits that European invaders (and the U.S. government, more specifically) had no rightful claims to lands that they expropriated from Native Americans, the argument seems to say that later generations of at least some of those European invaders gained land rights based on the premise that under conditions of scarcity, resources must be shared by all occupants of a territory. Yet the fact is that such conditions of scarcity would, so far as history informs us, have not likely existed if not for the doings of the European invaders themselves! There was certainly significant land and resources (buffalo, for instance, and other food sources) for the millions of Native Americans prior to the invasion of North America by Europeans and prior to the massacres of various Native Americans by the U.S. military. Nor is there uncontroversial evidence to suggest that there is a high probability that there would have been a scarcity of such resources among Native Americans absent natural disasters and European invaders. So in effect the argument seeks to ground the future generations of European invaders' putative moral claims to the lands on which they reside on the fact that those whose ancestors by and large created a problem of resource scarcity have a moral claim to the lands over and above those who once possessed the land without scarcity of resources. But why not infer from history and morality a rather different conclusion, namely, that at best current non-Native Americans possess trumping or overriding moral claims to whatever property they legitimately own which is *on* the land belonging to the descendants of those from whom the European invaders expropriated it? Is this not the more intuitively sensible inference, given historical circumstances? How, then, can we say that the violations against Native Americans are superseded?

Simply because such evils occurred long ago? Neither the laches defense nor statutes of limitations seem plausible, morally speaking. Would we dare infer that a thief who breaks into my home, takes me hostage and resides there for months on end, eating my food, making himself "at home" in various other ways in turn somehow gains a right to the home, even if he should assume some of the household chores (after all, he is a rather tidy thief, and doesn't like to live in a messy place)? Would we not say that he is a thief, and that no matter how much he makes himself at home, that he has made himself at home in *my* home, and that he is to be arrested, tried, and if found guilty by way of a fair trial, then he is to be punished and made to compensate me for damages? Why, then, do we not conclude similarly in the case of reparations to Native Americans? I say "similarly" in that those who currently reside on U.S. lands do so while they themselves are not causally responsible for the crimes perpetrated against Native Americans by the U.S. military. Thus compensation, not punishment, is what is at issue regarding reparations to Native Americans. The Supersession of Historic Injustice Objection, then, surely has little to recommend it.

The Counterfactual Objection

There is a final concern with policies of reparations to Native Americans. Waldron notes a counterfactual difficulty regarding reparations:

> The present surely looks different now from the way the present would look if a given injustice of the past had not occurred. Why not therefore change the present so that it looks more like the present that would have obtained in the absence of the injustice? . . . The trouble with this approach is the difficulty we have in saying what would have happened if some event (which did occur) had not taken place.[52]

Waldron adds that the problem of reparations becomes even fuzzier when we factor into the rectificatory scheme the matter of human choice. For given the fact that humans do have some choices, this makes it quite problematic to figure out how the present situation might be readjusted to best approximate the scheme of things had a particular injustice not taken place. Besides the matter of whether or not such human choices can rightly have normative import and to be non-arbitrary, argues Waldron, "Ultimately, what is raised here is the question of whether it is possible to rectify particular injustices without undertaking a comprehensive redistribution that addresses all claims of justice that may be made. . . ."[53] I shall refer to this as the *Counterfactual Objection*.

In reply to Waldron's concerns about counterfactual aspects of reparations, it might be argued that it hardly counts against the moral requirement of reparations to, say, Native Americans that the subsequent redistributive scheme of compensatory justice would lead to a proliferation of rights claims to historic injustices pertaining to the settlement and development of North America. Even if it were true that few such claims could or would be settled adequately, this does nothing to count against the claim that reparations are morally required as a matter of moral principle. Nor does it somehow render senseless the multidimensional aspects of the expressive functions of reparations to Native American nations. Furthermore, in the case of Native American nations, there are records of leaders of such nations declaring their unambiguous aversion to and despising of most anything to do with "manifest destiny" and other social, political, and cultural features of the "American experiment." Historical records provide a keen understanding of the culture and beliefs of Native American peoples, and we can be sure that what is important to them is at least the returning of their land to them, even though the land is hardly in the condition in which it was seized from them. That it is impossible to return to Native American nations what was once theirs and in the same condition as it was when it was taken from them by force and fraud is not a good enough reason to think that it is not morally required to return such lands to them.[54] Moreover, there is nothing in Native American history or culture to suggest that Native Americans would have freely chosen to give up their lands to anyone who would do to the land what European settlers by and large did to it.

Although the counterfactual approach to reparations is indeed a problem for reparations policies, it says nothing about the moral requirement of reparations themselves, except that, like matters of punishment and compensation in general, rectificatory justice is at best imprecise. The Counterfactual Objection against reparations to Native Americans would seem to imply that punishment and compensation are too problematic even for most contemporary courts to handle, as evidence and argumentation are rarely unambiguous in interpretation. Yet this is surely an implication few would find plausible. Imprecision and Herculean cases are hardly excuses for the law's turning its head from the need for justice. So the Counterfactual Objection against reparations to Native Americans does not show that reparations are not morally required, or that they are not feasible as a legal means of compensating (to some significant extent) those who deserve them.

If the objections to reparations to Native Americans are specious for at least the reasons noted, and if the Principle of Morally Just Acquisitions and Transfers is plausible and applicable to the Native American experiences, then the balance of reason suggests at least the *prima facie* plausibility of some policy of reparations to Native Americans. Moreover, it is incumbent on the supporter of such reparations to devise a plausible policy of reparations. Although a full-fledged theory and policy of reparations to Native Americans is beyond the scope of this chapter, a few points can be noted along the lines of how reparations to Native Americans might accrue.

It should be acknowledged that the various nations which constitute Native Americans as a broad set of ethnic groups have varying degrees of experiences with oppression at the hands of the European invaders, and that a principle of proportionality must be used to distinguish variant levels of reparations to different Native American nations, that is, where history is clear about the differences in evil experienced by them. In general, however, whether it be the Navajos, the Cherokees, the Mohawks, the Six Nations, the Senecas, or other Native American nations, sufficient evils have been perpetrated against them by the U.S. government that would require some form of compensatory reparations of a significant measure. One obvious reason for this is noted by G. Sher: "In the case of . . . Indians, . . . we may indeed have enough information to suggest that most current group members are worse off than they would be in the absence of some initial wrong."[55] Yet it is unnecessary to impose a standard of strict proportionality that the law cannot uphold even in much easier cases. After all, one possible strategy is to argue that even if compensating for such wrongs would not restore full justice to Native Americans, it would at least bring Native Americans substantially closer to justice than they are currently.

A Possible Reparations Policy

What sorts of specific compensatory measures ought to be imposed and against whom? Short of complete restoration of lands and/or compensation for personal injuries of Native Americans, there lies another proposal. It is the partial but significant restoration of lands to Native Americans, lands that have, it is argued, never played an important role in the economic viability of the United States. Thus the restoring of such lands to Native Americans by way of reparations would pose no real threat to the U.S. economy. This is what has been referred to as the "Buffalo Commons" proposal:[56]. . . What you end up with is a huge territory lying east of Denver, west of Lawrence, Kansas, and extending from the Canadian border to southern Texas, all of it "outside the loop" of United States business as usual.

The bulk of this area is unceded territory owned by the Lakota, Pawnee, Arikara, Hidatsa, Mandan, Crow, Shoshone, Assiniboine, Cheyenne, Arapaho, Kiowa, Comanche, Jicarilla, and Mescalero Apache nations. There would be little cost to the United States, and virtually no arbitrary dispossession or dislocation of non-Indians, if the entire Commons were restored to these peoples.[57] The reasons given in favor of this proposal are twofold. First, it provides Native Americans a means of tangible self-determination. Secondly, it provides "alternative socioeconomic models" for possible adaptation by those who are not Native Americans.

Of course, this proposal, however reasonable in its attempt to not disrupt the lives of U.S. citizens, is grossly inadequate as a form of reparations for the remainder of the territories taken by force and fraud from Native Americans. Nor does it begin to compensate Native Americans for the murders and other personal injuries inflicted on them by the United States. Nonetheless, the Buffalo Commons proposal is a reasonable attempt to balance the practical attempt to honor the unreasonable application of some plausible principle of utility to current U.S. society[58] over against the demand for rectification for injustice. Although reasonable, the Buffalo

Commons proposal is insufficient as a means for providing adequate reparations to Native Americans. However, if the Principle of Morally Just Acquisitions and Transfers is correct in regards to the Native American experiences, then one is hardly in a moral position to deny the plausibility of at least something akin to the Buffalo Commons proposal.

Conclusion

If the arguments against reparations to Native (North) Americans in the United States are defeasible for the reasons given herein, then the presumptive case in favor of reparations to Native Americans gains strength. Barring further argumentation that would render morally problematic such reparations, then, a case for such reparations has been made along the following lines. To the extent that history is unambiguous concerning the extent of guilt, fault, wrongdoing, and the identities of perpetrators and victims of historic injustices, policies of reparations to Native Americans should be enacted according to some fundamentally sound principle of proportional compensation.

If the foregoing analysis is sound, then one hope that the United States has of dragging itself out of the mire of its own perpetration of historic injustices against Native Americans is for it to institute adequate policies of reparations to Native Americans. Even so, such policies must receive far more commitment by the U.S. government than the treaties made by the U.S. government with Native American nations had received in the past. What is also needed is a national sense of shame-based guilt[59] and collective remorse[60] for the roles that the U.S. government and its citizenry played in founding the United States. Yet if such shame requires a higher-level self-consciousness,[61] this might well be precisely what U.S. society lacks, providing its critics with ammunition for claims of the fundamental immorality of the United States in general. For a society that is based on unrectified injustice is itself unjust. But a society that simply refuses to admit its unjust history toward others not only remains unjust on balance, but serves as a stark reminder of the unabashed arrogance of its unspeakable badness.

NOTES

Introduction

I am grateful to my colleagues in the Philosophy Department at the University of Hawai'i at Mānoa, the University of Hawai'i Foundation, and the University of Hawai'i University Research Council for supporting this project. Thanks are also due to Chris Framarin and Virginia Suddath for their invaluable assistance in preparing the manuscript, to J. Angelo Corlett for his comments on the Introduction and Chapter 1, and to my editor Phyllis Korper for proofreading the bulk of the penultimate manuscript.

1. As I try to show in Chapter 1, if retribution (punishment) is required by justice, then it may be properly conceived as a part of rectification. However, in using the term here I wish to emphasize the sense of making things right which rectification entails, not punishment for the wrongdoer. Moreover, I want to emphasize restoration, apology, and other victim-centered concerns of rectification. See Ch 1, II.4.
2. Robert C. Solomon and Mark C. Murphy, eds., *What Is Justice?: Classic and Contemporary Readings,* 2nd ed., New York: Oxford University Press, 2000, from the back cover.
3. Solomon and Murphy, *What Is Justice?,* p. 4. The editors do, however, note two important rectificatory questions: the question of whether the history of injustice ought to play a role in our thinking about what is just now (p. 7), and the question of whether descendants of victims of injustice deserve compensation (p. 4).
4. Solomon and Murphy, *What Is Justice?,* p. 279.
5. Charles Mills makes the point that "*questions of racial justice, and what is necessary to redress the legacy of slavery in this country*", for example, "*is simply not an issue of major concern to whites, even in the cases—professional intellectuals whose subject matter is questions of justice—where one would think that there is the highest probability of finding some systematic reflection on the subject.*" ("Under Class Under Standings", *Ethics* 104:4 (July 1994): 874, emphasis in the original).

   Mills observes that, in contrast to "the world of mainstream (i.e., white) ethics and political philosophy, preoccupied with discussions of justice and rights in the abstract", Native American and African American political thought (among others) have "historically focused on issues of conquest, imperialism, colonialism . . . reparations . . . etc. These issues hardly appear in mainstream political philosophy, but they have been central to the political struggles of the majority of the world's population. Their absence from what is considered serious philosophy is a reflection not of their lack of seriousness but of the color of the vast majority of Western academic philosophers (and perhaps *their* lack of seriousness)" (Charles W. Mills, *The Racial Contract,* Cornell University Press, 1997, p. 4, emphasis in the original).

This dominance is echoed by Leonard Harris. According to Harris, "American Philosophy can be said to maintain an appropriately honorable status peopled almost exclusively by whites, a fact to be explained not by the antecedents of rape, murder, child abuse, exploitation, racial elitism, nepotism, xenophobia, nativism, provincialism, cultural chauvinism, or the treatment of minorities as exotic instantiations of inferior natures but by intelligence and support of the right canonical figures" ("'Believe it or Not' or The Ku Klux Klan and American Philosophy Exposed", *The American Philosophical Association Newsletter on Philosophy and the Black Experience* 95:1 (Fall 1995), <http://www.apa.udel.edu/apa/archive/newsletters/v95n1/ black.asp>).

6. See, for example, William Banner, "Compensatory Justice", Bill Diggs, "Banner on Compensatory Justice", and Richard Ray, "The Foundations of Compensatory Justice", *Journal of Social Philosophy* 6:2 (April 1975). For a more recent discussion, see Chapter 7 *infra*.
7. Immanuel Kant and John Locke, for example. Kant held that perpetrators of injustice ought to try to "remedy" their injustice, or apologize when that is not possible (*Lectures on Ethics,* Louis Infield, trans., Indianapolis, Indiana: Hackett, 1963, pp. 131, 214), and Locke posited a right to reparation (*Two Treatises of Government,* Peter Laslett, ed., Cambridge: Cambridge University Press, 1988, chap. II, sect. 8, 10, 11).
8. From the first half of the century, see W. D. Ross, *The Right and the Good* (Oxford: Clarendon Press, 1930), generally cited for Ross's notion of a *prima facie* duty of reparation; and W. D. Lamont, "Justice: Distributive and Corrective", *Philosophy* 16:61 (January 1941).

   From the 1960's, see Morris Ginsberg, "The Concept of Justice" *Philosophy* 38:144 (April 1963); Joel Feinberg, "Justice and Personal Desert", in *Doing & Deserving: Essays in the Theory of Responsibility,* Princeton, New Jersey: Princeton University Press, 1970, originally published in *NOMOS VI: Justice,* Carl J. Friedrich and John W. Chapman, eds., New York: Atherton Press, 1963; and Joel Feinberg, "Duties, Rights, and Claims", *American Philosophical Quarterly* 3:2 (April 1966).
9. For example, James W. Nickel, "Discrimination and Morally Relevant Characteristics", *Analysis* 32:4 (March 1972) sparked a discussion which included: J. L. Conan, "Inverse Discrimination", *Analysis* 33:1 (October 1972); Roger A. Shiner, "Individuals, Groups and Inverse Discrimination", *Analysis* 33:6 (June 1973); Paul W. Taylor, "Reverse Discrimination and Compensatory Justice", *Analysis* 33:6 (June 1973); Michael Bales, "Reparations to Wronged Groups", *Analysis* 33:6 (June 1973); and Philip Silvestri, "The Justification of Inverse Discrimination", *Analysis* 34:1 (October 1973). Nickel replied in "Should Reparations Be To Individuals Or To Groups?", *Analysis* 34:1 (October 1973). For a rectificatory discussion by Nickel which is not focused on "discrimination", see his "Justice in Compensation", *William and Mary Law Review* 18:2 (Winter 1976).

   Robert Nozick, *Anarchy, State, and Utopia* (New York: Basic Books, 1974) was probably the most popular book of the decade claiming to address rectificatory concerns. The book suggests a historical entitlement theory which includes the rectification of injustice, characterizes rectification as a "major topic", and raises several important rectificatory questions. Unfortunately, Nozick doesn't know "of a thorough or theoretically sophisticated treatment of such issues", and refers his readers to Boris Bittker's "useful book" of the previous year (p. 152, citing Boris Bittker, *The Case for Black Reparations* (New York: Random House, 1973) at p. 344 Ch 7 n.2). Indeed, as Robert Litan notes, Nozick's theory of rectification is "the single most important issue Nozick admits leaving untreated" (Robert E. Litan, "On Rectification in Nozick's Minimal State", *Political Theory* 5:2 (May 1977): 233, citing *Anarchy, State, and Utopia*, p. 152).

Also see D. N. MacCormick, "The Obligation of Reparation", *Proceedings of the Aristotelian Society* 78 (1977–78), and George Sher, "Compensation and Transworld Personal Identity", *The Monist* 62:3 (July 1979).

10. See Christopher Arnold, "Corrective Justice", *Ethics* 90 (January 1980); George Sher, "Ancient Wrongs and Modern Rights", *Philosophy & Public Affairs* 10:1 (Winter 1981); Christopher Morris, "Existential Limits To The Rectification of Past Wrongs", *American Philosophical Quarterly* 21:2 (April 1984); Onora O'Neill, "Rights to Compensation", *Social Philosophy & Policy* 5:1 (Autumn 1987); Mari J. Matsuda, "Looking to the Bottom: Critical Legal Studies and Reparations", *Harvard Civil Rights-Civil Liberties Law Review* 22:2 (Spring 1987); and Robert Goodin, "Theories of Compensation", *Oxford Journal of Legal Studies* 9:1 (Spring 1989).

    Books include: Elizabeth H. Wolgast, *The Grammar of Justice,* Ithaca, New York: Cornell University Press, 1987 (esp. chap. 6), and Richard Swinburne, *Responsibility and Atonement,* Oxford: Clarendon Press, 1989 (esp. chap. 5 and chap. 6).

11. See Judith Shklar, *The Faces of Injustice,* New Haven: Yale University Press; John W. Chapman, ed., *NOMOS XXXIII: Compensatory Justice,* New York: New York University Press, 1991; Bernard R. Boxill, *Blacks and Social Justice,* rev. ed., Lanham, Maryland: Rowman & Littlefield, 1992; Thomas W. Simon, *Democracy and Social Injustice: Law, Politics, and Philosophy,* Lanham, Maryland: Rowman & Littlefield, 1995; George Sher, *Approximate Justice: Studies in Non-Ideal Theory,* Lanham, Maryland: Rowman & Littlefield, 1997; George Schedler, *Racist Symbols and Reparations: Philosophical Reflections on Vestiges of the American Civil War,* Lanham, Maryland: Rowman & Littlefield, 1998; Howard McGary Jr., *Race & Social Justice,* Malden, Massachusetts: Blackwell, 1999, and Roy L. Brooks, ed., *When Sorry Isn't Enough: The Controversy Over Apologies and Reparations for Human Injustice,* New York: New York University Press, 1999.

    See also Jean Hampton, "Correcting Harms Versus Righting Wrongs: The Goal of Retribution", *UCLA Law Review* 39:6 (August 1992); Robert Ginsberg, "The Future of Past Injustices", in *Horizons of Justice,* J. Ralph Lindgren, ed., New York: Peter Lang, 1996; Samuel C. Wheeler III, "Reparations Reconstructed", *American Philosophical Quarterly* 34:3 (July 1997); and Andrew Askland, "A Justification of Compensation to the Descendants of Wronged Parties: An Intended Analogy", *Public Affairs Quarterly* 12:4 (October 1998).

12. Discussion of "preferential treatment" for African Americans had already begun before President Johnson's Executive Order 11246 (1965), the event many consider the birth of affirmative action. See, for example, the Constitutional argument in Richard Lichtman, "The Ethics of Compensatory Justice", *Law in Transition Quarterly* 1:2 (Spring 1964).

13. For some earlier work, see Graham Hughes, "Reparations for Blacks?", *New York University Law Review* 43:6 (December 1968), and Mark Green, "Reparations for Blacks: The Question of Effective Equality Through Preferential Treatment", *Commonweal* 90:13 (13 June 1969). Also the following by Howard McGary Jr.: "Reparations and Inverse Discrimination", *Dialogue* 17:1 (1974), "Justice and Reparations", *The Philosophical Forum* 9:2–3 (Winter-Spring 1977–78), and "Reparations, Self-Respect, and Public Policy", *The Journal* (MBPI, vol. 1, 1984). The latter two are reprinted in his *Race & Social Justice* (Malden, Massachusetts: Blackwell, 1999).

14. For example, Louis P. Pojman, "The Moral Status of Affirmative Action", *Public Af-*

fairs Quarterly 6:2 (April 1992), and Stephen Kershnar, "Are the Descendants of Slaves Owed Compensation for Slavery?", *Journal of Applied Philosophy* 16:1 (1999).

15. In his discussion of a recent book on bioethics, Dan Brock notes that "a relatively distinctive feature of [Bernard Gert's] treatment of bioethics' issues—indeed, it is distinctive in applied ethics generally—is the explicit development of positions on bioethics' issues from a general moral system. This is a clear strength of the book in a field in which many treatments of concrete issues are ad hoc and ungrounded in any more general moral system." Dan W. Brock, Review of *Bioethics: A Return to Fundamentals* (Bernard Gert, Charles M. Culver and K. Danner Clouser, eds., New York: Oxford University Press, 1997), *Ethics* 110:3 (April 2000): 615.
16. George Sher, *Approximate Justice: Studies in Non-Ideal Theory,* Lanham, Maryland: Rowman & Littlefield, 1997, p. 5. Sher uses the term "compensatory justice" here. I make my case for "rectificatory justice" in Chapter 1.
17. The only collection at all similar to the present volume is *NOMOS XXXIII: Compensatory Justice* (John W. Chapman, ed., New York: New York University Press, 1991). This volume in the American Society of Legal and Political Philosophy yearbook series emerged from the meeting of the society held in 1989 in conjunction with the annual meeting of the Association of American Law Schools.
18. Marcus G. Singer, ed., *Morals and Values: Readings in Theoretical and Practical Ethics,* New York: Charles Scribner's Sons, 1977, p. vii.
19. Thomas W. Simon, *Democracy and Social Injustice: Law, Politics, and Philosophy,* Lanham, Maryland: Rowman & Littlefield, 1995, p. 12.
20. For additional commentary, see Nancy Davis, "Rights, Permission, and Compensation", *Philosophy & Public Affairs* 14:4 (Fall 1985), and Peter Westen, "Comment on Montague's 'Rights and Duties of Compensation'", *Philosophy & Public Affairs* 14:4 (Fall 1985). See Montague's reply in "Davis and Westen on Rights and Compensation", *Philosophy & Public Affairs* 14:4 (Fall 1985).
21. Kathleen Gill notes in her essay that she has "only been able to find one article in the philosophical literature specifically on apologies" (n. 1), *viz.,* Louis Kort's. Richard Joyce was writing on apology at about the same time as she. See Richard Joyce, "Apologizing", *Public Affairs Quarterly* 13:2 (April 1999).
22. For a discussion of the Manifesto by Foreman himself, see "Control, Conflict and Change: The Underlying Concepts of the Black Manifesto", in *Black Manifesto: Religion, Racism, and Reparations,* Robert S. Lecky and H. Elliott Wright, eds., New York: Sheed and Ward, 1969. Other books inspired by the Manifesto include Arnold Schuchter, *Reparations: The Black Manifesto and its Challenge to White America,* Philadelphia & New York: J. B. Lippincott, 1970, and the legal analysis by Boris I. Bittker in *The Case for Black Reparations,* New York: Random House, 1973. In the year following its publication, James W. Nickel described Bittker's book as "the most comprehensive discussion of black reparations and related issues now available" (*Ethics* 84:2 (January 1974): 180). For a brief discussion of Schuchter and Bittker, see Derrick Bell, *Race, Racism, and American Law,* 2nd ed., Boston, Massachusetts: Little, Brown & Co., 1980, pp. 44–47.

    A recent forum discussion by four class-action lawyers on the idea of a lawsuit seeking reparations for slavery can be found in "Making the Case for Racial Reparations: Does America Owe a Debt to the Descendants of its Slaves?", *Harper's* (November 2000). Work which takes an economic perspective on demands for rectification include: Robert S. Browne, "The Economic Basis for Reparations to Black America", *The Review of Black Political Economy* 2:2 (Winter 1972)); Norman Girvan, "The Question of Compensation: A Third World Perspective", *Race* 16:1 (July 1974); Richard F. America, *The Wealth of Races: The Present Value of Benefits from Past Injustices,* Westport, Connecticut: Greenwood Press, 1990; Tyler Conan, "Discounting and Restitution", *Philosophy & Public Affairs* 26:2 (Spring 1997); and Randall N. Robinson, *The Debt: What America Owes to Blacks,* New York: Plume, 2001.

1. *"Justice and Rectification: A Taxonomy of Justice," by Rodney C. Roberts*

1. This is J. O. Urmson's interpretation of Aristotle, *Nicomachean Ethics* (1130a 8–13). J. O. Urmson, *Aristotle's Ethics,* Oxford: Blackwell, 1988, pp. 71–72.
2. D. D. Raphael, *Problems of Political Philosophy,* 2nd ed., Atlantic Highlands, New Jersey: Humanities Press, 1990, p. 117.
3. W. D. Lamont, "Justice: Distributive and Corrective", *Philosophy* 16:61 (January 1941): 12.
4. Raphael, *Problems of Political Philosophy,* p. 119.
5. Raphael, *Problems of Political Philosophy,* p. 120.
6. Judith Shklar finds the entire enterprise of distributive justice problematic. She thinks that what is usually taken to be justice is in fact unjust by its own standards. On Shklar's view: "normal justice does not and cannot reach its own ends. Neither equal nor proportionate deserts can be distributed when no one even knows what constitutes human worth. No one gets or gives what is owed and no one arrives at the balance, psychic or social, that justice is supposed to establish. That is what ignorance is bound to bring" (*The Faces of Injustice* (New Haven: Yale University Press, 1990, p. 23).
7. Bill Diggs, "Banner on Compensatory Justice", *Journal of Social Philosophy* 6:2 (April 1975): 7–8.
8. Bernard Boxill, "The Morality of Reparation", *Social Theory and Practice* 2:1 (Spring 1972): 117 [p. 127. inf.]
9. Joel Feinberg, "Wrongful Life and the Counterfactual Element in Harming", *Philosophy and Law,* Jules Coleman and Ellen Frankel Paul, eds., Oxford: Blackwell, 1987, p. 146.
10. I realize that the notion of commensurability can be extremely problematic, especially between cultures, e.g., rectifying injustices involving land and indigenous peoples invariably bring claims of incommensurability to the fore. On incommensurability generally, see Ruth Chang, ed., *Incommensurability, Incomparability, and Practical Reason,* Cambridge, Massachusetts: Harvard University Press, 1997.
11. According to Aristotle, currency, "by making things commensurate as a measure does, equalizes them; for there would be no association without exchange, no exchange without equality, no equality without commensurability. And so, though things so different cannot become commensurate in reality, they can become commensurate enough in relation to our needs. Hence there must be some single unit fixed [as current] by a stipulation. This is why it is called currency; for this makes everything commensurate, since everything is measured by currency" (*Nicomachean Ethics,* Terence Irwin, trans., Indianapolis, Indiana: Hackett, 1985, p. 131 (1133b 20).
12. Ralph Barton Perry, "The Definition of Value", in Tom L. Beauchamp, *Philosophical*

Ethics: An Introduction to Moral Philosophy, New York: McGraw-Hill, 1982, p. 341, emphasis in the original, from Perry's *Realms of Value: A Critique of Human Civilization,* Cambridge, Massachusetts: Harvard University Press, 1954.

13. Robert Goodin draws a similar distinction between two kinds of compensation, calling one "means replacing" and the other "ends displacing". However, Goodin does not suggest (as I do) that both may usually be required in order for compensation to be affected ("Theories of Compensation", *Oxford Journal of Legal Studies* 9:1 (Spring 1989), esp. p. 60).
14. On what she calls rational belief-mediated feelings, see Judith Jarvis Thomson, *The Realm of Rights,* Cambridge, Massachusetts: Harvard University Press, 1990, p. 250 ff.
15. Christopher Arnold, "Corrective Justice", *Ethics* 90 (January 1980): 182.
16. John Stuart Mill, *Utilitarianism,* chap. V, in *John Stuart Mill: Utilitarianism, On Liberty, Essay on Bentham,* Mary Warnock, ed., New York: Meridian, 1974, p. 316.
17. Immanuel Kant, *The Metaphysical Elements of Justice,* John Ladd, trans., Upper Saddle River, New Jersey: Prentice-Hall, 1965, reprinted in *Justice,* Jonathan Westphal, ed., Indianapolis, Indiana: Hackett, 1996, p. 151.
18. Kant, *The Metaphysical Elements of Justice,* p. 151.
19. Kant, *The Metaphysical Elements of Justice,* p. 152.
20. Cf. Chapter 8 *infra*.
21. Joel Feinberg, *Doing & Deserving: Essays in the Theory of Responsibility,* Princeton, New Jersey: Princeton University Press, 1970, p. 74, emphasis added. I take it that what Feinberg means by "moral equilibrium" is something like John Kekes's definition, *viz.*: "the state in which the benefits and harms an individual receives are proportional to what is warranted by the significant fact in the individual's past" (*The Oxford Companion to Philosophy,* Ted Honderich, ed., Oxford: Oxford University Press, 1995, p. 193).
22. Feinberg, *Doing & Deserving,* p. 76, emphasis added.
23. Feinberg, *Doing & Deserving,* p. 75.
24. Gerald Gaus, "Does Compensation Restore Equality?", in *NOMOS XXXIII: Compensatory Justice,* John W. Chapman, ed., New York: New York University Press, 1991, pp. 60, 75, emphasis in the original [pp. 94, 104 inf.].
25. Gaus, "Does Compensation Restore Equality?", pp. 67, 70 [pp. 99, 100 inf.].
26. J. R. Lucas, *On Justice,* Oxford: Clarendon Press, 1980, p. 7, emphasis added, cited in Gaus, "Does Compensation Restore Equality?", p. 70 [p. 101 inf.]. In contrast to Lucas's view, Gaus notes (p. 80, n.76) [p. 179, n. 76 inf.] that, according to David A. J. Richards, "resentment is appropriate if you have been wronged, while indignation is the appropriate response to a wrong to others (*Theory of Reasons for Action,* Oxford: Clarendon Press, 1971, p. 253). However, whether indignation or resentment is the appropriate moral feeling when one has been wronged, the point is that whichever emotion is at work, it serves as ground for a legitimate complaint on the part of the victim, the addressing of which is required by justice.
27. Richard Swinburne, *Responsibility and Atonement,* Oxford: Clarendon Press, 1989, p. 82. It seems that for Swinburne, reparation means restoration. He thinks of "making reparation" as "removing the former harm", and uses the following example. "If I steal your watch and have not sold it, I can return it to you". He then gives an example of compensation, saying that: "Sometimes I can only make things rather similar to the way they were, so that the victim is almost equally happy with the new state. I can com-

pensate him adequately, that is." Swinburne also recognizes the need to compensate for intangible losses, saying that: "If I smash up your car, I can pay for repairs. The harm done by stealing, injuring, and similar acts is not only the physical damage, but the inconvenience of temporary loss and the trauma and anxiety resulting from it, and for these too compensation is needed."

28. Swinburne, *Responsibility and Atonement,* p. 82; emphasis added.
29. Swinburne, *Responsibility and Atonement,* p. 82.
30. Swinburne, *Responsibility and Atonement,* p. 88.
31. It strikes me as at least plausible that forgiveness by the victim may be both a sufficient and a necessary condition for full rectification. Since the victim can absolve the wrongdoer of all moral culpability, it seems that, even without compensation or an apology, forgiveness by the victim may be sufficient for full rectification.
32. Mill, *Utilitarianism,* chap. V, pp. 303–304.
33. Hugo Adam Bedau, "punishment", *The Oxford Companion to Philosophy* , Ted Honderich, ed., Oxford: Oxford University Press, 1995, p. 732.
34. Lamont, "Justice: Distributive and Corrective", p. 14. If the *Encyclopedia of Philosophy* (7:29, Paul Edwards, ed., New York: MacMillan, 1967) is any indication, it would seem that, if not pain, at least suffering is a necessary part of punishment. According to Stanley I. Benett: "Clearly punishment is unpleasant. It is inflicted on an offender because of an offense he has committed: it is deliberately imposed, not just the natural consequence of a person's action (like a hangover), and the unpleasantness is *essential* to it, not an accompaniment to some other treatment (like the pain of the dentist's drill)" (p. 280, emphasis in the original).
35. Bedau, "punishment", p. 732.
36. Bedau, "punishment", p. 732. For example, W. G. Maclagan in his essay "Punishment and Retribution" (*Philosophy* 14 (1939)), holds that "the retributive infliction of pain and only the retributive infliction of pain constitutes punishment" (p. 283), and argues that punishment so construed is indeed justified.
37. Randy E. Barnett, "Restitution: A New Paradigm of Criminal Justice", *Ethics* 87:4 (July 1977).
38. For example, according to Lamont, the principle aim of punishment is "*to influence behaviour, through the will, so as to induce the person punished and others to refrain from acts which violate rights*" ("Justice: Distributive and Corrective", p. 16, emphasis in the original). Similarly, Lucius Garvin thinks that, according to what he calls "the reform theory", "the offender, perceiving that society disapproves his act and that it has adopted the way of punishment as a sign to him (and to others) that it does disapprove it, is minded thereby of the evil of his act and repents of it" ("Retributive and Distributive Justice", *The Journal of Philosophy* 42:10 (May 1945): 277).
39. Michael S. Moore, "The Moral Worth of Retribution", in *Responsibility, Character, and the Emotions: New Essays in Moral Psychology,* Ferdinand Schoeman, ed., Cambridge: Cambridge University Press, 1987, p. 181, emphasis in the original. Moore notes (n. 1) that his use of the phrase "moral culpability" does not "presuppose that the act done is morally bad, only that it is legally prohibited. . . . Usually, of course, most serious crimes are also serious moral breaches."
40. Mill, *Utilitarianism,* chap. V, p. 313.
41. John Locke, *The Second Treatise of Government,* chap. II, Thomas P. Peardon, ed., New York: Macmillan, 1952, p. 9.

42. I am indebted to Jennifer O'Beirne for our conversations regarding a possible duty on the part of individuals to in some way aid in the rectification of injustices, even if all we mean is a duty to assist in creating awareness that an injustice has in fact occurred.
43. For example, see Allen Buchanan, "Liberalism and Group Rights", in *In Harms Way: Essays in Honor of Joel Feinberg,* Jules L. Coleman and Allen Buchanan, eds., Cambridge: Cambridge University Press, 1994; and *Groups and Groups Rights,* Christine Sistare, Larry May, and Leslie Francis, eds., Lawrence, Kansas: University Press of Kansas, 2001.
44. Cf. Dan Brock's comment, Introduction, n.15.
45. I begin to address the moral psychology of rectification for groups in Rodney C. Roberts, "Why Have the Injustices Perpetrated Against Blacks in America Not Been Rectified?", *Journal of Social Philosophy* 32:3 (Fall 2001): 357–373.

3. *"'The Laborers in the Vineyard' and Other Stories," by Phillip Montague*

1. *The Anchor Bible,* trans. W. F. Albright and C. S. Mann (New York: Doubleday and Co., Inc., 1971), XXVI, p. 236.
2. "The denarius was the average day's wage, on which an agricultural worker could expect to provide himself and his family with necessities of life." *Ibid.,* p. 237.
3. From another perspective the householder might be viewed as having violated the principle that relevantly dissimilar cases ought to be treated dissimilarly. Focusing on this last principle rather than P would not substantially alter the discussion which follows.
4. "Justice, Reasonableness, and the Similar Handling of Similar Cases," *Philosophy and Phenomenological Research,* XXXIII, 1972, pp. 90–99.
5. The example is Joel Feinberg's. The view that an injustice would be involved in giving money to only one of the beggars is, I believe, also his.
6. It might be argued that if the beggars need the money then I am obligated to give it to them; and if I am obligated to give it to them, then they have a right to it. But even if this line of reasoning is sound, it is beside the point at issue here, since any injustice implicit in failing to give money to one or more of the beggars would have nothing to do with the differential treatment of those involved.
7. Cf. William K. Frankena, "The Concept of Social Justice," *Social Justice,* ed. Richard Brandt (Englewood Cliffs, N.J.: Prentice Hall, Inc., 1962), pp. 1–29; Marcus George Singer, *Generalization in Ethics* (New York: Alfred A. Knopf, 1961), esp. p. 46; Chaim Perelman, *Justice* (New York: Random House, 1967), Ch. ii; R. M. Hare, *Freedom and Reason* (Oxford: The Clarendon Press, 1963), pp. 32–33, 118–119.
8. Perelman, *op. cit.,* p. 20.
9. *Loc. cit.,* pp. 96–97.
10. This is not to deny that there are other ways in which one might be regarded as behaving unreasonably—e.g. acting according to a rule, but an unreasonable one.

4. *"Corrective Justice and Property Rights," by Jules L. Coleman*

1. To clarify: You have no right to them in the best theory of distributive justice. The purpose of this essay is to determine the conditions under which you would have a certain

kind of "right" to the property: a right that is sustainable by corrective justice, even if it is not one that follows from the best theory of distributive justice.

2. See Section II for an argument against this claim.
3. It is a little misleading to refer to forced transfers as "mutually advantageous," even when full compensation is paid. That is because the victim does not ordinarily gain from the transfer, even when he is fully compensated. Instead, he is made indifferent between his *ex ante* and *ex post* positions. This problem can be easily fixed in either of two ways: To insure that forced exchanges are in fact mutually advantageous, compensation should exceed what it would take to render a victim indifferent between his *ex ante* and *ex post* positions by epsilon (or one dollar, say); or instead of referring to forced, but fully compensated, transfers as mutually advantageous, we might simply refer to them as welfare-enhancing transfers in which no one is made worse off.
4. A voluntary exchange that involves many bargainers all capable of behaving strategically can be more socially costly than a forced transfer in which compensation is not subject to negotiating and is instead set by a third party.
5. Jules L. Coleman, *Risks and Wrongs* (New York: Cambridge University Press, 1992), esp. chs. 16–20.
6. It does not matter for my immediate purposes which formulation—welfare or well-being—we use, nor does the general account presuppose any particular conception of what is to count as the appropriate baseline.
7. Since wrongs are invasions of rights, we have to understand what it is to have a right in order to understand what it is to commit a wrong. In understanding rights, the important distinction is between their *content* and their *structure*. The structure is the analysis of rights, an account of what is analytically true of rights—what it means, in other words, to have a right. Some (like Joel Feinberg) hold that rights are *valid claims;* others (like Joseph Raz) argue that rights are *normative grounds of duties;* still others (like Ronald Dworkin) claim that rights are *trumps in political arguments*.

Suppose that Feinberg is correct; what is true of rights analytically (that is, as part of their structure) is that they are valid claims. It is one thing to note that rights are claims; it is another to reveal the particular claims individuals have. That will depend on the *content* of the specific rights individuals have and the substance of the particular claims associated with each individual right or with rights of certain types. The kinds of valid claims that comprise rights will range over various domains. Thus, if someone has a property right of a certain kind, that will entail that he has valid claims regarding, among other things, the terms of its transfer. The terms of transfer specify the conditions that must be satisfied in order for transfers of resources to comply with the constraints imposed by rights. The terms of transfer constitute what I call the *transaction domain*.

Whereas the structure of rights is given by a philosophical account of what it is to have a right, the content of rights is given a *normative* theory of rights that specifies, among other things, the terms of legitimate transfer. If I have a right to a resource of some sort, say, a painting, part of what that means, *its structure,* is that I have certain claims with respect to the painting. This tells me nothing yet about the specific claims or powers I have with respect to the painting. I might have the power to exclude others from viewing the painting other than on terms agreeable to me; or I might only have the power to charge people a fee for viewing it. I might have the power to set that fee, or I might have to accept a fee set by an agency of some sort. I might have the power to sell the painting and to exclude others from taking it without my consent. Or I might have the power to sell the painting, but not to exclude others from taking it, provided they compensate me. I might have the power to determine the level at which compensation is to be set, or I might have to accept compensation determined by an art agency. And so on. All of these possibilities are compatible with the claim that I have a right to the painting. They differ with respect to the content of that right, the powers the right confers on me, and the constraints it imposes on others.

The content of rights depends on the underlying normative theory of rights. Suppose that the point of having rights is to promote welfare understood in, broadly speaking, utilitarian terms. Rights are valuable to the extent they are welfare maximizing. The norms governing transfer of rights will then reflect the goal of welfare maximization. Thus, the constraints imposed by rights, the powers and claims conferred by them, will be sensitive to empirical conditions and their possible impact on utility.

8. 109 Minn. 456, 124 N.W. 221 (1910).
9. If, however, your car rear-ended mine (due to my faulty brake-lights), then my negligence would have been responsible for *that*.
10. The relationship between community standards, custom, and criminal statutes, on the one hand, and negligence (or unreasonable risk-taking), on the other, is unsettled and quite controversial. Should custom, for example, *constitute* the standard of reasonable care? Or instead, should it establish the prima facie standard of reasonable care? Does it establish a rebuttable presumption of care? Or strong evidence of it? Or simply evidence? Or does it have no special claim at all? My point is that the content of even general norms can have an important "local" dimension in the sense that the duties the general norm imposes on individuals differ depending on the norm's content, and its content often depends on local understandings and practices.
11. See Robert C. Ellickson, *Order without Law* (Cambridge: Harvard University Press, 1989).
12. Coleman, *Risks and Wrongs,* esp. ch. 21.

5. *"Rights and Compensation," by Judith J. Thomson*

This chapter was written during my tenure of an NEH Fellowship and a sabbatical leave from MIT. Many people made helpful criticisms and suggestions; I am especially grateful to Charles Fried.

1. All quotations from Feinberg are of passages in Joel Feinberg, "Voluntary Euthanasia and the Inalienable Right to Life," *Philosophy and Public Affairs* 7(1978): 93–123.
2. A similar point, about an example similar to Feinberg's, was made in Judith Jarvis Thomson, "Self-Defense and Rights," *The Lindley Lecture,* University of Kansas Press, 1976./if150. I have preferred, for a number of reasons, to use Feinberg's example here rather than my own.
3. See Robert E. Keeton, "Conditional Fault in the Law of Torts," *Harvard Law Review* 72(1959): 401.
4. See H. A. Prichard, "Exchanging," *Moral Obligation* (Oxford: The Clarendon Press, 1949).
5. The following principle is stronger than (P_3):

   '[$\text{Prom}_{A,B}$ ($p \rightarrow q$)] & p' entails '$\text{Prom}_{A,B}$ q'.

Is it acceptable? I think not. "I promise you that if you go, I'll go," I say; and you do go. No doubt you have a claim against me that I go, but I do not think I at any time promised to go. It is an interesting question what is 'the internal logic of promising'—if anything merits so grand a name.

'$\text{Prom}_{A,B}$ (p & q)' entails '$\text{Prom}_{A,B}$ p',

for example, is surely plausible enough. But since (CP_2)—see the text, below—is not at all plausible, the 'logic' is at best slim.

6. *"Rights and Duties of Compensation," by Phillip Montague*

1. W. D. Ross, *The Right and the Good* (Oxford: The Clarendon Press, 1930), p. 21.
2. Judith Thomson, "Rights and Compensation," *NOUS* 14 (1980): 3–15 [chap. 5 sup.]; Joel Feinberg, "Voluntary Euthanasia and the Inalienable Right to Life," *Philosophy & Public Affairs* 7 (1978): 93–123.
3. Thomson states quite explicitly that the property rights of concern to her are Hohfeldian ("Rights and Compensation," p. 3) [p. 67 sup.]; and it is clear from the rest of his account that Feinberg too has Hohfeldian rights in mind when he discusses the case in question.
4. Thomson, p. 4 [p. 67 sup.]; Feinberg, p. 102. In fact, Feinberg characterizes actions like A's as *justified* rather than permissible. As I'll suggest later, Feinberg may wish to *deny* that A's action is permissible.
5. Thomson, p. 14 [p. 75 sup.].
6. Feinberg, p. 102.
7. Ibid.
8. See Feinberg's *Social Philosophy* (Englewood Cliffs, New Jersey: Prentice-Hall, Inc., 1973), p. 58; "Duties, Rights, and Claims," reprinted in *Rights, Justice, and the Bounds of Liberty* (Princeton, New Jersey: Princeton University Press, 1980), p. 131. That Feinberg is not completely comfortable with this version of the correlativity thesis is indicated in his "The Nature and Value of Rights," reprinted in *Rights, Justice, and the Bounds of Liberty,* p. 149.
9. This same result would follow from versions of the correlativity doctrine which do not *identify* rights with duties, but which imply that statements about rights entail statements about duties and conversely. See, for example, Ruth Macklin, "Moral Concerns and Appeals to Rights and Duties," *The Hastings Center Report* 6 (1976), p. 35.
10. According to Feinberg, "to say that I lack a duty to refrain is to say that I have a liberty or privilege to do so" *(Social Philosophy,* p. 58). This evidently implies that A cannot be permitted to burn B's furniture if he has a duty to not do so. I think the only way for Feinberg to escape inconsistency here is by maintaining (as was suggested in an earlier note) that A's action is *justified* but *not permissible.* This kind of maneuver strikes me as rather implausible, however.
11. I am using the expression "x has a duty to do y" with less care than some might claim is required. In particular, I have taken no pains to distinguish fulfilling duties from such things as fulfilling obligations, doing what is right, and doing what ought to be done. Perhaps by paying greater attention to possible differences among these concepts it would be possible to resolve some of the issues being raised here, but I doubt it. I think that however we sort out the concepts just referred to, we will conclude that B cannot

have a (Hohfeldian) right to not have his property destroyed by A if A's doing so is permissible.

12. The converse is almost certainly false, however.
13. y should be thought of here as ranging over action-kinds rather than individual actions, but this point is not important for my purposes.
14. This definition of general prima facie duties is patterned after W.D. Ross's account in chap. 2 of *The Right and the Good* (Oxford: The Clarendon Press, 1930).
15. See, for example, Ruth Marcus, "Moral Dilemmas and Consistency," *The Journal of Philosophy* 77 (1980): 121–36.

7. *"Does Compensation Restore Equality?," by Gerald F. Gaus*

In thinking about these matters, I have greatly benefited from discussions with Bob Evans and Loren Lomasky. I also benefited from the comments of Sharon Beattie, John Chapman, Eve Cole, Jim Fetzer and Doc Mayo. My thanks to Linda Hatten for her research assistance.

1. Aristotle, *The Ethics,* J.A.K. Thomson, trans. (Harmondsworth, Middlesex: Penguin, 1955), 148–149.
2. John Rawls, *A Theory of Justice* (Cambridge: Harvard University Press, 1971), 246.
3. Ibid., 100.
4. John Passmore, "Civil Justice and its Rivals," in Eugene Kamenka and Alice Ehr-Soon Tay, eds., *Justice* (London: Edward Arnold, 1979): 25–49 at p. 42.
5. "Now the principle of redress has not to my knowledge been proposed as the sole criterion of justice, as the single aim of the social order. . . . It is thought to represent one of the elements in our conception of justice. Rawls, *A Theory of Justice,* 101.
6. *Ibid.* Nevertheless, I think William T. Blackstone is right to interpret Rawls as essentially endorsing the principle of redress. "Reverse Discrimination and Compensatory Justice," *Social Theory and Practice* 3 (Spring 1975): 253–88 at p. 281.
7. Herbert Spiegelberg, "A Defense of Human Equality," *Philosophical Review* 53 (March 1944): 101–24 at p. 111. Emphasis in original.
8. *Ibid.,* 114. Cf. Blackstone, "Compensatory Justice," 281.
9. David Gauthier, "Justice and Natural Endowment: Toward a Critique of Rawls' Ideological Framework," *Social Theory and Practice* 3 (Spring 1974): 3–26 at pp. 15–16.
10. Rawls, *A Theory of Justice,* 104.
11. I am leaving aside here Rawls's controversial claim that we do not deserve the fruits of our talents because we do not deserve those talents. *A Theory of Justice,* 103–4.
12. Spiegelberg, "Human Equality," 114. Emphasis added.
13. Rawls, *A Theory of Justice,* 102.
14. For a criticism of presumptive principles, see Joseph Raz, *The Morality of Freedom* (Oxford: Clarendon Press, 1986), 8–12.
15. Joel Feinberg, *Harm to Others* (New York: Oxford University Press, 1984), 14–16. See also his *Social Philosophy* (Englewood Cliffs, N.J.: Prentice-Hall, 1973), 21.
16. I have tried to do so elsewhere. See my *Value and Justification: The Foundations of Liberal Theory* (Cambridge: Cambridge University Press, 1990), sec. 24; see also my "Contractual Justification of Redistributive Capitalism," in John W. Chapman and J. Roland Pennock, eds., *NOMOS XXXI: Markets and Justice* (New York: New York University Press, 1989), 89–121 at pp. 97–101.

17. John Locke, *Second Treatise of Government,* in Peter Laslett, ed., *Two Treatises of Government* (Cambridge University Press 1960), 287 (sec. 4). Emphasis in original.
18. S. I. Benn and R. S. Peters, *Social Principles and the Democratic State* (London: George Allen & Unwin, 1959), 110. Emphasis in original.
19. *Ibid.,* 111.
20. See Richard E. Flathman, "Equality and Generalization: A Formal Analysis," in J. Roland Pennock and John W. Chapman, eds., *NOMOS IX: Equality* (New York: Atherton Press, 1967), 38–60; Isaiah Berlin, "Equality as an Ideal," in Frederick A. Olafson, ed., *Justice and Social Policy* (Englewood Cliffs, N.J.: Prentice-Hall, 1962), 128–50; and William K. Frankena, "The Concept of Social Justice," in R. B. Brandt, ed., *Social Justice* (Englewood Cliffs, N.J.: Prentice-Hall, 1962), 1–29. For a dissenting view see Richard Norman, *Free and Equal* (Oxford: Oxford University Press, 1987), 57–58.
21. J. R. Lucas, "Against Equality," in Hugo A. Bedau, ed., *Justice and Equality* (Englewood Cliffs, N.J.: Prentice-Hall, 1971), 138–51 at p. 139. See also Raz, *The Morality of Freedom,* chap. 9.
22. See Robert Brown, *Analyzing Love* (Cambridge: Cambridge University Press, 1987).
23. See my *Value and Justification,* sec. 14.
24. Stanley I. Benn, "Human Rights—for Whom and for What?" in Eugene Kamenka and Alice Erh-Soon Tay, eds., *Human Rights* (New York: St. Martin's Press, 1978, 57–73 at p. 67. Emphasis in original. See also Flathman, "Equality and Generalization," 39; Berlin, "Equality as an Ideal," 131, 133.
25. See my "Subjective Value and Justificatory Political Theory," in J. Roland Pennock and John W. Chapman, eds., *NOMOS XXVIII: Justification* (New York: New York University Press, 1986), 241–69 at pp. 255–58.
26. For such a criticism of Benn's egalitarianism, see Les Holborow, "Benn, Mackie, and Basic Rights," *Australasian Journal of Philosophy* 63 (March 1985): 11–25. In his final work, Benn weakens his Egalitarian Principle so as not to undermine the Liberal Principle. See *A Theory of Freedom* (Cambridge: Cambridge University Press, 1988), 117–21.
27. See Albert Weale, *Equality and Social Policy* (London: Routledge and Kegan Paul, 1978), 19; and Robert Nozick, *Anarchy, State and Utopia* (New York: Basic Books, 1974), 223.
28. It seems, then, that both *E* and *L* migrated from legal and political to moral contexts. I argue here that in the case of *E* this migration took a distinctly illiberal turn.
29. Stanley Benn and I have considered these issues more thoroughly in our "Public and Private: Concepts and Action," in S. I. Benn and G. F. Gaus, eds., *Public and Private in Social Life* (New York: St. Martin's Press, 1983), 3–27, esp. pp. 9–10.
30. Blackstone, "Compensatory Justice," 255.
31. Compensatory justice thus presupposes a theory of distributive justice. Blackstone, I think, rather suggests this. *Ibid.*
32. See here Jules Coleman, "Justice and the Argument for No-Fault," *Social Theory and Practice* 3 (Fall 1974): 161–80, esp. pp. 174ff. I consider penal sanctions briefly in section 4.5.
33. See Jules Coleman, "The Morality of Strict Tort Liability," in his *Markets, Morals and the Law* (Cambridge: Cambridge University Press, 1988), 169.
34. Coleman, "Justice and No-Fault," 175. Emphasis in original.
35. *Ibid.,* 176.
36. Judith Jarvis Thomson, "Preferential Hiring," in William Parent, ed., *Rights, Restitution and Risk* (Cambridge: Harvard University Press, 1986), 149.

37. See here Robert K. Fullinwider, "Preferential Hiring and Compensation," *Social Theory and Practice* (Spring 1975): 307–20, esp. pp. 310–11.
38. I return to this problem below, section 4.2.
39. Nozick, *Anarchy, State and Utopia,* 57.
40. Blackstone, "Compensatory Justice," 268. For an analysis of some practical implications of the "proportionality principle," see Robert Simon, "Preferential Hiring," *Philosophy & Public Affairs* 3 (Spring 1974): 312–20.
41. Nozick, *Anarchy, State and Utopia,* 57; and David Gauthier, *Morals by Agreement* (Oxford: Clarendon Press, 1986), 211.
42. Jules Coleman, "Corrective Justice and Wrongful Gain," in his *Markets, Morals and the Law,* 187–88.
43. In this connection notice that Nozick's account of compensation does identify who is to do the compensating.
44. Coleman, "Corrective Justice and Wrongful Gain," 188.
45. Thomson, "Preferential Hiring," 151.
46. *Ibid.,* 152. See also Bernard R. Boxill, "The Morality of Preferential Hiring," *Philosophy & Public Affairs* 7 (Spring 1978): 246–68.
47. It could be maintained that we all have a duty to rectify all injustices, perhaps individually or *qua* members of the polity. I shall not pursue here the implications of this strong principle.
48. Jules Coleman, "Corrective Justice and Wrongful Gain," 187–88.
49. Note that I focus here on the redistribution of resources, and so exclude penal sanctions; see section 4.5.
50. Kurt Baier, *The Moral Point of View,* abridged ed. (New York: Random House, 1965), 154. For other neo-Hobbesian justifications of morality, see Gregory S. Kavka, *Hobbesian Moral and Political Theory* (Princeton: Princeton University Press, 1986); and James M. Buchanan, *The Limits of Liberty* (Chicago: University of Chicago Press, 1975).
51. I shall not defend characterization of rights in terms of claim rights. For a standard account, see Feinberg, *Social Philosophy,* chap. 4. For sustained criticism of this view, see Alan R. White, *Rights* (Oxford: Clarendon Press, 1984).
52. See Gauthier, *Morals by Agreement,* 211.
53. On this distinction, see Guido Calabresi and A. Douglas Melamed, "Property Rules, Liability Rules and Inalienability: One View of the Cathedral," *Harvard Law Review* 85 (April 1972): 1089–1128.
54. *Ibid.,* 1126.
55. For criticism of the economic analysis, see Alvin K. Klevorick, "On the Economic Theory of Crime," in J. Roland Pennock and John W. Chapman, eds., *NOMOS XXVII: Criminal Justice* (New York: New York University Press, 1985), 289–309. See also the commentaries that follow by Richard Posner and Jules Coleman.
56. Loren E. Lomasky, *Persons, Rights, and the Moral Community* (New York: Oxford University Press, 1987), 143.
57. *Ibid.,* 142. Emphasis in original.
58. The following discussion, and all quotations, draw on Lomasky, *Persons, Rights,* 142–46.
59. From this, it would seem that Lomasky presents an agent-relative account of value and value-based reasons to act. His position, however, is somewhat more complicated. See *ibid.,* 159. For a discussion, see Eric Mack, "Against Agent-Neutral Value," *Reason Papers* (Spring, 1989): 82–92.

60. Lomasky puts great emphasis on this incommensurability thesis, providing the basis for criticism of the use of indifference curves in moral theory. Although he does not say that they are useless, he thinks that indifference curves imply a commensurability Lomasky seeks to deny. *Persons, Rights,* 143–44.
61. Although it adds complications, it is important to stress that the choice is not simply between whether end E1 is to be preferred to E2 or *vice versa.* Rather, in any given situation Alf will be able to do more or less to advance an end; in one case it may be rational for Alf to forgo an opportunity to advance El to a low degree in order to advance E2 to a high degree, even though generally Alf cares more for the former than the latter. Stanley Benn examines the implications of this point in *A Theory of Freedom,* chap. 3.
62. Lomasky, *Persons, Rights,* 144.
63. In terms of indifference analysis, we can say that such a person has a preferred threshold: no trade-offs that take him below a certain level of physical fitness are acceptable. For an extensive analysis of thresholds, see Benn, *A Theory of Freedom,* 56ff.
64. Bernard Williams, "Conflicts of Values," in his *Moral Luck* (Cambridge: Cambridge University Press, 1988), chap. 5 and Stuart Hampshire, "Public and Private Morality," in his *Morality and Conflict* (Oxford: Basil Blackwell, 1983), chap. 5.
65. Williams, "Conflicts of Values," 77.
66. Benn, *A Theory of Freedom,* 48–49. Emphasis added.
67. On knowing the evaluative comparisons of others, see David Milligan, *Reasoning and the Explanation of Action* (Brighton, Sussex: Harvester Press, 1980), chap. 6.
68. Lomasky, *Person, Rights,* 144.
69. As I said above, in some cases we may have no trade-off rates for grave harms to a central value.
70. It has been put to me that she did not violate your privacy since, after all, you *let* her in; you could have just let her freeze. But this seems to me too simple a view of our rights to privacy. Someone who puts you in a position in which you can enjoy your privacy only by allowing her to incur injury is making the option of enjoying your right too costly; it seems tantamount to a threat. And it seems the same holds true on less bitterly cold nights, when your colleague is seeking to increase the costs of your enjoyment of privacy in other, somewhat more subtle, ways. If you refuse to let her in, you know you are apt to have an unpleasant day at work tomorrow.
71. See Kavka's discussion of "rule egoism" in *Hobbesian Moral and Political Theory,* chap. 9.
72. J. S. Mill, *A System of Logic* (London: Longman's Green, 1947), bk. VI, chap. xii, sec. 2. I consider Mill's view in more depth in "Mill's Theory of Moral Rules," *Australasian Journal of Philosophy* 58 (September 1980): 265–79.
73. Mill, *Logic,* bk. VI, ch. xii, sec. 3.
74. J. S. Mill, "Thornton on Labour and its Claims," in J.M. Robson, ed., *The Collected Works of John Stuart Mill* (Toronto: University of Toronto Press, 1963), 5: 659.
75. Gregory Kavka tries to reply to a rather different charge of rule worship in *Hobbesian Moral and Political Theory,* 378–84.
76. According to David A. J. Richards, resentment is appropriate if you have been wronged, while indignation is the appropriate response to a wrong to others. See his *Theory of Reasons for Action* (Oxford: Clarendon Press, 1971), 253.
77. J. R. Lucas, *On Justice* (Oxford: Clarendon Press, 1980), 7. For further consideration of the moral emotions, see my "Commitment to the Common Good," in Paul Harris, ed., *On Political Obligation* (London: Routledge, 1990), 26–64, esp. pp. 36–46.
78. I develop this argument more fully elsewhere. See my *Value and Justification,* section 24.

79. See Dan Brock, "Paternalism and Promoting the Good" in Rolf Sartorius, ed., *Paternalism* (Minneapolis: University of Minnesota Press, 1983): 237–60.
80. Charles Fried, *Contract as Promise: A Theory of Contractual Obligation* (Cambridge: Harvard University Press, 1981), 99.
81. *Ibid.,* 101. This again points to the illiberal nature of the principle of redress, which seems to give others rights to our talents and what we make of them.
82. This relates to the claim by natural law thinkers that one's *summ* can be extended. See Stephen Buckle, *Natural Law and the Theory of Property* (Oxford: Clarendon Press, 1991).
83. I have argued for this notion of ownership in my "Contractual Justification of Redistributive Capitalism," 106–8. Cf. C. B. Macpherson, "Human Rights as Property Rights," in his *Rise and Fall of Economic Justice* (Oxford: Oxford University Press, 1987), 82.
84. See further Gerald F. Gaus and Loren E. Lomasky, "Are Property Rights Problematic?" in *The Monist* 3,4.
85. Cf. Richard A. Epstein, *Takings: Private Property and the Power of Eminent Domain* (Cambridge: Harvard University Press, 1985).
86. A temptation here is to assume that if a person is wronged, then somewhere there *must* be a sort of harm that can be compensated. We would do well to follow Wittgenstein's advice. "Don't say: 'There *must* be' . . . look and see. . . ." G.E.M. Anscombe, trans., *Philosophical Investigations* (London: Macmillan, 1953), section 66.
87. Hence the inadequacy with proposals to base criminal justice simply on the provision of restitution. See Randy E. Barnett, "Restitution: A New Paradigm of Criminal Justice," *Ethics* 87 (July 1977): 279–301. For a more adequate view, see Roger Pilon, "Criminal Remedies: Restitution, Punishment, or Both?" *Ethics* 88 (July 1978): 348–57. Barnett replies in the "The Justice of Restitution," in Jan Narveson, ed., *Moral Issues* (New York: Oxford University Press, 1983), 140–53.
88. It is unclear whether this is Blackstone's view. See "Compensatory Justice," 254.
89. C. L. Ten criticizes this view of punishment in his *Crime, Guilt and Punishment* (Oxford: Clarendon Press, 1987), 38–42.
90. Joel Feinberg, "Voluntary Euthanasia and the Inalienable Right to life," *Philosophy & Public Affairs* 7 (Winter 1978): 93–123 at p. 102.
91. *Ibid.*
92. Most famously, Judith Jarvis Thomson in "Rights and Compensation," in William Parent, ed., *Rights, Restitution and Risk,* chap. 5 [chap. 5 sup.]. See also Coleman, "Corrective Justice and Wrongful Gain," 186.
93. Phillip Montague, "Rights and Duties of Compensation," *Philosophy & Public Affairs* 13 (Winter 1984): 79–88 at p. 84 [p. 79 sup.]. See also the comments by Nancy Davis and Peter Westin, and Montague's reply in *Philosophy & Public Affairs* 14 (Fall 1985).

8. "What Is an Apology?," by Louis F. Kort

1. Austin, J.L., *How To Do Things With Words,* J.O. Urmson ed. (New York, Oxford University Press, 1965), pp. 45–47.
2. Goffman, E., *Relations In Public* (Harmondsworth, Middlesex England, Penguin Books Ltd., 1971), pp. 138–149.
3. Goffman, p. 139.

4. Goffman, p. 139
5. Goffman, pp. 144–145.
6. Goffman, p. 149.
7. Goffman, p. 143.
8. In J.L. Austin's terms, they are different 'illocutionary acts'.

9. *"The Moral Functions of an Apology," by Kathleen A. Gill*

Thanks are due to my colleague Carla Johnson for her very helpful comments on an earlier draft of this chapter.

1. I have only been able to find one article in the philosophical literature specifically on apologies. Louis F. Kort, "What Is an Apology?", *Philosophy Research Archives* 1 (1975): 80–87 [chap. 8 sup.]. Kort takes Goffman's analysis as a starting point.
2. Erving Goffman, *Relations in Public: Microstudies of the Public Order* (New York: Basic Books. 1971), 95–187. Goffman began writing on this topic as early as the mid-1950s. Erving Goffman, "On Face-Work," *Psychiatry: Journal for the Study of lnterpersonal Processes* 18 (1955): 213–31.
3. Goffman, *Relations in Public,* 183.
4. These four categories are defined systematically in Ritsu Itoi, Ken-Ichi Ohbuchi, and Mitsuteru Fukuno, "A Cross-Cultural Study of Preference of Accounts: Relationship Closeness, Harm Severity, and Motives of Account Making," *Journal of Applied Social Psychology* 26 (1996): 913–34. Goffman identifies three basic types of remedial work: accounts, apologies, and requests *(Relations in Public,* 114).
5. The distinction between a justification and an excuse, along with an examination of the language of excuses, can be found in J. L. Austin, *Philosophical Papers* (London: Oxford University Press, 1961), 123–52. Austin does not use the term "accounts."
6. Marvin B. Scott and Stanford M. Lyman, "Accounts," *American Sociological Review* 33 (1968): 46.
7. Evidence for this claim may he found in Barry R. Schlenker and Bruce W. Darby, "The Use of Apologies in Social Predicaments," *Social Psychology Quarterly* 44 (1981): 271–78. Schlenker and Darby claim that a "more full blown" apology may include offers to help the injured party or make restitution, and direct attempts to obtain forgiveness. Compensating victims and asking for forgiveness are certainly related to apologizing, but I will assume in this essay that they are distinct types of action.
8. Janet Holmes, "Apologies in New Zealand English," *Language in Society* 19 (1990): 162.
9. Itoi et al., "A Cross-Cultural Study of Preference of Accounts", 913.
10. Goffman, *Relations in Public,* 113. Note that the offering of an apology typically invites a response on the part of the addressee. It is then that the remedial work becomes an "interchange." Acceptance of the apology signals the completion of the interchange, and this "usually, but not inevitably, will leave the participants in a position to act as if the issue can be dropped" (Goffman, *Relations in Public,* 120).
11. Hiroshi Wagnisuma and Arthur Rosett, "The Implications of Apology: Law and Culture in Japan and the United States," *Law & Society Review* 20 (1986): 482. According to Wagaisuma and Rosett, "Apology is not a defense to a criminal charge, but in both Japan and the Unites States the codes and rules permit apologetic behavior to be

considered in mitigation of punishment" (479). Reports on criminal cases in newspapers frequently note the expression of an apology, or the absence of one. See, for instance, "Racist Sentenced to Death," *Minneapolis Star Tribune,* 26 February 1999, and "Former Justice Official Sentenced for Wrongly Representing Indians," *Minneapolis Star Tribune,* 4 June 1997.

12. Wagatsuma and Roselt, "The Implications of Apology," 478–81.
13. Kort, "What Is an Apology?" G-11 [p. 109 sup.].
14. Recognizing the pervasive desire to keep the workload of the courts to a manageable level, John Haley describes how programs that emphasize the importance of apologizing help prevent litigation and criminal charges. John O. Haley, "Comment: The Implication of Apology," *Law and Society Review* 20 (1986): 504–06.
15. This apology came to my attention through a full-page ad carried in a regional newspaper, which announced in large, bold print that Philip Morris accepted the apology. *Minneapolis Star Tribune,* 27 August 1995.
16. See for instance David T. Risser, "The Social Dimension of Moral Responsibility: Taking Organizations Seriously," *Journal of Social Philosophy* 27 (Spring 1996): 189–207.
17. Roy L. Brooks, ed., *When Sorry Isn't Enough: The Controversy over Apologies and Reparations for Human Injustice* (New York: New York University Press, 1999), 4.
18. *Ibid.,* 3.
19. This point is made by Haley, "Comment: The Implications of Apology," 503.
20. "Southern Baptists Reaching Out to Blacks," *Minneapolis Star Tribune,* 26 June 1999.
21. The announcement of a three-year recruitment initiative in 1999 was described as "an extension of a 1995 public apology by the Southern Baptist leadership for the convention's past policies . . . 'we have to show that while in the past Southern Baptists have refused to minister to people because of their race, today we're talking about sharing gospel that sees no color.'" Meanwhile, the resolution passed calling on President Clinton to rescind his ambassadorial appointment of James Hormel because Hormel is homosexual suggests that future Southern Baptists will be called on once more to apologize for past actions of the church.
22. The social commentator Russell Baker is one prominent source. See "Between Nostalgia and Apologies, We've No Time for the Future," *Minneapolis Star Tribune,* 8 October 1997. Baker complains that "the apologizer comes away feeling like a splendid human being—and it doesn't cost him a nickel." The resolution to apologize for slavery submitted by Rep. Tony Hall generated a wide range of negative reactions, with "many prominent civil-rights leaders" cited as seeing it as "a cheap political gesture." See "Furor over Forgiveness," *Minneapolis Star Tribune,* 5 August 1997. For cynical reactions to ABC's apology to Philip Morris, see Michael Schudson, "A Lot More Apologies on Tobacco Needed," *Minneapolis Star Tribune,* 6 September 1995, and Jeff Cohen and Norman Solomon, "In Disneyland, Journalism Means Saying You're Sorry," *EXTRA!* 8 (Nov./Dec. 1995): 20.
23. Queen Elizabeth issued a formal apology in 1993, and New Zealand issued an apology in 1996 (Brooks, *When Sorry Isn't Enough,* 511). The U.S. government officially apologized to native Hawaiians for the 1883 overthrow of the Kingdom of Hawai'i. The apology is expressed in U.S. Public Law 103–150, 103rd Congress, 23 November 1993.
24. Although both the Maori and native Hawaiians have found ways to unify, there seem to be significant divisions within each group. The question of identity among native Hawaiians is addressed by David J. Baker, "*Ea* and Knowing in Hawai'i," *Critical Inquiry* 23 (Spring 1997): 640–59. Problems of unity and identity among the Maori are described

in Andrew Sharp, *Justice and the Maori: The Philosophy and Practice of Maori Claims in New Zealand since the 1970s,* 2d ed. (Auckland: Oxford University Press, 1998).

25. Difficulties surrounding compensation for historical injustice are seen as virtually insurmountable by Ellen Frankel Paul, "Set-Asides, Reparations, and Compensatory Justice," in *NOMOS XXXIII: Compensatory Justice,* ed. John W. Chapman (New York: New York University Press, 1991), 97–139. Examples of popular resistance may be found in the transcript of NPR's "Talk of the Nation," "Government Apologies" (Largo, Md.: Federal Document Clearing House, 20 January 1998). One poll found that two-thirds of the black respondents thought the federal government should both apologize and pay money to them to compensate for slavery, while two-thirds of the white respondents resisted the idea of an apology, and 88 percent of whites rejected paying reparations (Brooks, *When Sorry Isn't Enough,* 343).
26. Nicholas Tavuchis, *Mea Culpa: A Sociology of Apology and Reconciliation* (Stanford, Ca.: Stanford University Press, 1991), 102.
27. Jerzy Jedlicki, "Heritage and Collective Responsibility," in *The Political Responsibility of Intellectuals,* ed. Ian Maclean, Alan Montefiore, and Peter Winch (Cambridge: Cambridge University Press, 1990), 53–76. According to Jedlicki, "What is most interesting is that as a rule actual disclosure is not the issue. The important facts are known to people either from their own experience or from foreign and illegal publications. The matter concerns *admission* or the act of accepting responsibility. Through such an act the psychological and political function of information changes rapidly, even if its content remains unchanged" (68).
28. A UN-sponsored Truth Commission released a report (February 1999) in which it concluded that the United States, especially through the CIA, had provided direct and indirect support for the Guatemalan army during the thirty-six-year civil war. According to newspaper reports, the Guatemalan army was found responsible for 93 percent of the 42,000 deaths the commission investigated. When the report was made public, U.S. Ambassador Donald Planty reiterated the long-standing denial of U.S. complicity. But one month later President Clinton admitted U.S. involvement, acknowledged that it was wrong. and promised not to repeat the mistake. See "Report Lays Blame on Guatemala," *Minneapolis Star Tribune,* 26 February 1999, and "Clinton Acknowledges U.S. Role in Guatemala Civil War," *Minneapolis Star Tribune,* 11 March 1999.
29. Olufemi Taiwo, ed., "Newsletter on International Cooperation," in *The American Philosophical Association Newsletters,* ed. Eric Hoffman, 98 (1999): 105–15.
30. Julius W. Pratt, *Expansionists of 1898: The Acquisition of Hawaii and the Spanish Islands* (Gloucester, Mass.: Peter Smith, 1959). John W. Foster, "The Annexation of Hawaii: An Address Delivered Before the National Geographic Society" (Washington, D. C.: Gibson Bros., 1897). Helena Allen, *The Betrayal of Liliuokalani: Last Queen of Hawaii, 1838–1917* (Glendale, Ca.: Arthur H. Clark Co., 1982).
31. Will Kymlicka, *The Rights of Minority Cultures* (New York: Oxford University Press, 1995), 5–6. George Hicks has pointed out that "changing attitudes towards women's rights" was an important factor in getting governments to address Japan's sex-slave operations during World War II. George Hicks, "The Comfort Women Redress Movement," in Brooks, *When Sorry Isn't Enough,* 114.
32. See, for instance, Daniel Norell and Thomas Walz, "Reflections from the Field: Toward a Theory and Practice of Reconciliation in Ethnic Conflict Resolution," *Social Development Issues* 16 (1994): 99–111. See also Arnold Epstein, *Ethos and Identity: Three Studies in Ethnicity* (Chicago: Aldine Publishing Co., 1978).

33. "A Declaration against 'The Citizen's Asian Peace Fund for Women,' a Non-governmental Charity Fund," issued by The Feminism Committee Questioning Japanese Modernization, 1995. See also Hicks, "The Comfort Women Redress Movement," 124.
34. Lisa Portmess, "Compensation *Ex Gratia* and the Vincennes Incident," *Public Affairs Quarterly* 6 (1992): 401–13.
35. See Jose Luis Morin, "Hawai'i: Stirrings in the Colony," *NACLA Report on the Americas* 31 (Nov.–Dec. 1997): 10–14. In a similar vein, one reason President Clinton is said to be opposed to issuing a formal apology for America's slave past is the fact that "it could increase legal, as well as moral, pressure for reparations to the descendants of slaves" (Brooks, *When Sorry Isn't Enough,* 352).
36. For an excellent account of one such struggle, see Richard H. Kohn, "History and the Culture Wars: The Case of the Smithsonian Institution's *Enola Gay* Exhibition," *Journal of American History* 82 (1995): 1036–63.
37. Holmes, "Apologies in New Zealand English," 159.

10. "The Morality of Reparation," by Bernard R. Boxill

I am deeply indebted to Professor Thomas Hill, Jr. for helpful criticisms of earlier drafts of this chapter.

1. Michael Harrington and Arnold Kaufman, "Black Reparations—Two Views," *Dissent,* 16 (July–Aug. 1969), 317–320.
2. John Locke, *Treatise of Civil Government and A Letter Concerning Toleration,* ed. Charles L. Sherman (New York: Appleton-Century Company, Inc., 1937), 9.

11. "Compensatory Justice and the Black Manifesto," by Hugo Adam Bedau

1. See, however, Murray Kempton, "The Black Manifesto," *New York Review of Books,* July 10, 1969, pp. 31–33; Michael Harrington and Arnold S. Kaufman, "Black Reparations—Two Views," *Dissent* (1969), pp. 317–320; Robert S. Lecky and H. Elliot Wright, eds., *Black Manifesto: Religion, Racism, and Reparations* (New York: Sheed and Ward, 1969); Arnold Schuchter, *Reparations* (Philadelphia: Lippincott, 1970).
2. The Manifesto, said Murray Kempton (p. 31), is "not so much argument as incantation; according to Michael Harrington, it is an "outlandish scheme" (p. 317), and an "impossible vision"(p. 318).
3. All page references are to the version published by Lecky and Wright, eds., pp. 114–126. The full text is also available in Kempton, and in Schuchter.
4. The chief difference between compensatory and distributive justice lies in whether the recipient deserves a benefit on account of, respectively, some injury he has suffered or on some other ground, e.g., his right to a fair share. Recent discussions of justice by Rawls, Rescher, Runciman and others have not adequately developed the relation between compensation and distribution. Indeed, thanks to the notion of redistributive justice, the contrast between the two may even seem to break down. See Bertrand de Jouvenal, *The Ethics of Redistribution* (Cambridge: Cambridge University Press, 1951).

5. Thus, Michael Harrington objected to The Black Manifesto mainly on the ground that taking it seriously would "divert precious political energies from the actual struggle" to remedy "unequal income distribution in America" (p. 318). Murray Kempton went even farther in the direction of repudiating the apparent burden of The Manifesto, for he insisted that its "indictment" was "not of a genuine deprivation but of a totally fancied reward" (p. 31). Arnold Kaufman, while emphasizing the legitimacy of its literal compensatory nature, endorsed the argument because he thought it would "strengthen . . . the political will to support vast enlargement of compensatory *governmental* programs" (p. 319; italics in original). Similarly, Calvin B. Marshall, chairman of the Black Economic Development Conference, has criticized the failure of the churches to respond to The Manifesto's appeal as evidence of their "refusing to consider human need . . ." (*New York Times,* June 10, 1970, p. 53). But "human need," like "unequal income distribution," and the rest, are not concepts central to an argument for *reparations* and *compensatory* justice.
6. Lecky and Wright, p. 126.
7. For a discussion of the difference between the idea of (criminal) guilt and the idea of (civil) liability, and of the need to confine corporate responsibility to the latter, see Joel Feinberg, "Collective Responsibility," in his *Doing and Deserving* (Princeton: Princeton University Press, 1970), pp. 231–233.
8. This point is persuasively argued by William Stringfellow, "Reparations and Repentance As a Necessity to Reconciliation," in Lecky and Wright, pp. 52–64.
9. The "Introduction" to The Manifesto does speak of "taking the wealth away from the rich people such as General Motors, Ford, Chrysler, the DuPonts, the Rockefellers, the Mellons . . ." (p. 117). The Manifesto continues, ". . . we are dedicated to building a socialist society inside the United States where the total means of production and distribution are in the hands of the State . . ." (p. 118).
10. ". . . The common image of Marx as a prophet of social justice is a false one. . . . To Marx's mind . . . socialists like Proudhon who preached social justice . . . were misguided because they failed to see the irrelevance of the idea of justice to the social problem." Robert Tucker, "Marx and Distributive Justice," in Carl J. Friedrich and John M. Chapman, eds., *Nomos VI: Justice* (New York: Atherton Press, 1963), pp. 309, 323.
11. See Schuchter, *passim,* and esp. Appendix B, "Slavery and the Churches."
12. Lecky and Wright, p. 126.
13. In the first year after it released The Manifesto, B.E.D.C admitted it had raised only 1/170 of the $500 million originally sought from the churches. It was also reported, however, that as much as one-third of the total had been pledged. *New York Times, loc. cit.*
14. Kaufman, p. 319.
15. I have tried to set out those principles in a general analysis of compensatory justice in a paper (unpublished), versions of which were presented to several audiences in conjunction with earlier versions of this chapter.
16. John W. Wade, *Cases and Materials on Restitution* (2nd. ed.; Brooklyn, New York: Foundation Press, 1966), p. 1198.
17. *Ibid.,* p. 1212.
18. *Ibid.,* pp. 455–456.
19. Lecky and Wright, p. 116; cf. p. 117.
20. See, e.g., Dee Brown, *Bury My Heart at Wounded Knee* (New York: Harper, Row and Winston, 1971) and Vine de Loria, ed., *Of Utmost Good Faith* (San Francisco: World Publishing Co., 1971). Much the same point has been made, along with other valuable

suggestions, in Graham Hughes, "Reparations for Blacks?" *New York University Law Review,* 43 (1968), pp. 1063–1074.

21. See Lecky and Wright, p. 50, and *New York Times, loc. cit.*
22. For evidence as to the wealth of the churches in the United States, see Lecky and Wright, p. 176, and Schuchter, pp. 175–178.
23. See, e.g., Eric Williams, *Capitalism and Slavery* (New York: Capricorn Books, 1966) and Robert S. Starobin, *Industrial Slavery in the Old South* (New York: Oxford University Press, 1971). [This note was designated 22a in the original. The remaining notes have been renumbered accordingly.]
24. If we were not required to use the model of unjust enrichment, we could take a very different approach to this question. It is clear from actual cases at law where compensation is successfully sought for incommensurables (e.g., an eye blinded in industrial accident, a reputation damaged by libel or slander), the injured party can accept a certain sum as his indemnity and it will be adequate to compensate him for his loss if he decides that it is. It does not follow from this that an eye is "worth" $10,000 or an unsullied reputation "worth" $50,000, because these sums are not to be construed as measures of the value of the thing lost, but only as compensation for injury to them, and an imperfect remedy at best.
25. Cf. Brian Barry, *Political Argument* (New York: Humanities Press, 1965), p. 113.
26. Cf. Joel Feinberg, "Justice and Personal Desert," in Friedrich and Chapman, eds., *Nomos VI,* p. 94.
27. Richard Lichtman, "The Ethics of Compensatory Justice," *Law in Transition Quarterly,* 1 (1964), 87; italics in original. Professor Lichtman has informed me that his current views on these issues are very different from what they were when he wrote this essay.
28. Earlier versions of this chapter were read before a number of audiences during 1970 and 1971. I am especially grateful for stimulus and criticism to many colleagues who discussed it with me at colloquia arranged by the Departments of Philosophy at the University of Waterloo and at the University of Michigan, by faculty at Boston College Law School, and at the Boston Area Political Theory Conference.

12. *"Wrongdoing, Reparations and Native Americans," by J. Angelo Corlett*

I am grateful to Robert Audi, Bernard Boxill, Anthony Ellis, Margaret Gilbert, Richard W. Miller, Jan Narveson, James Nickel, Michael Slote, Burleigh Wilkins and Clark Wolf for incisive comments on earlier drafts of this chapter. Parts of this chapter in earlier draft forms were presented at the Canadian Society for the Study of Practical Ethics, Canadian Learneds Society, 1997, and at the Conference on War Crimes: Legal and Moral Issues, University of California, Santa Barbara, 1997.

1. Similar points might well apply to Native Americans in Central and South America. Indeed, Native Americans in (former) island nations of the Americas, for example, the Hawaiian islands were victimized (accompanied in the end by threat of military force) by unjust takings by the U.S. and others (see Michael Dougherty, *To Steal a Kingdom: Probing Hawaiian History* (Waimanalo: Island Style Press, 1992)). That Hawaiian culture was significantly affected by the intrusion of Europeans is noted in Martha Beckwith, *Hawaiian Mythology* (Honolulu: University of Hawai'i Press, 1976).
2. William L. Anderson, ed., *Cherokee Removal* (Athens: University of Georgia Press,

1991); Garrick Bailey and Roberta Glenn Bailey, *A History of the Navajos* (Santa Fe: School of American Research Press, 1986); Robert Berkhofer, Jr., *Salvation and the Savage* (New York: Atheneum, 1965); Dee Brown, *Bury My Heart at Wounded Knee* (New York: Henry Holt and Company, 1970); Angie Debo, *A History of the Indians of the United States* (Norman: University of Oklahoma Press, 1970); *And Still the Waters Run* (Norman: University of Oklahoma Press, 1989); John Ehle, *Trail of Tears* (New York: Anchor Books, 1988); Grant Foreman, *Indian Removal* (Norman: University of Oklahoma Press, 1932); Michael D. Green, *The Politics of Indian Removal* (Lincoln: University of Nebraska Press, 1982); Robert V. Remini, *The Legacy of Andrew Jackson* (Baton Rouge: Louisiana State University Press, 1988); David E. Stannard, *American Holocaust: The Conquest of the New World* (Oxford: Oxford University Press, 1992); Ian K. Steele, *Warpaths* (Oxford: Oxford University Press, 1994); Clifford E. Trafzer, *The Kit Carsen Campaign* (Norman: University of Oklahoma Press, 1982); Peter H. Wood, Gregory A. Waselkov and M. Thomas Hatley, eds., *Powhatan's Mantle* (Lincoln: University of Nebraska Press, 1989); Grace Steele Woodward, *The Cherokees* (Norman: University of Oklahoma Press, 1963).

3. Other philosophers who have written on reparations, but concerning the African-American experience, include J. L. Cowan, "Inverse Discrimination," *Analysis,* 33 (1972); Alan H. Goldman, "Reparations to Individuals or Groups?" *Analysis,* 35 (1975); Howard McGary, "Justice and Reparations," *The Philosophical Forum* (1978), 250–263; James W. Nickel, "Discrimination and Morally Relevant Characteristics," *Analysis,* 34 (1973); "Should Reparations Be Made to Individuals or to Groups?" *Analysis,* 34 (1974); Roger A. Shiner, "Individuals, Groups, and Inverse Discrimination," *Analysis,* 33 (1973); Philip Silvestri, "The Justification of Inverse Discrimination," *Analysis,* 34 (1973); Paul W. Taylor, "Reverse Discrimination and Compensatory Justice," *Analysis,* 33 (1973). The main philosophical work which focuses on reparations to Native Americans is David Lyons, "The New Indian Claims and Original Rights to Land," *Social Theory & Practice,* 6 (1977), 249–72. Other philosophers have written on the problem of reparations to Aboriginals in Australia, see Janna Thompson, "Land Rights and Aboriginal Sovereignty," *Australasian Journal of Philosophy,* 68 (1990), 313–29; John Bigelow, Robert Pargetter and Robert Young, "Land, Well-Being and Compensation," *Australasian Journal of Philosophy,* 68 (1990), 330–46.
4. I assume that Native Americans are indigenous and aboriginal peoples to North America, and that even if they are not so indigenous or aboriginal, that they acquired the lands on which they resided in North America in ways that did not violate the Principle of Morally Just Acquisitions and Transfers, discussed below.
5. James Tully, "Aboriginal Property and Western Theory: Recovering a Middle Ground," *Social Philosophy & Policy,* 11 (1994), 153.
6. A. John Simmons, "Original Acquisition Justifications of Private Property," *Social Philosophy & Policy,* 11 (1994), 63–84; Jules L. Coleman, "Corrective Justice and Property Rights," *Social Philosophy & Policy,* 11 (1994), 124–38 [chap. 4 sup.]; Gary Lawson, "Proving Ownership," *Social Philosophy & Policy,* 11 (1994), 139–52. It is assumed herein that the concept of property rights is itself an important part of a plausible political philosophy.
7. "Reparation 'sets things straight' or 'gives satisfaction' . . . for redress of injury" (Joel Feinberg, *Doing and Deserving* (Princeton: Princeton University Press, 1970), 74–5.
8. Note that nothing in this conception of reparations requires that the reparations be "paid" or rendered by the perpetrators of wrongdoing only (compare the conception of reparations set forth in D. N. MacCormick, "The Obligation of Reparations,"

Proceedings of the Aristotelian Society, LXXVIII (1977–78), 175). Contrast this notion of reparations with one articulated by Bernard Boxill: "... Part of what is involved in rectifying an injustice is an acknowledgment on the part of the transgressor that what he is doing is required of him because of his prior error". Bernard Boxill, "The Morality of Reparation," in *Reverse Discrimination,* Barry R. Gross, ed. (New York: Prometheus, 1977), 274.

9. Sanford Levinson, "Responsibility for Crimes of War," *Philosophy & Public Affairs,* 2 (1973), 250.
10. Feinberg, *Doing and Deserving,* Chapter 5.
11. That reparations also recognize the personhood of victims is argued in Mari Matsuda, "Looking to the Bottom: Critical Legal Studies and Reparations," in Kimberle Crenshaw, Neil Gotanda, Gary Peller and Kendall Thomas, eds., *Critical Race Theory* (New York: The New Press, 1995), 74.
12. Feinberg, *Doing and Deserving,* 76.
13. Jeremy Waldron, "Superseding Historic Injustice," *Ethics,* 103 (1992), 6.
14. A. John Simmons, "Historical Rights and Fair Shares," *Law and Philosophy,* 14 (1995), 150–1.
15. Of course, this claim is unproblematic in cases involving murder, as the United States itself recognizes no legal statute of limitations in murder cases.
16. MacCormick, 179.
17. Lyons, 252. Indeed, it is an historical, rather than an end-state, argument for reparative justice.
18. These acts amount to a series of intentional actions that were crimes, torts and/or contract violations.
19. For a discussion of the concept of corrective justice that is helpful in the context of reparations, see Jules L. Coleman, "Corrective Justice and Wrongful Gain," *Journal of Legal Studies,* 11 (1982), 421–40.
20. Will Kymlicka, *Liberalism, Community, and Culture* (Oxford: Oxford University Press, 1989), 165. Discussions of Kymlicka's argument are found in John Tomasi, "Kymlicka, Liberalism, and Respect for Cultural Minorities," *Ethics,* 105 (1995), 580–603; Robert Murray, "Liberalism, Culture, Aboriginal Rights," *Canadian Journal of Philosophy,* 29 (1999), 109–38.
21. John R. Danley, "Liberalism, Aboriginal Rights, and Cultural Minorities," *Philosophy & Public Affairs,* 20 (1991), 172.
22. Another reason might concern factors of distributive justice: the continual failure or refusal of a government to recognize in the form of compensation its harms against some of its constituents often results in the social alienation and violence that erupt in society as a result (at least in part) of such non-recognition. For such non-recognition of a government's harms leads many to believe that the government supports the status quo of what happened to the victims.
23. For a discussion of hard cases in the context of law, see Ronald Dworkin, *Taking Rights Seriously* (Cambridge: Harvard University Press, 1978), Chapter 4.
24. A version of the Argument From Historical Complexity seems to be articulated by Loren Lomasky when he writes: "... It is undeniably the case that virtually all current holdings of property descend from a historical chain involving the usurpation of rights. It does not follow that those holdings are thereby rendered illegitimate, morally null and void" (Loren Lomasky, *Persons, Rights, and the Moral Community* (Oxford: Oxford University Press, 1987), 145). A similar view is articulated, but not endorsed, in

A. John Simmons, "Original Acquisition Justifications of Property," *Social Philosophy & Policy,* 11 (1994), 74–75.

25. This assumption will be taken up in discussing the Objection to Collective Responsibility, below.

26. This principle bears a keen resemblance to the principle of just acquisitions, transfers and rectification found in Robert Nozick, *Anarchy, State, and Utopia* (New York: Basic Books, 1974), 150. However, the Principle of Morally Just Acquisitions and Transfers makes no particular theoretical commitments to Nozick's entitlement theory or its implications.

Writing on the recovery or repossession of stolen or lost property, Immanuel Kant argues that those who acquire such property have a responsibility to "investigate" the historical chain of acquisitions and transfers of the property, and if, unbeknownst to her, the property she deemed she purchased legitimately was the actual possession of another, then "nothing is left to the alleged new owner but to have enjoyed the use of it up to this moment as its possessor in good faith" (Immanuel Kant, *The Metaphysical Elements of Justice,* 302 in Kant, *The Metaphysics of Morals,* Mary Gregor trans. and ed. (Cambridge: Cambridge University Press, 1996), 82).

27. Note that the matter of property *ownership* is not at issue here. Rather, *sovereignty* over land, a notion consistent with Native American worldviews, is at issue. For more on property and sovereignty, see Thompson, 313–29.

28. For descriptions of examples of the taking of Native American lands by force and violence, see Debo, *A History of the Indians of the United States,* 47,87, 96, 118, 297, 304–05, 317, and 320.

29. For descriptions of examples of the taking of Native American lands by fraud, see Debo, *A History of the Indians of the United States,* 89, 106, 118, 207, 261, 320–21, and 379.

30. For descriptions of examples of the taking of Native American lands by misunderstanding, deliberate or otherwise, see Debo, *A History of the Indians of the United States,* 76, 190–91.

31. For discussions of the concept of collective responsibility, see J. Angelo Corlett, "Collective Responsibility," in Patricia Werhane and Edward Freeman, eds., *Encyclopedic Dictionary of Business Ethics* (London: Blackwell, 1997), 117–120; "Collective Moral Responsibility," in A. Jokic, ed., *From History to Justice* (Dordrecht: Kluwer Academic Publishers, forthcoming); Joel Feinberg, *Doing and Deserving* (Princeton: Princeton University Press, 1970), Chapter 8; Peter French, *Corporate and Collective Responsibility* (New York: Columbia University Press, 1984); *Responsibility Matters* (Lawrence: University of Kansas Press, 1990); Virginia Held, "Can a Random Collection Be Morally Responsible?" *The Journal of Philosophy,* 67 (1970), 471–80; "Corporations, Persons, and Responsibility," in Hugh Curtler, ed., *Shame, Responsibility, and the Corporation* (New York: Haven, 1986); Larry May, *The Morality of Groups* (Notre Dame: Notre Dame University Press, 1987); *Sharing Responsibility* (Chicago: University of Chicago Press, 1992); Burleigh T. Wilkins, *Terrorism and Collective Responsibility* (London: Routledge, 1992).

32. Joel Feinberg argues that there is a kind of collective responsibility, namely vicarious responsibility, which derives from the process of authorization (see Joel Feinberg, *Doing and Deserving* (Princeton: Princeton University Press, 1970), 226). Thus when former U.S. President Andrew Jackson, duly elected by the U.S. citizenry, commands the U.S. Army to conduct the policy of "Indian removal" even by violent force, vicarious responsibility accrues to the United States and its citizens. Presumably, such

responsibility, insofar as it entails culpability, would accrue at least until adequate reparations are made to the various Native American nations that were victimized by the said policy and others akin to it.

33. For discussions of corporate responsibility, see J. Angelo Corlett, "Corporate Responsibility and Punishment," *Public Affairs Quarterly*, 2 (1988), 1–16; "Corporate Punishment and Responsibility," *Journal of Social Philosophy*, 28 (1997), 86–100.
34. For a distinction between weak and strong forms of compensation, see Bigelow, Pargetter and Young, 336–7. Bigelow, Pargetter and Young argue for compensation in a strong sense as a reply to the Argument From Collective Responsibility.
35. John Locke, *Second Treatise on Government*, sections 34, 37, 40–43. For an assessment of Locke's view, see Tully, 161f.
36. That considerations of social utility might *favor* (rather than disfavor) reparations to those deserving of them is argued in Matsuda, 74f.
37. This argument is set forth and defended in Lyons, 252f.
38. See Locke. For a helpful discussion of Locke's positions on rights and other political concepts, see A. John Simmons, *The Lockean Theory of Rights* (Princeton: Princeton University Press, 1992); *The Edge of Anarchy* (Princeton: Princeton University Press, 1993). Locke's line of reasoning has been plausibly refuted in Robert Nozick, "Distributive Justice," *Philosophy & Public Affairs*, 3 (1973), 70f. See also Jeremy Waldron, *The Right to Private Property* (Oxford: Oxford University Press, 1988), Chapters 6–7; "Two Worries About Mixing One's Labor," *The Philosophical Quarterly*, 33 (1983), 37–44.
39. Lyons, 254f. Lyons argues, astonishingly, that the genuinely compensable wrongs against Native Americans by the U.S. government might be more recent acts of discrimination against them, rather than the historical injustices of murders and illegitimate takings of their lands (Lyons, 268–71).
40. Waldron, "Superseding Historic Injustice," 17.
41. Christine M. Korsgaard, "Taking the Law Into Our Own Hands: Kant on the Right to Revolution," in Andrews Reath, Barbara Herman and Christine M. Korsgaard, eds., *Reclaiming the History of Ethics: Essays for John Rawls* (Cambridge: Cambridge University Press, 1997), 307.
42. That inheritance is justly and fairly delimited by principles of justice is argued in John Rawls, *A Theory of Justice* (Cambridge: Harvard University Press, 1971), 277f.; *Collected Papers*, Samuel Freeman, ed. (Cambridge: Harvard University Press, 1999), 142f.
43. A similar point is found in Waldron, "Superseding Historic Injustice," 15.
44. As noted above, U.S. law recognizes no statute of limitations in cases of murder. Thus neither the statute of limitations objection to reparations to Native Americans (rejected earlier) nor the *Laches* doctrine count against reparations to Native Americans in instances where murders of Native Americans were perpetrated by the U.S. government and representatives of its agencies in the fulfilling of their duties as official representatives of the U.S. government.
45. See Locke, *Second Treatise on Government*, section 27; Robert Nozick, *Anarchy, State and Utopia* (New York: Basic Books, 1974), 175–82; A. John Simmons, *The Lockean Theory of Rights* (Princeton: Princeton University Press, 1992), 278f.
46. Furthermore, it has been argued that it is reasonable to hold that the Iroquois indeed acquired rights to some North American lands, and on a Lockean basis! See John D. Bishop, "Locke's Theory of Original Appropriation and the Right of Settlement in Ir-

oquois Territory," *Canadian Journal of Philosophy*, 27 (1997), 311–38. See also Naomi Zack, "Lockean Money, Indigenism, and Globalism," *Canadian Journal of Philosophy (Supplementary Volume)*, 25 (1999), 32f.

47. See Thompson, 320–1.
48. Waldron, "Superseding Historic Injustice," 24.
49. Waldron, "Superseding Historic Injustice," 25.
50. Waldron, "Superseding Historic Injustice," 25.
51. Waldron, Superseding Historic Injustice," 25–26.
52. Waldron, "Superseding Historic Injustice," 7–8.
53. Waldron, "Superseding Historic Injustice," 13.
54. For a discussion of how reparations might accrue in such circumstances, see Tyler Cowen, "Discounting and Restitution," *Philosophy & Public Affairs*, 26 (1997), 168–85.
55. G. Sher, *Approximate Justice* (Totowa: Rowman & Littlefield, 1997), 15.
56. Ward Churchill, *From a Native Son* (Boston: South End Press, 1996), 528–30.
57. Churchill, *From a Native Son*, 529.
58. Recall the discussion of the Objection From Social Utility, above.
59. For an account of collective feelings of guilt, see Margaret Gilbert, "Group Wrongs, Guilt Feelings," *The Journal of Ethics*, 1 (1997), 65–84. For a more recent account of the concept of collective guilt, see Margaret Gilbert, *Sociality and Responsibility* (Totowa: Rowman & Littlefield, 2000), Chapter 8.
60. For an account of collective remorse, see Margaret Gilbert, "Collective Remorse," in Alexandar Jokic, ed., *War Crimes and Collective Wrongdoing* (London: Blackwell, 2000); Gilbert, *Sociality and Responsibility*, Chapter 7.
61. Gabrielle Taylor, *Pride, Shame, and Guilt* (Oxford: Oxford University Press, 1985), 67

CONTRIBUTORS

HUGO ADAM BEDAU

Professor of Philosophy, Tufts University

BERNARD R. BOXILL

Professor of Philosophy, University of North Carolina, Chapel Hill

JULES L. COLEMAN

Wesley Newcomb Hohfeld Professor of Jurisprudence and Professor of Philosophy, Yale University

J. ANGELO CORLETT

Professor of Philosophy, San Diego State University, and founding Editor-in-Chief of *The Journal of Ethics*

GERALD F. GAUS

Professor of Philosophy, Tulane University, an Editor of the *Australasian Journal of Philosophy*, and Co-editor of *Politics, Philosophy and Economics*

KATHLEEN A. GILL

Professor of Philosophy, St. Cloud State University

LOUIS F. KORT

Formerly Assistant Professor of Philosophy, University of North Carolina, Greensboro

PHILLIP MONTAGUE

Professor of Philosophy and Chair of the Department of Philosophy, Western Washington University

RODNEY C. ROBERTS
Assistant Professor of Philosophy, University of Hawai'i at Mānoa

JUDITH J. THOMSON
Professor of Philosophy, Massachusetts Institute of Technology

ANTHONY D. WOOZLEY
University Professor Emeritus of Philosophy and Law, University of Virginia

INDEX OF AUTHORS

What follows is an index of authors who have contributed to this book, and authors who are quoted in extended quotations. Page numbers of contributions are in **bold face,** page numbers of extended quotations are in light face.